Me & Issy

A Four Seasons Romance

Rosalie Wise Sharp

AUTHOR'S NOTE

Excerpts have been included from *Four Seasons: The Story of a Business Philosophy*, Isadore Sharp, 2009, Penguin, and *Rifke*, Rosalie Wise Sharp, 2007, ECW Press. All paintings by the author.

Copyright © Rosalie Wise Sharp, 2022
Published by ECW Press
665 Gerrard Street East
Toronto, ON M4M 1Y2
416-694-3348 / info@ecwpress.com

LIBRARY AND ARCHIVES CANADA CATALOGUING IN PUBLICATION
Title: Me & Issy : a Four Seasons romance / Rosalie Wise Sharp.
Other titles: Me and Issy
Names: Sharp, Rosalie, author.
Identifiers: Canadiana (print) 20220186502 | Canadiana (ebook) 20220186812 |

ISBN 978-1-77041-712-0 (Hardcover)
ISBN 978-1-77852-059-4 (ePub)
ISBN 978-1-77852-060-0 (PDF)
ISBN 978-1-77852-061-7 (Kindle)

Subjects: LCSH: Sharp, Rosalie. | LCSH: Sharp, Isadore. | LCSH: Sharp, Rosalie—Marriage. | LCSH: Sharp, Rosalie—Family. | LCSH: Jewish women—Ontario—Toronto—Biography. | LCSH: Jews—Ontario—Toronto—Biography. | LCSH: Four Seasons Hotels & Resorts—History. | LCGFT: Autobiographies.
Classification: LCC FC3097.9.J5 S53 2022 | DDC 971.3/5410049240092—dc23

Cover design: Rosalie Sharp
Text design: Tania Craan
Typesetting: Troy Cunningham

This book is funded in part by the Government of Canada. *Ce livre est financé en partie par le gouvernement du Canada.* We acknowledge the support of the Canada Council for the Arts. *Nous remercions le Conseil des arts du Canada de son soutien.* We acknowledge the support of the Ontario Arts Council (OAC), an agency of the Government of Ontario, which last year funded 1,965 individual artists and 1,152 organizations in 197 communities across Ontario for a total of $51.9 million. We also acknowledge the support of the Government of Ontario through Ontario Creates.

PRINTED AND BOUND IN CANADA

PRINTING: FLASH   5   4   3   2   1

*For Isadore, our children,
and our children's children*

Candles and kepas for Shabbat blessings, 51" x 61".

TABLE OF CONTENTS

INTRODUCTION   7

CHAPTER ONE
Snooping around
in the Past   11

CHAPTER TWO
Girl Meets Boy   29

CHAPTER THREE
Paths across the Sky   49

CHAPTER FOUR
Growing Up the Hard Way   69

CHAPTER FIVE
None of the World's Goods   95

CHAPTER SIX
The Wind in the Willows   117

CHAPTER SEVEN
The Lost Genes   129

CHAPTER EIGHT
High School Capers   141

CHAPTER NINE
Go Together like a
Horse and Carriage   155

CHAPTER TEN
Our Dream House   173

CHAPTER ELEVEN
What Flower Is That?   203

CHAPTER TWELVE
Disaster at Its Worst   209

CHAPTER THIRTEEN
Not a Decorator   219

CHAPTER FOURTEEN
A Train across India   239

CHAPTER FIFTEEN
Our Last House   253

CHAPTER SIXTEEN
260 Oil-on-Canvasses   269

ACKNOWLEDGEMENTS   279

Isadore and Rosalie Wise Sharp, September 6, 2021.

INTRODUCTION

BY ISADORE SHARP

Just a few words from me, "the husband of," on my life with Rosalie, my companion of 69 years. I believe the Covid pandemic has brought many of us to search our early lives for answers about how we got from there to now.

That first night we met, Rosalie told her best friend, Merle, that she had found the man of her dreams, and I do believe that first meeting was providential.

So let me explain. It was 1952 and reluctantly I had to go to my cousin's wedding and, for those who knew my mother, you know what I mean — I "had to go."

Well, I noticed this beautiful young bridesmaid and at that time of my life, of course, I would try to make out.

So, I asked her to dance, got her telephone number, and here we are 69 years later.

And had I not attended that wedding we never would have met, because our lives and interests were poles apart.

As I have said many times, I know that my success is directly related to having married Rosalie because she has always been satisfied and happy with whatever we've had — even managing to do everything on my salary of $40 a week when we got married.

And over these many years she has always been unconditionally supportive.

Most important, of course, was by filling in for me in raising our four boys.

She was always there for them — like putting her professional career on hold because, as she told me then, "I want to be there when the kids come in and yell 'Mom, what's for lunch?'" But also supportive in my work, because she was never, ever negative and was always in my corner.

So, when Rosalie said, "My most valuable contribution to his success has been my silence," that meant that if things didn't work out, she was ready to face the problems together. And, yes, she has been my unfailing helpmate for 69 years, who has enriched my life in so many ways.

And I never cease to be in awe of her paintings, her out of-the-ordinary table decorations, and her great sense of personal style. She surprises me daily with her knowledge, whether it's about antiques, opera, books, art, ceramics, or some esoteric term on TV that *I've* never heard of.

All borne out of a compulsive curiosity. Who else would knock on doors of strange houses and ask for a tour?

She was both school bright and disciplined. On beginning her fourth year of high school, she decided to take two languages that she hadn't taken before. So, every day during lunch hour Rosalie taught herself three years of Latin, and two years of German; she wrote the final fourth-year exams and passed with honours in both subjects, with no classrooms and no teachers. Her oil-on-canvas works are of every genre from abstract to portrait. And her handwriting is calligraphic. When she was in grade school spelling bees, she was the last man standing.

To list a few of her achievements: in 1969 she graduated with the Lieutenant Governor's Award as the top student at OCAD, became a successful interior designer, ran her company Rosalie Wise Design for more than 20 years, and has written five books.

And her writing skills were best recognized in 1975 when she received a six-page response to a six-page letter she wrote to the author V.S. Naipaul about his book *An Area of Darkness*.

He ended by writing: "My dear lady, stop reading, start writing."

And, as our son Tony once said when he was about 14 years old, and I quote: "Dad, how are you ever going to keep up with Mom?" Well Tony, I'm still trying.

So, this is a great opportunity for me once again, to thank and praise my remarkable Rosalie — who can't wait to start each day, and always with that brisk resolve in her step.

2020

Self-portrait, 2015, 51" x 61".

CHAPTER ONE

Snooping around in the Past

Snooping around in our childhood is our day's occupation during this year of the pandemic 2020. We are after answers. How did it happen that my husband and I are still best friends and lovers after 69 years? How did our random journeys from childhood fit each other as easily as my Apple earbuds slide seductively into their sleek white case? How did it happen that Isadore has become a global hero both to us and to his 40,000 employees? And why do we fly first class in a private plane and live in a rather nice house? Maybe the answer can be found in patching up the past, probably a regular pastime of all of us old fogeys although we don't admit to being old, just "older." Isadore and I come from similar privileged beginnings. Not moneyed but rich as only an immigrant household can be. Our parents took to the new opportunities with daring, a steady focus, and unremitting self-reliance. Toronto was the "goldene medina," Yiddish for golden country, where everything denied to Jews in Poland was possible. Here you could own land, borrow money from the bank, be a landlord, and send your kids to college. The two of us are the last generation where Yiddish was spoken, food was kosher, grandmothers lived upstairs, clothes were scarce, and gentiles were hostile. Me and Issy had these things in common.

We spoke Yiddish to our grandparents, but our kids know hardly a word of a language spoken in all generations before theirs. These days, I usually say at family get-togethers, "Let's sing just one Yiddish song," as my mother and I did in the car all the way to Montreal and back on our annual visit to her brother. In 1930s to '50s Toronto, Issy and I lived a life just a few steps from the Polish shtetl, those thousands of small Jewish towns. Some had escaped from the Spanish Inquisition or were expelled from too many other countries to name.

Our parents practised a life they knew from their parents, and their parents' parents, defined by the Jewish rites of passage — circumcision, bar mitzvah, wedding under a chuppah (canopy), and by Friday night dinners, the high holidays, and the Old Testament. Theirs was a fierce work ethic. It is told that Max Sharp, Issy's dad, stayed home for his honeymoon and didn't head out for work until 9 a.m.

Max was a sweetheart. He moved gently through life with never an unkind word or a prejudice. He wasn't tall — we were eye to eye — with blondish Ashkenazi complexion and a slim build, with an interest in keeping that way. He was the most agreeable person known to man. He faced every hardship with an unruffled equanimity. A bombshell would hardly disturb his poise. He said yes to everything I ever suggested. Yes to reading Pearl S. Buck, yes to a speech I wrote for him, and yes to compose his own geometric designs in his needlepoints (instead of the stamped store-bought patterns). He produced at least 50 of these, and I have a stool in my dressing room covered in a "Max original" Vasarely-like geometric.

One time, Max and I dropped into a Gucci shop in Palm Springs and I suggested he buy a pair of bright red loafers. Not one to say no, he tried them on and as we were checking out at the cash I said, "Max you know these are quite expensive."

"How much can they be? Shoes are shoes," he replied.

However, I noticed his surprise as he paid the amount — $500. When

Max died, many of his grandsons competed for those shoes. I think they had to draw straws.

Max came from a long line of rabbis and personified the Mosaic morality of the shtetl. Material things should neither be praised nor disdained. A Jew should never boast, exhibit undue enthusiasm, give the exact number of his grandchildren, or kiss his wife in public; all exhibitions of emotion are bad form. So, Max with his verbal economy never used superlatives. When I asked him if he enjoyed one of my brown rice salads, he answered, "There's nothing wrong with it," which I knew to be praise indeed. With his slim build he preferred light fare, but he dutifully ate the resident heavy Jewish cooking. I remember him sitting downcast, staring at the tablecloth, resigned to his fate, fork and knife raised at the ready as Lil dropped yet another plate of schmaltzy food before him. Papa Max was tolerant in the extreme and embraced the modern dysfunctional family as if he was born to it. When his granddaughter Wendy told him she was pregnant — no husband — he gave her a big "mazel tov." When a friend recommended a diet of no coffee, carbs, sugar, or alcohol, he adopted it for life.

MAX WAS BORN IN 1902 in the shtetl of Oshpitzim, famously Auschwitz in German. Yes, Auschwitz was a Jewish town. Our own family of 11 visited that town and the Auschwitz cemetery in 2011 and signed a visitor's book in the "Sharf" family mausoleum. We looked at the list of names and found Asher J. Sharf, 52nd Street, New York, obviously a relative, but no one we knew. This mausoleum and a written description of their three-storey house in Oshpitzim indicates that they were prosperous and also VIPs in town because the great-grandfather Rabbi Moishe Yankel had been a leader of the Galician Hasidim for 50 years, and Max's father was the "wise man" in this town.

Max, Mottel in Yiddish, was the middle of 11 children, seven boys and four girls, most of whom immigrated to Palestine except his two sisters, Chaya and Leah, who died in the Holocaust. His great-grandfather Chief Judge Moishe Yankel, born 1787, wrote two books, one on the Talmud and one on the Torah, that we have seen, bound in red leather, *The Paths of Propriety*. Kalman, the oldest brother, died in the First World War. He had been a strong swimmer and jogged twice a day, after morning prayers and before evening prayers. Max's traits of honesty and reliability were carefully taught by his mother, Gittel Green, and his pious father, Rabbi Moishe Yankel. From the age of four, Mottel, sidelocks in place, would have studied in the Yeshiva from 8 a.m. till five (no play for youngsters), which brings me to imagine an old masters painting in burnt umber, of a dark room and tiny boys bent over desks writing on their tablets in the persimmon glow of a fireplace. One of my favourite Yiddish songs, "Near the Fireplace," is a ballad about the rabbi teaching tiny children their ABC's (Aleph Bets) around a warm hearth. A sad song because children like Mottel were delivered into the hands of the rabbi and the bondage of school at just four years old. The song explains, "Children, as you grow older you will understand how many tears lie among the Hebrew letters, and when you suffer prejudice and privation you will derive strength from Hebrew texts." Maybe that's why we Jews are known as "the people of the book." Max once told me an Oshpitzim story, with laughter in his eyes. One Shabbat as he and their Polish Catholic maid were returning from shopping for the Sabbath challah (braided egg bread) and the kosher chicken, a friend of Teresa's approached for a chat. Quickly Teresa threw her shawl over the food because kosher food becomes treif (non-kosher) when looked on by a goy. Teresa knew.

Isadore seems to have inherited many traits of his forbears, the Oshpitzim rabbis. I imagine Issy standing on the shoulders of a chain of rabbis dating back to the writing of the Bible, each meting out fairness in the same considered way — models of humanity and learning through the ages. Issy has also inherited a kind of glandular optimism and sees the best in people, sometimes better. And he has the tzedakah gene, that Jewish version of charity which implies that giving is both an ethical obligation and a privilege. Tzedakah dictates that one should give away about one third of one's means to the needy. Partly for which Isadore was inducted as an Officer of the Order of Canada in 1992.

MOTTEL AND LATER HIS brother Lazar were the first to leave Oshpitzim. Max arrived in Palestine just after Sukkot in 1920. With the blithe strength of the chalutz (pioneer), Max helped build one of the first kibbutzim, Deganya. The brothers struggled together with their valiant co-pioneers — fighting the English, the Arabs, and the malaria, whilst raising trees from the deserts and rescuing fields from the swamps.

Issy's mom, Lillie Godfrey (formerly Gotfried), came from the neighbouring shtetl of Ostrowietz. Her oldest known forbear was her great-great-great-grandfather Baruch Gotfried, born about 1785. Her older brother Max brought everyone to Toronto and would never let them forget it. Max Godfrey is worth a mention. He and his sister, Issy's mom, have so much in common — they looked alike, had the same big presence in a room. He is said to have been so charismatic that he could summon a chair and have "the chair come to him." Issy has inherited some of his uncle Godfrey's genes, particularly Max's self-confidence and compelling charm. Recently Max's son Irvin told me his father was very kind, "he was an angel." One summer when the Godfreys and Sharps shared a cottage at Crystal Beach, Uncle Godfrey took his twin sons to the amusement park. When they took a ride on the Octopus, and they started screaming for help, their dad demanded of the attendant, "Stop this immediately or I will kill you!" The machine was duly halted. Rides were forbidden in my family, but it so happened that my first ever ride when I was 16 was on the same Octopus, which was so horrible. "Uncle Godfrey — help — where are you?" Why, I wondered, was anyone ever attracted to these rides? And all those years I thought I had missed something. We last saw dear Max Godfrey in his declining days at age 94 with a full head of black hair, just a few strands of grey.

Back in 1925, it had been Max Godfrey's idea to bring his sister Lil and his sister Rose's brother-in-law Max Sharp to Toronto and arrange their marriage. In Jewish tradition fathers chose the mates for their daughters and provided a dowry, which was sometimes a bargaining tool, and a big strain on the family's finances. This responsibility fell to Max G. since his father had died. So, two brothers Sharp married two sisters Godfrey, and Max S. and Lil had a love affair till the end. He worshipped her. Maybe this is why Isadore is excessively fond of me. Max Sharp had started as a plasterer for $15 a week and when they wouldn't give him a raise, he opened his own business and went broke when he miscalculated a job by misreading a set of plans. He had been given a mirror image of half the building so his quote was off by half. But Max lived up to his agreement and finished the job, which put him in debt for several years. They struggled through the 1929 Depression by selling pinball machines. But the family's fortunes improved slowly when he became a builder of houses in 1938. He excavated basements with a horse and plow and once broke his shoulder, but kept on working. He built the original Shaarei Shomayim Synagogue on St. Clair Avenue as well as the current one on Glencairn to which he walked for years every Saturday, his kippah on his head and prayer book and prayer shawl in a purple velvet bag under his arm. In 2015, we made a donation to the synagogue and the main hall is now named the Max and Lil Sharp Sanctuary.

LIL WAS A FULL partner in the business decorating the houses and planting the gardens. Never getting down and digging but giving directions to a labourer while, I picture her, wearing her hat. In business and in life it was a honeymoon to the end, made the more romantic since she was three inches taller and somewhat wider. Lil was exceedingly pretty with Sephardic dark eyes, curly hair, and an especially shapely nose and full lips, both of which Issy inherited. Once when I came into their penthouse from our place downstairs, it was quiet, and no one answered when I called out, but when I went down the hall to their bedroom, I saw them asleep coupled together, blankets to the chin, from which poked only two forearms, hands clasped. When Lil died in 1983, we all stood around her hospital bed and witnessed Max pronounce the indelible words, "Doctor, isn't she beautiful."

But back in the early years Lillie Sharp was the matriarch running a big house with four kids and a dog, while caring for her mother, Crayndl, who lived with them. Crayndl was an entrepreneur. She had a prosperous coal business in Ostrowietz and would travel back to Poland to manage it. Shtetl wives typically were the breadwinners, while the men spent their days studying the Torah. So, Lillie followed her mother's example and was a strong advocate in Max's plastering business. She was a force. I was a witness because Issy and I lived a floor below the Sharp penthouse in the iconic (at the time) apartment house built by Isadore under the banner of Max Sharp and Son Construction Company, which became a two-man company when he joined his dad after his architecture course at Ryerson Institute of Technology. Max then stepped back and trusted Isadore, the graduate, to run the show. When Issy poured three concrete steps to a house he had designed for his sister Bea, Max watched knowing a height was wrong but said nothing. He subscribed to the edict "never give advice unless asked." Whenever I manage *not* to give advice, I say I'm doing "a Papa Max."

Issy remembers from his early Max Sharp and Son days, two major mistakes he made. When he was excavating Northview Terrace in 1953, there was a hurricane force rainstorm. We were dating at the time, so I clearly remember that the yellow brick six-storey building closely bordering the property looked like it was on a cliff and could topple into the three-storey gaping hole of the excavation. Issy's retaining wall was too flimsy, so he stayed up well into the night in the pouring rain, reinforcing it, with the help of his workers. And then Isadore himself laid out the footings of this 12-storey building with his surveyor's transit and his Ryerson know-how when he should have had it done, he says, conventionally and safely by a professional surveyor, as he would always do after that. Which brings to mind the condo building in Miami that collapsed recently.

From his high school days he worked with his dad and remembers unloading the bricks and blocks and carrying the hods of plaster, alongside the workmen Vito Pisano and Pete Sienco. The carpenter Morris Gotlieb once said, "Issy never stopped saying 'Good Morning,'" implying as the boss's son, he could ignore the pleasantries. Morris always had a dour look because he was on his second family — he witnessed his first family ushered into the line that went to the gas chambers. Morris needn't have worried because Issy has a native graciousness even when he was top of the heap. While he was CEO he began making New Year's phone calls to the top brass of the company. At first there were six, but by 2010 there were 120 annual calls. And I remember whenever someone was promoted to general manager, I would hear Issy on the phone with smiles and mazeltovs — these calls he still makes. There are many great stories of employees who, for example, started out as a part-time bartender and 15 years later became a GM. (About the same time it takes to be a brain surgeon.) Someone should record these "upward mobility" stories.

WHENEVER I REFLECT ON Isadore's fine character, I am reminded of his mom, Lillie, the consummate Yiddish mother, who, like a mama bear, would swat her pups when they misbehaved, or smother them with crushing hugs. She lived not for herself, but for her children. She had little time for the nonsense of humour or irony. Lillie was a lady with absolutely no self-doubt, which speaks to the confidence in her four children, Edie, Bea, Issy, and Nancy — none of whom drinks much, smokes, has left a mate, or seen a shrink. Bea says they were given a lot of freedom. Questions like "where were you?" were never asked. When Issy was 18, he, Rudy Bratty, and Gerry Bender drove to California, sleeping in the car or budget motels. They stopped in Las Vegas and played the dice tables. Visited Catalina Island and the usual tourist haunts. One night they went to Tijuana to see a bull fight. Afterward while drinking in a local bar, three sailors befriended them and said, "Why not join us? We're off to a great party." So the three just-out-of-high-school innocents followed the sailors. As they were walking, it seemed to Issy that the streets were getting narrower and darker, and his canny intuition kicked in. "Quick, Rudy, these guys are going to roll us — get out that souvenir switchblade you bought today." Rudy confronted them, said something like, "Listen — don't mess with us!" and whipped out the knife. The sailors duly slinked away.

When the boys returned to Toronto three weeks later, they dropped Rudy off first, his mother welcoming him with tears of joy as did Gerry Bender's mother, "Oh Gerrila, my Gerrila," with cheers and hugs, but when Issy arrived home his mother smiled, nodded, and just carried on raking the lawn. And once when Isadore came in at breakfast time from a night of carousing, Lil just said, "Sit down, eat." Also, in the matriarchal tradition of the shtetl, where women were the breadwinners, Lil firmly believed that women were just a little brighter than men. Men were to be humoured and handled. This was a boon for Issy, who was never catered to or treated like a prince, even if he was the only son. But Lil indulged her three girls with women's lib freedoms. Edie and Bea took the train to Buffalo a few times — Bea took ballet at the Banff Centre for the Arts when she was 16, and at 19 went to Israel alone, followed by London, and even rode a bike from Paris to Versailles. When Edie brought home a boyfriend from the Catskills, Lil made up the living room couch. In my own family growing up I was not allowed even to sleep at a friend's house.

When Issy was five he had a cinder fight in the lane behind his house with a boy who called him "a dirty Jew." He ran in tears to his mom with a cut above his eye and blood on his clothes. His mom took one look, slapped him across the face, wiped off the blood, and said, "Look what you did to your shirt!" and sent him back out to play. Another time he came to her saying, "I'm late for school, and I'm afraid to go because I'll get the strap," so Lil took him to school and explained he was sorry to be late. He got the strap.

The classroom for Issy was just an interruption from his life in sports. He longed to be outdoors playing football or hockey or whatever sport was in season. With all the illusions of a nine-year-old, he resolved to be a champion pole vaulter. In the backyard his sister Bea would hold up a broom handle for an hour while he repeatedly ran across the lawn with his pole (a rake), gathering speed to leap over the broom. Such single-minded ambitions changed with the years, but not his optimism and confidence. Next he hoped to join the Marines because he worshipped older boys who offered their lives for the cause. Later, when interviewed about who were his mentors growing up, Issy cites those principled men who volunteered for the army during the war. Also the Poem "If" by Rudyard Kipling resonated with Isadore. "If you can make one heap of all your winnings/ and risk it on one turn of pitch-and-toss" (which he did on the first Four Seasons), "if you can talk with crowds and keep your virtue/ or walk with Kings — nor lose the common touch" (which Issy does every time he negotiates a deal or addresses his 40,000 employees).

Growing up, for his first business deal, he begged for a nickel so he could be partners in a balsa wood model airplane, but his mother said no; and there was the time he played hooky from Hebrew school and she dragged him off the baseball field. Finally he learned the Hebrew Torah portion he would recite from memory at his bar mitzvah. It was 1943 and the war was raging in Europe, so the rabbi wrote a patriotic speech for Issy to deliver, which apparently drew tears from the audience. His mother demanded that Max should take Issy downtown to record it (portent of later success at the microphone). Lil Sharp played the 78-shellac record so often that by the time I inherited it there were no grooves, just static. After the recording on Yonge Street, Max asked, "What would you like to do now?" Issy answered, "Let's go to a movie," and of course Max inimitably never said no so they walked down the street to the Imperial Theatre and saw *Arsenic and Old Lace* with Cary Grant. Although this day was the only time Issy remembers he spent just him and his dad, he feels he was never deprived of love.

At age 12 he needed skates to try out for the hockey team. "You'll use your sister's skates," said his dad.

"But those are white figure skates," said Issy.

"No problem, we'll dye them black," which he did but they came out a kind of blue black. So Issy made the team maybe *because* of his blue skates.

Issy remembers pushing the heavy square floor polisher (not electric), a Friday night ritual when his mother rolled her stockings in circles around her ankles, laid newspapers down on the freshly waxed floor, and then lit the Shabbat candles. At mealtime, cutlery always in a glass in the centre of the table, and Lil would slap the four kids to attention and say, "Now — eat."

The Sharp household played host to many — there was a war refugee who came to stay for a year and two Israeli cousins, Uri and Ruthie Scharf, who each spent a year at Forest Hill Collegiate Institute. And there was a wedding hosted for poor relatives. Lil later became very much a Canadian. She was a born fundraiser for causes like cancer: I remember passing the pastries at teas she would hold in her grand penthouse, and Lil was a leader in the Pioneer Women, a labour Zionist group that became a force in Jewish Toronto.

Isadore was named for Lil's father as was the son of Lillie's sister, Sarah Weinzweig. Izzy Weinzweig was a math genius who worked with Einstein and told us an awe-inspiring story at dinner one night which goes like this: In the War of Independence in 1948 Israel needed an anti-aircraft gun. One of these stood on display outside the armouries on Jarvis Street in Toronto. So Izzy W. and cohorts stole this in broad daylight, took it apart, then sent it in pieces to Israel by ship in barrels, the gun parts covered in grease so the customs officials wouldn't look too closely. Izzy then took the year off from the University of Toronto to fight in the Israeli war, jumping onto the backs of tanks, because they had no rear view, and throwing Molotov cocktails. He returned in time for the final exams and borrowed notes from a friend. When he sat for the exam, he found he had studied the wrong notes, but he got an *A* anyhow. There would have been a third Isadore Sharp in the family. This was the second son of Rose and Lazar who died as a baby. The three Godfrey sisters, Sarah, Rose, and Lil, all named a son after their father, who was named for *his* grandfather, Avraham Ytzhak Gotfried, born 1870 according to the family tree. And because two brothers married two sisters, their progeny have many genetic similarities. Rose's granddaughter, Leah Fogel, looks very much like my granddaughter Julia. They are both fair, of similar height and shape, with sisterly slim-nosed faces and blue eyes.

Later, after Issy and I were married, I would often run the one flight up from our apartment to visit Nanny Lil in the penthouse and watch her in action in the kitchen. She was large but moved gracefully. She didn't walk — she glided, like the prow of a sailing ship breasting a wave — same as she danced a smooth foxtrot. The four Sharp kids inherited her nimble coordination. They all can dance and all excel in sports. Edie was club champion of Oakdale Golf Club for 39 years and in 2015 was inducted into the Ontario Golf Hall of Fame; Bea is a good skier and tennis player; and Nancy was a cheerleader. Isadore has played every ball game available — a three-letter man at Forest Hill Collegiate Institute, and named athlete of the year at Ryerson, the only student to play all three sports. I enjoy watching him on the tennis court when he arches to deliver his shapely serve, like Shapovalov.

And in his aerobics class he didn't take a back row to the ladies. At parties he's in demand because so many husbands don't dance.

As well as athletics, he won a silver medal for scholastic proficiency at Ryerson because his English teacher had whetted his interest in academia finally and for the first time.

Oddly, unlike Lil, Max is not well coordinated but took up golf in his late 60s, played almost every day, and had a hole in one at age 90. His two companions had neither heard nor seen the ball landing because one was deaf and the other nearly blind. Once when Max was at Issy's office for his weekly visit, and had his usual coffee with Nan, Max said to Issy, "It's late and I need to go and meet the boys at the golf club."

"But Dad," said Issy, "it's pouring rain."

"Yes," said Max, then in his 90s, "but they might not be there tomorrow."

One day when Papa Max was driving the golf cart with his friend Harry, he took too sharp a turn and his friend fell out. Rubbing his shoulder, nothing was said, and Harry climbed back in. The next day Max answered the door to a police officer who handed him a summons from Harry (which he later cancelled). Harry and Max didn't speak for five years although they sat together at synagogue every week. Finally, one day as they were sitting side by side having breakfast after shul, Harry looked at Max eye to eye and said, "So how long is long?" and they shook hands.

In his 90s Max's driving became somewhat erratic. When he drove into the parking lot at the office, the staff would say, "Look out — Mr. Max is coming in for a landing." When Max and I were driving one day, I suggested a detour to avoid a busy intersection. He replied, "Di best vay to go is straight," which is a metaphor for the way he lived. I often remember those words as an imperative for good decisions. Finally, Issy's sisters called him, as usual for family problems, imploring him, "Please Issy — Get Daddy a driver," so Nan's husband, Richard Wilkins, was duly hired.

And another story. Issy's sisters Neddy and Bea called one day with a problem. "Issy, you've got to speak to Maria (she was Max's live-in care-giver). Can you believe Maria's now driving a Mercedes and her mortgage has been paid and she's dressed like Yentl at her divorce?"

"Okay," said Issy, "I'll talk to her."

When Maria and Max arrived for their weekly visit, he was dapper in a fine blue suit and matching tie and happy as a lark. While Max and Nan were having their coffee, he motioned for Maria to come into his office and closed the door. "Maria," he said, "you're doing a wonderful job, my dad's looking great, keep up the good work."

When Bea called to ask, "Did you read Maria the riot act?" Issy replied, "It went very well, not to worry, it's all been handled."

Isadore's assistant, his girl Friday, Nan Wilkins, has been with him for 41 years. Nan has become part of our family. She's coming to Isadore's 90th birthday dinner here this Friday. She has made Isadore a modern executive, preparing three-ring trip files with dividers specifying each day's programs and photos of the top staff with personal details. Previously Issy had just winged it. If you ask Nan for some data that happened 20 years ago, she will pluck it from her files, no problem. Nan, in her spare time, is a lyric soprano like Julie Andrews, once singing "Climb Ev'ry Mountain" standing at our garden pond — the sound resonating across the water, at a staff party of a hundred. Nan Mccracken Wilkins was born in Glasgow in 1936 and moved to Horwich, England, in 1941 where her mother, Betty, became the town's mayor for some years during the '80s and '90s. And Nan seems to have inherited her mother's diplomacy and work ethic.

Back in the days of our early marriage, I would sometimes watch my mother-in-law Lil in motion preparing the weekly Sabbath dinner for the family. She would stir fricassee on the stove, while deep-frying chicken wings breaded in flour heavy with garlic salt rife with MSG. She would toss noisy baking pans in and out of the oven with the deftness of a juggler, no oven mitts. Everyone would be present for Friday dinner — or else. Nanny

24

Lil cooked for 30, with one oven and no help. The menu included every-one's favourites: gefilte fish for Eddie, chicken soup for Siggy, cheesecake for Issy, and brisket and chicken and more for everybody else. Purist snob that I am, I would sniff at her ketchup-based sauces. After dinner, each of us took home boxes of leftovers that lasted halfway to the next Friday. Every box held chicken soup with added instant soup powder with more MSG, and spaghettini noodles in huge glass jars labelled "Hoover Carpet Shampoo" saved for her by the superintendent of the apartment house. Because the noodles absorbed most of the soup, the jar was white and heavy to lift out of the fridge, taking up half a shelf — "no thanks" was not an option.

Lil had taken me to the Y for a steam bath and my first massage when I was 18. She had a surprising lack of vanity, which I found admirable. Although she was overweight, she ran around in the nude with no self-consciousness while I covered my perfect young body with a towel. Lil could wash her very short frizzy hair under the kitchen faucet in seconds, and surprised me once while towelling her hair, with her comment, "It's too bad you have such straight hair." She would often speak her mind, but no one took offence because the lady bred no malice. At a Friday dinner when Issy arrived late and we were already seated, she said, "Who do you think I am — Rosalie?" I went on quietly eating my soup for a few seconds hop-ing I could disregard the comment but no, I was impelled to get up from the table and went to the den to cry. Max came in, I was surprised that he noticed, and managed to coax me back to the table and suggested maybe I should apologize to Lil? No, I didn't make this up.

Nanny Lil was the undisputed head of the family. In business and social affairs, her word reigned. When Max built two identical houses side by side, the family moved into one and put the other up for sale. Along came a buyer who preferred the house the Sharps were living in. "Done," said Lil. "You like this one better? No problem. It's yours. We'll move." And move they did — 15 times, each house farther from the Jewish ghetto and with one more bathroom, all by the build-design team of Max and Lil — he built, she decorated, and sold the house to not the highest bidder, but to the first offer. A lesson I should have learned since we sold our former house for half the price of the first offer. Once when the Sharps had sold their house and the next one not quite built, they arrived, with little notice, at Lil's sister Sarah's three-bedroom house and stayed for six months, each family six people and a dog, all sharing one bathroom. Issy was about 10 years old at the time.

Later when he was 16 and they had moved to their 15th and grandest house at 11 Manitou Boulevard, he remembers two incidents. Winters, when Max and Lil were in Florida, Issy hosted parties in the rec room above the dining room. One night while they were jitterbugging, they heard a crash from the room below. One of the 12 arms of the venetian glass chandelier had crashed onto the dining room table. "Not to worry," said Issy as they swept up the shards, "she'll never notice one arm missing."

When the Sharps returned home, Lil was heard to exclaim famously, from the open door, "Vot heppen to di chundelier?"

And when Issy hosted all night poker games and the boys descended in the morning, Lil would prepare a breakfast and say, "Sit down boys, eat."

I never heard Lil whine or waste time gossiping; she was always busy doing her job. Every morning she would administer the insulin shot for her mother's diabetes.

When Blackie, the pet cocker spaniel, gave birth in the night to six pups of various colours, Lil was there to midwife for seven hours and dock the tails. Snooky the German shepherd had a harder life. He fought with another dog and was banished by Lil to a farm near St. Catharines. The dog escaped and returned to the last duplex that Max had built, probably to avoid Lil, and sat in the driveway there, waiting for Max. Sadly, this time they gave him away to a more distant place.

Which brings to mind our oldest son Jordy's super dog Okanagan of family fame. He was better looking than Benji, so personable and popular that he was invited to sit in at the company board meetings, and someone remarked that "he was the only one who didn't say something stupid." Jordy had found him at the pound, the only dog resting his chin on his paws while all the other dogs were screaming "take me — take me!" Okanagan would relieve himself politely by backing into a bush, no clean-up required, unlike his brother Tony's dog, Sam, who presents his turds as a triumph, front and centre on the lawn. One night someone rang at midnight to say, "Your dog is sitting alone on Bloor Street." (Okanagan's tag had our phone number.)

"Thank you for calling," I said. "Would you mind putting him in a cab and sending him to this address?" Later we learned that Okanagan had been waiting obediently for Jordy in front of a restaurant.

When the dog died, Jordy sat shiva for him in the Jewish tradition and received callers at home, with photos on the coffee table, to remember and praise Okanagan. I will always remember the sweetness of that moment.

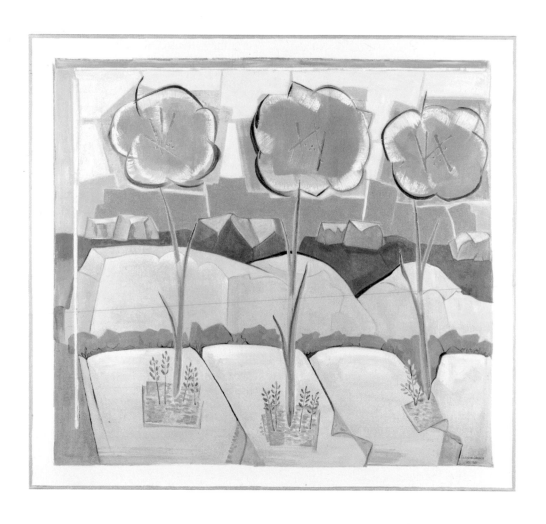

Three's a Crowd, 2010, 43" x 39".

CHAPTER TWO

Girl Meets Boy

Back when I was in high school, I remember that indelible night I met Isadore. I was almost 17. He was tall and tanned, with copper blond-streaked hair, and I was attracted to his slim body, his low voice and quiet way, the very opposite to my frenetic personality. I did most of the talking, but his words made an impact. When we danced, I felt a pull towards his body, which I still do. My diary states the next day:

> Nov. 15, '52. Dear diary, couldn't wait to get to school today to tell Merle the news. I finally found her in front of her locker. "Merle," I said, "it's happened. I'm hopelessly in love. I'm crazy about this guy I met at Pearl's wedding. I just know I'll never love anybody else and I'm sure he'll never call." Merle said, "Don't be a ninny. Of course, he'll call."

He did. And we remain best friends 69 years later, since we first met Sunday, November 15, 1952, at 8 p.m. Just a chance event because our paths would never have crossed. He was 21 and we were a dubious union. He was a poor risk because he was a Casanova who I had to share with other girls. My parents were not impressed because he wore rubber boots and was in the construction business. My father was expecting a doctor or a lawyer. In fact, at the time, I was dating a few very good candidates — Steve

Borins who became a judge, Ray Levin a doctor, and Harry Arthurs, a leading labour law scholar, who became president of York University.

Unlike my father, Issy's mom was very pleased with me. I was Jewish, and her boy loved me, and that was all she needed to know. I remember the first time Lil and I met. I came into the house and there she was, standing on the landing at the top of the curved staircase. A house dress as big as a tent flowed to the floor over her tall, more than substantial, figure. When Issy said, "Mom, this is Rosalie," she practically lifted me off the floor, clasping me to her soft bosom, and said, "Velkom to di femily."

Issy and I had a traditional dinner-dance wedding at the Club Kingsway. Soon after the wedding, the place burned down, which I took to be like breaking the champagne glass after a pledge. Five hundred guests attended, mostly invited by the Sharps — as my mom would point out often, because my dad footed the bill for everything. The Sharps paid for the flowers only, which my mom thought was stingy, even though traditionally the bride's father paid for the wedding. The truth is, I would have found it more romantic and relaxing to elope. I don't enjoy having to smile on cue and be a social success, although lately I'm quite good at it. At the wedding, however, it was so stressful, I couldn't appreciate the moment we took our vows.

Just before we were married, since he was denied the opportunity to be a war hero, Issy drifted into the business world. Under the aegis of Max Sharp and Son Construction, Issy was building a strip motel for clients. We met with Jack and Anne Gould who had just sold their small Spadina Avenue shmata (clothing) business, Townley Frocks, and were investing in a mom-and-pop 14-room motel. The plan was the typical "drive your car to the door" place, with seven rooms each side. Like the Bates Motel of *Psycho* fame, it was hard to find — not right on the highway, but near the junction of Highway 27 and the Queen Elizabeth Way. So, during construction, Issy changed Gould's life. "Jack, why not build the place twice as large, with 28 rooms instead of 14, and leave half the rooms unfinished? It won't cost much more, and that way you'll get twice as much cottage roof to display a large neon 'Motel 27' sign."

Jack, who was in his fifties took the advice of the 22-year-old Isadore, and business became so brisk that the extra 14 rooms were finished off immediately after the motel opened. Well, seeing this instant success, Isadore began to dream about building his own motel, but in a downtown location.

Now, as I write this in 2021, Issy is still chairman of Four Seasons Hotels and Resorts, which manages 126 hotels, 57 residences, and employs 40,000 people around the globe. Issy, in his earnest, evangelical style, still preaches to his employees his mantra of "The Golden Rule" since he first incorporated it in his mission statement of 1967. Isadore has always been a dreamer, even now. He skipped skepticism and avoided "let's be sensible." People called him naïve — they still do. But naïveté and trust in people have served him well. Trust and integrity have been the foundation of the company. He was an unusual leader with no notions of the prescribed MBA tenets of how to run a business. He made a lot of brash decisions against the trends and the pundits, trusting in his own intuitions. Isadore has a zealous belief that ethics is the religion that unites and motivates his people. "The only thing you can control," he says, "is your attitude." He has great confidence in his beliefs. Bucking the naysayers can be lonely, but from his parents he learned how to accept responsibility. Over the years I've had the pleasure of watching his mind work. In bed, at first light, I sometimes find him with arms crossed behind his head, gazing at the ceiling, weighing possibilities. Business books credit him with "a talent for innovation" and "the mind of an integrative thinker." Roger Martin applauds Issy's capacity for "holding two opposing ideas" while simultaneously producing "a synthesis that is superior to either . . . idea." I almost get this concept.

An early example of Isadore's integrative thinking is borne out in a story of one of his first jobs for Max Sharp and Son Construction. They had an option on a city block off Brimley Road to build nine bungalows for sale, but they needed to borrow the money. Straight from the job, still wearing his "building" clothes, Issy went to speak to Ted Hemmons, the manager at the Toronto Dominion Bank at Bathurst and Eglinton. Ted listened to the request for financing and said, "What equity will you put up for this loan?"

"Well, Mr. Hemmons, the value of the land we have under option has gone up in value which should serve as our equity."

Apparently, Mr. Hemmons was very impressed with Issy's "integrative" approach and said, "Isadore, you should take off those rubber boots and move into high finance."

Which he did so successfully. He credits many of his successes to his aptitude for solutions that appear magically and just when needed.

Here's Isadore himself to tell his tale:

So much of long-term success is based on intangibles.

Beliefs and ideas. Invisible concepts. People often ask me about my original vision for Four Seasons. Well, the truth is that there was no vision or grand scheme.

In 1961, when I built my first hotel, I knew nothing about the hotel business. My only professional experience was in building apartments and houses. I was just a builder, and the hotel was just another real estate deal. I never thought this was going to be a career, nor did I ever imagine I would one day find myself building and managing the largest and most prestigious group of five-star hotels in the world.

I approached the business of innkeeping from a customer's perspective. I was the host, and the customers were my house guests. I decided what to build and how to operate by asking myself: What would the customers consider important? What will the customers recognize as value? Because if we give them good value, they will unhesitatingly pay what they think it's worth. That was the first strategy, and it continues to this day.

The company evolved slowly at first, and I'll admit I made a few mistakes along the way. But I never made the mistake of putting profit ahead of people, and I believe part of Four Seasons' worldwide acclaim is built primarily on the strong relationships I've built over the years with owners, partners, and board members who shared my standards, and with the thousands of employees, managers, and executives who helped make the company such a success.

Looking back over the last 60 years, I've identified the four key strategic decisions that formed the rock-solid foundation of Four Seasons:

FIRST: "We will only operate medium-sized hotels of exceptional quality with an objective to be the best."
SECOND: "True luxury will be defined not by architecture or décor, but by service. So we must make the quality of our service our distinguishing feature and a competitive advantage."
THIRD: "We will create a work ethic based on the Golden Rule to give our people a framework to pursue a superior service culture."
FOURTH: "We will grow as a management company and build a brand name synonymous with quality."

These are now known as the four pillars of our business model.

Over the years, we've initiated many new ideas that have been copied and are now the norm in the industry. But the one idea that our customers value the most cannot be copied: the consistent quality of our exceptional service. That service is based on a corporate culture, and a culture cannot be mandated as a policy. It must grow from within, based on the actions of the company's people over a long period of time.

Four Seasons is the sum of its people — many, many good people.

IN THIS, THE YEAR of the pandemic, Issy has been rooting around in his past to understand his success. Why did he never have a fear of failure? What were the way posts? Recently Issy's high school friend Herb Noble came to dinner bringing a binder full of items describing why Isadore was the most popular kid at school. This was a shock to Issy, who has never had, he says, any "ego." Why was it that the principal of Forest Hill Collegiate Institute asked *him* to be the spokesperson to garner student support for an indoor skating rink? And the day my father locked me out, Issy instinctively acted responsibly by speaking to him immediately and making such a winning case, maybe because his parents taught him to do what needed to be done, as soon as possible. Issy credits this visit to my father as another of the landmarks for his success that he's just dug up from his youth.

It took five years of begging, borrowing, and debating, to produce the first hotel, which happened only because of Issy's persuasive charisma, which to him is a mystery he's trying to figure out now that there is a lull. Perhaps it's his self-confidence just short of loftiness rather like Lil Sharp, or maybe it's the low-key appeal that makes him so likeable. Sometimes while we were driving around the city, instead of paying attention to the road, he would be craning his neck out the car window, looking for possible sites. Now he had two jobs: building apartment towers all day, and at night sitting at a typewriter in our spare room with one finger pecking out proposals for hotels on various sites he had on hold. These three-page prospectuses would then be packaged in a colourful cardboard folder, and the next hurdle was to find investors. So Issy would park himself regularly on the doorstep of Cecil Forsythe, of Great-West Life Insurance, and pester him for money. After three years of proposals, Forsythe — who of course had taken a liking to Issy — finally caved in and pledged half the financing. With the promise from the trades to hold off on their pay, and with $90,000 each from Issy and two partners — his brother-in-law Eddie Creed and a friend, Murray Koffler. Another friend, Wally Cohen, to his everlasting regret failed to invest.

Isadore was up at 6 a.m. and on the job. He would help his construction workers with menial jobs, and I remember him walking along planks in the air with no safety net. There was a camaraderie between him and the merry band of Italian and Polish workers who called him "Mister Issy" and appreciated his fairmindedness. One of his workmen, Ciro Rappachietti, recounts that God sent him to Mister Issy because he got off the bus at the construction site of 2515 Bathurst Street when he noticed men were still working in the rain and not only was he hired but became an overseer. Isadore, the construction boss, was so handsomely athletic and dapper even in his work clothes. His arms were tanned below rolled-up shirt sleeves, and his body was hard from the physical work he enjoyed. His lean torso rivalled Michelangelo's statue of David and, I blush to say, still does. How did I end up with a guy in construction wearing rubber boots when my other boyfriends had been lawyerish shirt-and-tie types? Not to mention that Issy modelled clothes for Simpsons department store every Saturday when he was the "Simpsons rep," the photo with this title on the inside cover of the school magazine. The Toronto radio station CKEY interviewed him at the time, and the announcer afterwards said: "Isadore, you have the right voice and delivery for radio — you should consider a career on the air." And at age 90 he still has the deep resonant voice and the power to keep an audience in his thrall.

The Four Seasons Motor Hotel on Jarvis Street was born, opening March 21, 1961, with little fanfare. Not likely a good location because Jarvis Street was the centre of the red-light district. But later it was to develop that at any location where there was a Four Seasons Hotel, the surrounding real estate tripled in value, so the hookers moved to another street. I could have made my fortune by buying the next-door piece of land in 40 countries. The Jarvis Street hotel became the hangout for the literati from the CBC-TV early headquarters across the street, and soon was the place to be seen because it was modern and fresh unlike the ancient monster hotels like the Royal York and the King Edward. Thanks to Issy's vision, probably influenced by his mother planting all the gardens around their real estate, the building surrounded a garden courtyard with pool and café so sheltered that guests might imagine they were swimming in the tropics.

One day a tall willowy girl with long blond Lady Godiva hair walked through the lobby and out the doors to the courtyard, shedding her clothes as she strolled to the swimming pool and dove in naked. She swam the length of the pool and back, picked up her clothes, and walked out and across the road to the CBC building, still naked. The next day the press noted the incident titled "the Naked and the Fled."

The second hotel, the Inn on the Park, was conceived in 1961. On a summer's day we drove up to the corner of Eglinton Avenue and Leslie Street in Toronto, to a hilly meadow of tall grass. "Here," said Issy, "is the site for the second hotel. What do you think?"

There was not another building in sight, trucks were turning in to a municipal garbage dump across the road, and just then a CPR freight train roared by the property. I thought, "What can he be thinking? Real hotels are always downtown, usually handy to the railway station, and have regal names like Royal York, King Edward, and Prince George."

At the time, there were no rural hotels other than beer halls like the Jolly Miller, and I could not imagine why any hotel guest would choose to sleep in suburbia. I remember the disquieting thought that if this new venture failed, we might have to sell the house and move to a three-room flat — in fact, our house was the collateral for the loan. But I kept my fears to myself. In this case, as usual, his suburban hotel was a roaring success. It's amazing how many times he has been right, even up to the present.

The Inn on the Park had Issy's same garden concept but on a huge scale. The courtyard was about 300 feet long with two swimming pools, a wooden bridge over a duck pond, mature trees bordering a wide meandering path that encircled the courtyard. This walkway became a skater's road in winter. The complex included a tennis court, gym, and three restaurants. The Inn on the Park became such a smashing success that Americans came there for long-weekend vacations. I remember there was often a row of orange Detroit licence plates in the lot. Our family of six would go on a Sunday, change into our swimsuits in Issy's office instead of a guestroom, and spread a towel on the grass to leave the chaise lounges for the guests.

One night at the Inn on the Park there was an incident following an Italian wedding in the Trillium banquet room. At the door stood a seven-foot 900-pound art nouveau bronze statue, *Bellona, the Goddess of War* by Jean-Léon Gérôme. When she was displayed in 1893 at the entrance to his Paris exhibition, it caused a sensation. Her ivory teeth were bared in a scream, her jade eyes wide in terror, a giant cobra in silvered bronze wound about her body. Issy had acquired her for a song when she didn't sell at an auction in the ballroom. The morning after the wedding — behold, *Bellona* was missing her head, so sadly, her body was moved by four men to a storeroom. Flash forward three months to New York when I'm taking my usual stroll down Madison Avenue past a shop, the Volpe Gallery (which turned out to be Tod Volpe's family), and I stop dead in my tracks. The head of *Bellona* on a base is centred in the window. I went in and asked the price and must have said something suspect and they said, "Sorry, it's not for sale." Tod Volpe later served 28 months in jail, having scammed some high-powered clients like Jack Nicholson and Barbra Streisand. So one wonders about the wedding. The body of *Bellona* is now in the Art Gallery of Hamilton in Southern Ontario. Isadore had finally, after much coaxing, sold the headless body to Joey Tanenbaum who had a new head made up, rather different than the original, and donated *Bellona* to the museum. The night detectives have many such movie-making tales to tell of the goings-on at our hotels.

THE THIRD HOTEL, IN London, England, was the beginning of the big time.

It's always been something of a mystery to Issy that he was so trusted and respected by strangers like Sir Gerald Glover and the McAlpine family during the acquisition of the London Hotel. Issy had no wherewithal, just his personality. He travelled back and forth across the ocean for four years until he convinced the McAlpines to give him that deal. Because he sold them on his plan to convert their proposed 320-room hotel to 230 while paying them the same rent, they called him "the crazy Canadian." Bucking the naysayers is a lonely responsibility that Isadore often experienced as a CEO. On his fifth trip over Sir Gerald asked: "My dear boy, would you come over for lunch to meet the Duke of Westminster and the McAlpine board?" So Issy took the red eye yet again, and in his jet-lagged condition submitted to the friendly interrogation of the grandiose Brits. Their upper crust jargon would have been clearer, says Issy, if only they had subtitles across their chests. Questions about Canadian politics were challenging, but he passed the test as Sir Gerald later said, "My dear boy, I knew you would do well, and please bring your wife over next trip."

Well, with the deal still unconfirmed after four years, we both came and visited with Gerald and Sue who by now had become friends, having visited Toronto. We had a lunch at their country estate, Pytchley, the typical patrician mansion overlooking the commoners in the nearby village valley. Issy asked Glover, while standing in the garden overlooking a vast velvet lawn sloping down to a curved dark umber stream, cut as if with a knife into the green of the hill, "How, Sir, do you keep the lawn so perfect?"

"No trouble at all my dear boy, you merely cut it every week for three hundred years."

I admired Lady Sue Glover, who ran a home for unwed mothers and then placed the babies in good homes. Amazingly for me, who can't ride a horse, I watched her canter away side-saddle into the distance on a black horse.

This reminds me of a story about Issy and a white horse. It was at dusk after a few glasses of wine at a friend's farm. Five of us were standing at a split rail fence admiring a group of grazing horses. Someone said, "Is, I bet you can't ride that white one bareback." Of course, he immediately straddled the fence and climbed on. Off they went but the horse was not pleased and decided to gallop off to the barn. "Oh no." The upper half of the barn door was closed. I covered my eyes in fright, but through my fingers, I saw the most incredible sight. While the horse was in full gallop, and just before he reached the barn door, Issy swung his leg over and jumped off the horse and remained standing, a vision which I never forget.

But back to the Glovers. Later that day, we visited their London townhouse off Park Lane where we faced a three-fork dinner and wondered about the extra spoon. When the dessert of gooseberry tart and clotted cream arrived, I watched, while I used my fork, the other guests used a spoon as well, which I quickly picked up. Ever since that moment, Issy always insists on both spoon and fork as if "to the manner born." After dinner when cigars were passed in the drawing room, Issy said, "No thank you," but when the waiter offered me one, I said, "Yes, thank you" and held it aloft until he came round with the lighter to which I said as I put the cigar in my purse, "I'll keep it for later" as the crowd burst out laughing. Issy told me afterwards he wondered jokingly whether the "yes" cigar meant a no-cigar deal.

Finally, the deal was done somehow, and the hotel was readied for the big opening party with the royal guests of honour, Princess Alexandra and Sir Angus Ogilvy, who I was seated beside at dinner. From then on, because of Issy's stature, I always draw the most important man in the room as dinner companion, including Pavarotti, Abba Eban, and Prince Alwaleed of Saudi Arabia. I'm told I'm good at this job, although in truth I'm a closet loner. I've enjoyed this year of solitude during the pandemic — so few demands for wit and charm and social responsibility, although when it's required, I do my duty happily.

THE LONDON HOTEL WAS to serve as the poster child for all future properties. Medium-sized, superb service, best hotel in town, which the hotel achieved when that first year, 1970, it was named "best hotel in Europe." And this London project was a turning point for Isadore. Before this he had continued building apartment houses, but this was the moment he knew he would focus on the hotel business only.

Several years after the hotel was opened, Issy asked Sir Gerald, "How could you have trusted me with such an important project when you knew if it failed, I couldn't have covered the costs?"

"My dear boy," he answered, "over time you make a judgement about people. You develop a belief and a trust." A dictum which Issy has incorporated since that time.

Over the years of building hotels, Isadore still heads up the design and construction wing of Four Seasons. He has a designer's eye, and most hotel plans have been modified by his vision. No architectural plans go by without his approval, and he has a knack for making consequential last-minute changes. Shortly before the London hotel opened Issy noticed that the huge window of the lobby's grand staircase had a dark steel spandrel across the centre. Since it was not structural, he had it removed. In 1978, we took over a Toronto Hyatt hotel with 600 rooms, which Isadore reduced to 460. I remember the new rooms were mini suites decorated in three colour schemes by Rosalie Wise Design Inc. Yes, me!

Then there was the case of the Chicago hotel, slated to be a 600-room Marriott when Four Seasons took over the project. Issy to the rescue, who again reduced the number of rooms to 340 and, this was his significant change, closed off the main lobby, so it no longer opened to the atrium of the Bloomingdale mall.

In 1981, there came the coup for Four Seasons to hit New York, by acquiring the Pierre Hotel. Issy had his hands full making that deal. There were 200 rooms and 75 co-op apartment residents, who owned the hotel.

The apartment owners' names read like a who's who of New York. We visited a few and their impressionist paintings were probably worth more than the building. The Pierre, built in 1930 by Charles Pierre and friends, was a 41-storey blond brick and stone tower. Issy and I were once out on the 40th floor balcony just below the steep slant of the 30-foot green copper mansard roof, à la Versailles. Fringed along the roof were carved stone vases and lintels like a wedding cake, and we had a view clear across Central Park. The most prestigious ballroom in town played host to high society weddings and debutante balls. When a client requested a roast chicken menu for a bar mitzvah, the catering manager Herb Rose replied, "Madame — we don't do chicken."

Isadore negotiated for the classy hotel contract with three upper crust members of the board: Serge Semenenko, Arthur Bienenstock, and Matthew Rosenhouse. One night at home with our boys Issy explained that finally we're about to have a deal in New York, the most important city for a hotel company.

"But Dad," they said, "how do you know for sure?"

"Well, the only thing that can go wrong now is that the board members who are about to sign the deal will suddenly die."

Incredibly, the following week Semenenko and Rosenhouse died. So Isadore had to start over convincing Bienenstock and now Joe Mailman to hire us. He offered them a scheme to reduce carrying charges that would create a tax benefit.

"Sounds okay," said Mailman, "but we'd like you yourself to be here every week."

"Mr. Mailman, if *I* need to be here every week, then the Four Seasons is not for you, but I *will* be here whenever needed."

"I like your answer," he replied, and the deal was done.

Whenever Issy flew to New York, I always went along to walk the Madison Avenue shops, hit the museums, and do the de rigueur staff dinners and Issy's talks. I mingled with the famous residents. I missed

Elizabeth Taylor — once saw Audrey Hepburn in the restaurant, scarily thin like an anorexic. And we visited with Dorothy Rodgers in her apartment (Richard had just died). There stood the white grand piano where I imagined Richard Rodgers just sat down after dinner one night and rattled off "The March of the Siamese Children" from *The King and I*. Yves St. Laurent had a penthouse apartment, and I asked the concierge for a tour while Yves was away. Then to my everlasting regret I decided it was too snoopy.

After the Pierre, there came the new opportunities for resort hotels, which I thought might not work as well because they are seasonal. Issy and I and Roger Garland, executive vice president of development, went to the Caribbean Island of Nevis to look over the opportunity. From Anguilla we took a four-seater plane that landed on a rough airstrip and taxied up to the one-room customs house. Roger and I were enthused as the three of us trudged along the sandy beach bordered by acacias, and while the meeting with owners went on, I walked the mile to town and had tea and a danish on the upstairs verandah of the coffee shop overlooking the town square and the constabulary headquarters with the white-uniformed police, sporting their helmets and gold epaulets. I walked through the small park which was the old Jewish burial ground. (Sadly, the tales of the banished therefore wandering Jews is true. I always seek out the Jewish cemetery wherever we travel — even Nagasaki.)

Isadore says that my enthusiasm for Nevis influenced his decision. The spread-out cottaged resort opened to rave reviews, was voted best hotel in the Caribbean and became the poster child for future resorts because we discovered that people with no experience can become leaders given the opportunity. John Stauss, the hotel manager, trained 500 locals who had never worked in a hotel. To quote John, "You need patience and understanding." He would send the waitresses home with a sample double-forked cutlery layout to practise, and he would encourage them to ask again if they didn't understand at first. Issy said he learned from John that we could open a hotel in any remote location because people everywhere, with the right attitude, can become successful.

THEN THERE WAS THE Maui hotel, which we built the same time as Nevis, which stood on a steep hill that backed onto the sea. The drawings showed the entrance on the main road at the top. "Why not," said Issy, "put in a driveway that curves down to the sea with the hotel entrance facing the water?"

"Not possible," said the architect, "it's volcanic rock."

"Good," said Issy and then the hill was duly blasted, and the dramatic reversal was done. The Four Seasons Maui continues to be the most successful hotel on the island.

Our owner in Hawaii, Takeshi Sekiguchi, was our entrée into the Japanese market, which then, in the 1980s was having its biggest boom. We met with many Japanese bigwigs about a huge five-star hotel opportunity in Chinzanso, flying there at least four times for interminable and mostly fruitless meetings. Then in 1987, Sekiguchi arranged a lunch with the most influential businessman in Japan, Kisaburo Ikeura, chairman of the Industrial Bank of Japan. Pleasantries were exchanged, through an interpreter, Ikeura waxed on about the local history of feuding warlords and that when the warring shoguns left their fortresses to fight rivals, they would exchange wives as hostages to ensure their own safe return.

After lunch Mr. Ikeura said, "Well, Isadore, next time I would like to meet your wife." Issy had probably been extolling my virtues as was his usual habit.

"I certainly will bring Rosalie, with one condition: as long as you promise not to hold her hostage."

There was a quiet moment while the interpreter explained. Suddenly, he burst into laughter, jumped up, grabbed Issy's hands and said, "Business, business, yes we will do much business you and me together."

And they did. With the bank chairman's stamp of approval, we were off, no more questions asked. Fast forward to the hotel in Chinzanso, on the outskirts of Tokyo, fronting an ancient 17-acre park. A Prince, Yamagata Aritomo, had built his palace there in 1877 and named it Chinzanso (house of camellias). Later a thousand-year-old pagoda was transferred to the garden from the Hiroshima Mountains and then a shrine from Kyoto. We saw the featured 500-year-old tree that measures 4.5 metres around its base. The proposed hotel overlooking this garden was to have 500 rooms which Isadore inimitably changed to 296 (as he had previously done in London, Toronto, and ten other hotels). He also added more space for banquets because the main business was weddings, three or four a day. I remember the window of a local photographer's studio with portraits of brides, half wearing traditional Japanese brocade robes, hair piled high in the ancient manner, and others in white Western dress with train, standing in front of the shrine or a camellia tree. The Japanese venerate flowers and foods in a way we can't comprehend. Once, I remember the price of a melon in a restaurant was $500. The food revenue in Japanese hotels is 70 percent, the rooms 30 percent, while in Western hotels the percentage is the reverse.

THE MOST ASTONISHING BUSINESS episode started with a chance event. Isadore was having a sauna at the gym at the Inn on the Park. He seldom had a sauna after a workout. In the gloom, he noticed an old *Time* magazine on the bench with a wrinkled cover photo of Harold Geneen, who at the time was America's foremost business guru, the head of ITT. The write-up mentioned that Geneen was looking to enter the hotel business by buying the Sheraton Hotel Company. It so happened that Issy had made a bid in the competition to build a hotel across from the new city hall on Queen Street. He didn't have the financing, but he had the support for his presentation from David Owen, among others. David was the man heading up the huge development of the Eaton Centre across the road, and he had clearly stated on the news that the project was untenable without taking down the Old City Hall. Well, it so happened that I was a member of the Toronto Architectural Conservancy group, and we campaigned for keeping the Old City Hall built by E.J. Lennox in the 1880s. Issy remembers that during his presentation for the hotel the TV was on and David said, "Issy isn't that your wife, the lady in the big hat, marching in the protest and carrying the placard 'Save the Old City Hall?'" It was so typical of Issy to let me be. Meanwhile Issy, Cecil Forsythe, Owen, and potential investors viewed the model of the massive hotel John B. Parker had designed for the site. They all declined to invest, and Cecil told Issy afterwards, "Forget it, Issy, you're out of your league on this one."

But now after the sauna, Issy called ITT, spoke to one of Geneen's minions, and persuaded him that here was a good opportunity to build a flagship hotel in Toronto. Next, he heard "Come down and we'll talk." So he flew to the huge intimidating ITT office building in New York. Slowly Issy pitched his idea to higher-and-higher-ups resulting in the next step — flying to Boston to tell the tale to the Sheraton bosses. Then 10 of the ITT people flew to Toronto in their private jet to view the two hotels in town. It was a summer day, and both hotels were flooded with guests in the garden courtyards. The Inn on the Park was a Norman Rockwell panorama — a lineup at the diving pool, the tennis court in play, the garden café serving chocolate sundaes to bikini-clad ladies by the pool, dogs on parade across the bridge by the duck pond — and at the downtown hotel, famous TV types interviewed by Elwood Glover who had a daily *Luncheon Date* program in the lobby bar, where celebrities smoked their Pall Malls overlooking the rose garden.

When ITT called to discuss a deal, Issy went down with his lawyer, Paul Henry, to face a dozen daunting lawyers and Harvard MBAs. Immediately they suggested he step out of the deal and settle for a payout of $2 million

45

because a $100 million building was out of his league, and as usual he had no money to put in. Issy made the case of why he deserved to be a 50 percent partner, and somehow he succeeded. After long negotiations with the forbidding group, it was finally agreed that we would invest $3.5 million, borrowed from the Bank of Nova Scotia. ITT would own 51 percent and our company 49 percent. Sheraton would run the 1,600 room hotel, but Isadore would have the top billing he wanted: "the Four Seasons Sheraton." As well, they offered him a big paying job at Sheraton, but Isadore was never about money. He's never been driven by opportunism or the best bottom line. Profit has always followed. His goals from the beginning have never changed. Always he was out to run a respected business, to share the wealth, and to boast the happiest employees.

Taking gambles was his game. And at the same time as this ITT foray, he was making those tiring crossings to London to make *that* deal. Not to mention getting up at 6 a.m. for his day job building the still respected Avoca condominiums, in those days known as cooperative apartments.

Where did he get all that energy and purpose? And why did he make such a good impression? He's still looking through the past to connect the genes or reflect on the forces, especially during this year of solitude when he's been peeling away the layers of his life from the 1930s until now. Isadore credits his parents with honing, not suppressing his skills. "My three sisters and I had the precious privilege of parents who taught us to be fair and principled. I inherited my father's low-key personality and like-ableness. I had my mother's lack of vanity and her brutal self-confidence. Like her I had the conviction to persevere with an unwavering belief in my own ideas with never a thought of failing, like Wallenda the high wire artist who performed with no net. So analyzing myself over this year has been revelatory, since I've never been to a psychiatrist. Perhaps Rosalie found me appealing for some of these traits the first night we met 69 years ago."

In the 1980s, although Issy's business was booming, he didn't bother buying a fancy car or other rich trappings. He has always had a unique attitude towards money. He seems not to notice it. There are no restrictions. He always says yes to anything I'd like to buy and warns me not to be the underbidder on the piece of china I'm after.

So that is the history of the first three hotels — blood, sweat, and tears. However, the next 127 hotels were easier and the challenges smaller. As our renown increased, so did many new opportunities. But then there was the matter of the seventh hotel in Vancouver. The business deal we had signed with three partners, Toronto Dominion Bank, Cadillac Fairview, and Eaton's, became untenable that year of 1974 when building costs escalated three times and we were liable for the extra money. On a handshake promise to restructure the deal, Issy continued to spend money he didn't have. Fortunately, they kept their word, so we didn't go bankrupt.

That was the landmark moment when Isadore changed the company's business model from ownership of real estate to a management company. Since 1974 Four Seasons has been recession-proof — even pandemic-proof.

Me and Issy, 2021, 54" x 60".

CHAPTER THREE

Paths across the Sky

If you ask Isadore what achievements he is most proud of, he will mention three.

Of course, the first is founding a company that is considered the foremost luxury brand globally.

Then he is pleased that his 40,000 employees around the world have a better life.

And the third is the Terry Fox Run he founded in 1978 just after our son Chris died.

Young Terry Fox lost a leg to cancer and pledged to run across Canada to raise funds to find a cure.

Here's Isadore at a typical Terry Fox rally at home office:

In 1980, we, as others, were in awe of Terry's inconceivable and unimaginable commitment to run across Canada to raise $1.00 from every Canadian for cancer research. So, I had a young lady, Bev Norris, who was working in our marketing department, keep tabs on his progress.

After a few weeks she reported back that it was not going well. People just didn't believe him, saying that it was some advertising stunt, a gimmick, and mocking him.

So, we decided to help. We committed $10,000, put ads in the newspapers inviting 999 other companies to join us, to make it a $10 million run.

Well, when Terry heard about it he called me. No cell phones then — a pay phone on his way. And with an emotional and breaking voice, said that he was ready to throw in the towel, but if we believed in him, he would fight on. And he did, and then things changed.

That was the first time I spoke to Terry.

And when he got to Toronto, we held a luncheon where he spoke to more than 400 business leaders.

My mistake was in not taping that speech. He spoke from the heart, no notes, dressed in a T-shirt and shorts. And the room was so quiet and intent while he spoke that you could hear the click of a paper clip that Terry was flicking as he spoke.

We met afterwards. And when I suggested that he should be organizing and preparing for Vancouver now because this was going to be a world event, he refused, saying he didn't want to think of that right now. And I thought then that he knew he wasn't going to make it, but that he would run until he couldn't. And he did, sacrificing himself to help others.

And when he had to stop, I sent him a telegram saying, "You started it. We will not rest until your dream to find a cure for cancer is realized."

Terry ran 26 miles a day for 143 days, covering 3,339 miles, and seeing the effort it took for each step and a hop makes it all the more remarkable. Doctors and scientists would say that's impossible. The human body can't stand up to that stress.

But he did it because I believe Terry had a unique strength for a higher calling. A higher calling for a meaningful purpose, because Terry became a symbol of hope and leadership.

Hope for others like him. Hope versus despair over a debilitating disease. And as a leader for others to open their hearts and minds to help others, as he did.

And that is what has happened. Tens of thousands of people in more than 50 countries wherever there's a Four Seasons, coming together each year to help others. And as we look ahead, Terry's legacy will continue, because Terry represents everything we admire: hope, optimism, an indomitable spirit, and the courage to dream of the possibilities. A young man who set out on an improbable journey and paid the ultimate price. But, as he once said, "I believe in miracles." And what he did was truly miraculous. And Terry did complete his mission.

He is like that shooting star that we sometimes see in the darkest of nights for a short time, but it continues forever. To date $750 million has been raised for cancer research.

And that is his legacy that you all honour by continuing to help others.

Thank you, and we look forward to another successful run on September 15.

Every mid-September we held the run at Wilket Creek Park, where our family and hundreds of others would share hope for cancer cures and the Four Seasons Hotel provided hotdogs and ice cream while recovered cancer patients told their stories while a band played on. As Betty Fox once said on TV, "Were it not for Isadore Sharp, there would not be a Terry Fox Run."

And Issy made it all happen with his usual unflagging belief, just as he's done in business.

WITH THE BURGEONING OF the hotel company, our lives changed, and we went from vacationing every five years to jet-setting every other month to visit Four Seasons Hotels around the world. We criss-crossed time zones where it was day for night, or the tropics for winter, and the mystical became commonplace. I'm good with the tedium and delays of overnight flights — I just open one of my stock of books or eat a piece of dark chocolate to enhance my mood. As for jet lag, I simply don't bother with it.

Travelling to the hotels was indeed exotic and strange. I went from speaking

Yiddish with my parents to struggling with pleasantries in Urdu, Arabic, and Japanese, and to the challenges of uncooked or unknown foreign foods. We ate cross-legged in our socks on a floor in Kyoto and dined on silk cushions in the company of camels in the desert near Riyadh. While the camel looked on, I was offered a cup of her warm milk. I pressed it to my lips and pretended to sip, then passed the milk to Issy. In the Tokyo fish market, we were served huge chunks of raw fish — beer and sushi at 7 a.m. Issy feigned difficulty handling his chopsticks and couldn't quite get a grip on the slippery fish. At Japanese business dinners we were always seated with the higher-ups, in the centre of a long banquet table, with everyone else descended from there so the least important people sat in the end chairs. Now when we entertain at home, we always sit in the centre rather than at the ends. We have hosted a hundred business dinners with Issy holding court, charming potential owners. Typically, he will call for everyone around the table to tell us a story about themselves, and I remember a banker who once recounted: "The sheep lived on the first floor of our house in the village." We have hosted sheiks and Persian princes and Russian oligarchs and heard fascinating "growing up" tales. Sometimes the day after one of these convivial dinners the principals will sign on the dotted line. And no need for me to satisfy my travel yen for the strange lands of my fantasies, when interesting foreigners are available at our dinner table. I simply dress and arrive from my bedroom to the dining room.

Abroad, I took to consorting with kings and princes as easily as with the grocer and mail carrier at home. It doesn't come naturally to me, but I make a good show of it. Issy and I enjoy the company of the Saudi Prince Alwaleed, a major investor in Four Seasons. The prince has brought Saudi Arabia into the modern banking world and made the Saudis an international player. He's a good-hearted young man, generous and forward-thinking, especially about women's rights — his pilot is a woman. He would probably speak out more strongly against civil disabilities in Arabia if it was safe and practical to do so. We met once when he and Issy were skiing in Jackson Hole. Isadore was seated next to Alwaleed, then my chair, then the other 12 of his retinue. The prince remarked, "Isn't it a small world. I'm meeting next week with Bill Gates and Warren Buffett."

I piped up, "Well yes, your highness, it *is* a small world, at the top."

This tickled his fancy and he roared with laughter and repeated it to anyone who would listen. We are often guests in his palace and his retreat outside Riyadh. He lives in an opulence rarely found in the West. Another of my favourite owners is Beni Sung Ong, a Malaysian Singaporean power broker who lives in a modern mansion on a high hill looking out the back picture window to the valley below, there is a house to the left and another to the right for his son and daughter and their families. I envy this cultural custom. BS Ong and I are kindred spirits according to Issy, and I enjoy BS's easy embrace and appreciation for the family of man. He owns 11 Four Seasons Hotels with three under construction and has been Issy's friend and supporter for 40 years. With his ready enthusiasm he always addresses me "Rosalie! Rosalie!" Together we like to hunt through foreign street fairs, and he always asks after our boys by name.

Now we finally have a state-of-the-art hotel in the tony Yorkville area of our hometown, Toronto, with 250 condominiums and 210 rooms. (A far cry from the first Four Seasons Motor Hotel on red-light Jarvis Street.) Today, as we drive down Mount Pleasant Road and come up the deep dip towards downtown, the latest iconic Four Seasons Hotel looms above us, the highest point in the city skyline. Shahid Khan, the owner, is a fascinating man and always has a twinkle of humour in his eye as if he owns some secret amusement. When he was 16, he arrived alone from Pakistan to Chicago in a blinding snowstorm (he had never seen snow) and his canvas shoes fell apart. After sleeping at the Y, he immediately found a job washing dishes for $1.20 an hour. This, he describes, as the American dream. He graduated from university in mechanical engineering and then was hired to sell auto parts at Flex-N-Gate. Later he bought the company and, in his engineering brilliance, invented a one-piece bumper now made in 69 plants in eight countries with 27,000 employees. Also, Khan owns, among other teams, the NFL Jacksonville Jaguars.

In the summer of 1989, magazine maven Malcolm Forbes invited us to Tangiers for his weekend birthday celebration. Malcolm flew us all there in two 727s. I was the only nobody in a lustrous crowd that included Walter Cronkite, Barbara Walters, and Henry and Nancy Kissinger. Elizabeth Taylor, wearing a roomy tent-like dress, was his hostess.

And I love our hotel openings in foreign places because I don't know anyone there, and I can move around unknown and watch the parade of moguls and their mates, all dressed in their best costumes. I can even audit their conversations — it's easier than making small talk.

On these many trips, I derive much naches (joy) from watching my husband in action, making speeches which embody the hallmarks of his personality: his grace, humility, appreciation, inclusiveness, understatement, and especially his naïveté, which has served him so well. And yesterday my friend Stephen Brown added, "The way Issy listens, he looks at you straight with an unflinching eye and listens with such a rapt attention."

I watch Isadore structure financial deals — he could write the book on negotiating. As he says, "You have to address the needs of the other guy." He has a remarkable facility for coming up with just what is needed, and on cue. He says that when he loses this timing he'll quit. He always keeps his cool — not me. Any small thing can drive me up the wall. Nothing drives Issy to distraction. And did I mention that he never takes no for an answer?

While negotiating the contract for the Las Vegas hotel with Clyde Turner, CEO of Circus Circus, among a roomful of owners and lawyers, there was an impasse of about one point. Four Seasons' typical contract fees for technical services was $500,000. Clyde said, "Sorry Issy, we'll give you $50K because *we* can do that job and we don't need you."

"But Clyde," Issy answered, "this is a standard clause in all our hotel agreements, so I must insist, but let's leave it and go on with the rest of the contract."

At the end of the meeting, Isadore remarked, "Back to that one point of disagreement, Clyde it's $500,000 or $50,000, it's your call."

"You son of a bitch," said Turner, laughing. "Okay, it's $500,000."

Isadore is imperturbable. His charisma derives from his dad, his uncle Max Godfrey, and his mom, Lil Godfrey Sharp — he is a benevolent governor with his father's gentle nature and respect for all others regardless of their station.

Which reminds me of an anecdote illustrating Issy's persuasive charm. I hired a couple, Thelma and Henry, as housekeepers ostensibly because she was ecstatic when she saw the flat that they would live in over the garage. But as it turned out they were not for us. I needed to fire them, so I sent Issy to do the job. He talked to them for a *long* time and later when Thelma came in with the dinner, she was as happy as if Issy had given her a promotion. Another time at a business crisis Issy's VP said it looked hopeless. "Issy, go in and work your magic," he told him, and as usual our Issy wins again.

And he never fails to win the respect of any crowd. Isadore has no enemies. There was Captain Nair's board meeting in India. Nair was offering us a hotel in Goa. Issy was negotiating and had to contend with one naysayer so irate that the man turned red and spluttered. Isadore continued quietly to frame his case till all on the board were won over.

And in every hotel he visits, Issy traditionally holds a town hall with all the employees. These talks have become the stuff of legend. To 40,000 employees Isadore is a rock star.

Yesterday we were in New Orleans for a board meeting at the new Four Seasons, and Greg, Tony, Joanne, and I were front row witnesses to Issy's town hall. He jogged up to the stage, amid riotous cheers from 300 staff in the audience. He half sat on a high stool, one leg bent resting on a rung, immaculately dressed as always, his slim build framed by a silver grey suit, open snow white shirt, (no tie in a bid to contemporary fashion), and his signature glossy black tasseled loafers.

He spoke to the staff as if they were close friends, took them into his confidence and shared the company's plans, just the way he would speak to his board of directors. He speaks with the charisma of a late night TV host. Even though I've heard much of it before, it has a power for me because I hear it through the ears of a new audience. And this is the gist of Issy's speech to the employees:

Town Hall Meeting — Four Seasons Hotel,
New Orleans, December 7, 2021

Thanks, Mali, and good afternoon everyone. It's a pleasure to be here because over the years visiting the hotels has always been one of the most enjoyable parts of my job.

And to visit a new hotel makes it even more special.

But this visit is also special because it's my first since my trips to the three Texas hotels on March 9, 2020. The pandemic began in March 2020. So it is truly a pleasure to be here.

First, to all the new Four Seasons people, thank you for joining the company, and I hope that over time it will prove to be a good decision as it has been for so many others.

Also, a special thanks to all the Four Seasons people who have moved here from our other hotels. And it's this concept of the combination of attracting new people and retaining many more that allows us to continue to grow and succeed.

And, as the opening team you will all have had the unique experience of solving all the challenges and problems inherent in a new building.

But there is one message that I'd like to share with you, and it's one I've said many times before. But the longer I'm in the business the more important I believe this message has become.

But the fact is: the success of the hotel will depend entirely on all of you, because it will be through your efforts, your attitude, your enthusiasm, and your honest concern for the customer that will make this hotel truly great.

Yes, we have this magnificent building and excellent location. It's the ideal situation and a good opportunity. But that's all it is — a good opportunity — because it's now up to you, the people who work here, to create that exceptional guest experience, that memorable experience because of the quality of your service. And that has become the trademark of the Four Seasons brand.

So this is the beginning and you can all look to the future that has unlimited possibilities.

And our objective will always be to get better as we get bigger, and to continue to raise that bar of "Barrier to Entry," which Warren Buffett believes is a company's greatest asset.

So, I believe we are at the threshold of the next great era of Four Seasons. And I say this because we have established a sustainable competitive advantage, which is our culture and our brand. And, unlike our many innovations that have been copied and are now industry norms, a culture cannot be copied, it must grow from within based on the actions of its people over a long period of time. Remember, we started in 1961, and over the past 60 years Four Seasons has earned the respect of many other companies, and there's one great example that stands out. In a book recently published called *The Apple Experience*, about how Steve Jobs created the Apple Store, Four Seasons is mentioned in the first chapter, which is the most important third-party endorsement we may ever receive. And I quote: "The story of the Apple experience did not begin with the opening of the Apple Store in 2001. It began 40 years earlier with the founding of another brand that would be credited with completely reinventing the customer experience — the Four Seasons."

When Steve Jobs first decided to enter the retail business, he hired former Target executive Ron Johnson. Jobs challenged Johnson with this question: Who offers the best customer service experience in the world? The answer was — "The Four Seasons Hotels."

The chapter goes on in some detail about some of our innovations, but the emphasis is on the importance of people's attitude and essentially the principles of the Golden Rule, which is most gratifying because it confirms and reinforces what we believe and how we've been operating from the beginning. And coming from Steve Jobs makes it very special.

As I said, we are now at the threshold of our next great era, and it's clear that the "Best is yet to come."

And yes, it's taken a long time to build a global brand name and sustain a corporate culture through the best and worst of times. But research over a 40-year period by the author Jim Collins has proven, and I quote: "What makes and keeps companies great are a strong set of core values. Values that you never compromise."

And that's what we've done for the past 60 years, and what we're well prepared to do for the next 60 years.

ISADORE NOW CALLS FOR questions from the employees. Here's question one only (of ten):

"Mr. Sharp which is your favourite hotel?" It's an oft asked question and Issy explains that the hotel he's in is the favourite that day because he's known this very Four Seasons for the five years it takes, from inception to opening, and he's had a major influence on every hotel's negotiations, floor plans, elevations, and interiors. Rather like a grandad treats his grandkids because he's known them from birth.

Whenever I have a workout in our gym, our current rec room, I am surrounded by plaques and trophies Issy has received from business groups, universities, newspapers, and charities, and on the wall in front of me are

14 framed magazine covers featuring his face. Respectfully, unlike me, he keeps them all. In 1992, he was honoured by the *Financial Post* as CEO of the Year, and for an unprecedented 23 years in a row, *Fortune* magazine has ranked Four Seasons as one of the "World's Best 100 Companies to Work For" — one of only nine companies to make the list every year.

I would like to claim I had a hand in my husband's great success, but if I did, it was only because time and again I kept quiet and didn't tell the truth about my fears for some of his schemes which is telling about my business acumen.

Throughout the years, I've watched in disbelief as Issy's aspirations have come to fruition. Early on, he made some very audacious statements that seemed like pipe dreams. He told me once that his aim was to make the name Four Seasons a worldwide brand, synonymous with luxury, like Rolls-Royce. "Sure," I thought, "with only about 10 hotels — hardly likely," but I didn't let on. My most valuable contribution to his success has been my silence.

This was not the first of his schemes that I didn't get. I remember when he built the first condos in Canada, then known as "cooperative" suites. It all began with two proposed rental towers at 575 and 581 Avenue Road at Heath Street.

The Hungarian real estate agent for the land, Andrew Czepely, contended that these should be for sale as cooperatives, which were so commonly popular in Budapest and Paris, etc. Issy bought into Andrew's scheme. But, privately, I could not understand why clients would buy an apartment when renting was cheaper and who would want to pay for *not* having a garden. Issy's investors felt the same way, but somehow he persuaded them that pride of ownership is both innate and elemental. Issy then proceeded to build other cooperative apartments, at 120 Dale Avenue in Rosedale, two towers on Avoca, followed by Granite Place. The success of these "owned" rather than rented apartments led the Canadian Government to take notice and create the *Condominium Act*, in 1998, and the condo option became endemic.

At this time when Issy claims he was just a builder, he was also building the first two hotels in Toronto, just as he says as "another real estate deal." But after London, the third hotel, when he became a proper hotelier, we began our business travel. For many years we have taken hotel to hotel trips. I marvel at Issy's physical and intellectual vigour, to be "on" every day in a new city, and to enjoy it. I swing along with the carefree comforts hotel life affords, as well as nightly dinners with so many admirable hotel managers who are a breed apart — from all walks of life, business people, poets, writers. Contrary to popular perception, though, staying in our hotels now is not as exciting for us as going backpacking might have been when we were young. It's true that when we stay at Four Seasons, we are treated to all the luxuries, but we are not guests in the usual sense. For us, visiting hotels is work, and staying home is the vacation.

IN JULY 1984 WE holidayed (no Four Seasons Hotels) in Communist Russia, hoping to pick up en route a few tribal rugs in Bukhara, Uzbekistan, since I was still into my carpet mania. We hit all the obligatory tourist stops — memorably Pavlovsk, the country seat of Catherine the Great's son Paul, and the tragic Tsarskoe Selo, the bucolic summer palace of Nicholas and Alexandra from which, on July 17, 1918, they and their family were summarily carted off to Yekaterinburg in Siberia to be executed. The five children had names straight from Tolstoy — Olga, Marie, Anastasia, Tatiana, and Alexei.

Whenever we were sightseeing, Issy was a reluctant tourist. He'd sooner hop around the world to his hotels, spending a day in each one, than sit on a bus tour to see the country houses of the tsars. Sometimes on our travels I feel guilty schlepping my ambivalent captive, who'd rather be working. Just as we arrived from Canada to our St. Petersburg hotel room, the first thing Issy did was consult his travel schedule to confirm by telephone our flight home. Then he cannily checked behind the curtains and under the bed, whispering that he was certain the room was bugged. In Russian airports he always cautioned me not to bring novels, which were confiscated: "They'll put us in jail and throw away the key," I heard more than once. In the streets and on the highways, everywhere we found road-wide images of Vladimir Lenin, statues in public parks and busts on buildings — Lenin canonized. There were banners across roads and highways with red-lettered slogans announcing the current Five-Year Plan — which gave Issy the idea to put a banner across Leslie Street advertising the Terry Fox Run.

In St. Petersburg, we walked every evening to a restaurant of *Fodor's* choice. When we pointed to our selection on the menu, the waiter explained, in broken English, that the foods listed comprised all the dishes that the place might offer over a year, but only one of these items was available daily. This was customary in every restaurant.

From Moscow we took the six-hour flight by propeller plane to Bukhara. Not an empty seat available. Everyone in Russia was entitled to fly almost free, but the wait for seats could be years. As soon as the seat-belt sign was turned off, there was an announcement, in Russian of course, and all the passengers folded down their tray tables in concert, on which the attendants dropped one wrinkled apple, stored from last year's crop. About five hours out, the seat-belt light went on and we guessed that the captain announced we were landing. On the ground, I was waiting for Issy to round up the luggage when he came rushing and said, "Quick, let's go, we have to run! The plane's leaving any minute — and this is not Bukhara, it's Tashkent." A soldier had alerted Issy by nudging him and pointing to a sign that read "Tashkent."

Bukhara, when we arrived there, was a big disappointment. Not only were there no rugs — we were told the best place to buy old Bukhara carpets was Hamburg — there was little trace of the low mud-brick buildings and native charm of the old market town. The place had been completely Russianized with tall concrete apartment houses providing evenly small quarters for all. Our hotel room was damp with one of the wallpaper strips unstuck and flapping in the breeze from the window air conditioner. Not only that, but the drainpipes in the bathroom floor were exposed in an opening in the floor. For the evening meal, we ordered mutton, which must have contained maggots or some other contamination, because the next morning I woke up with the runs. As I came out of the bathroom, Issy was just on his way for a morning run. I said to him, "Is, you better get going because you don't have much time." He answered that he never bothered with germs, but 20 minutes later he returned and hurried straight into the bathroom, without a word.

The next day, back in Moscow for the last night before our trip home, we called the doctor because Issy was feeling quite ill. Enter Dr. Anna Bukhanovsky, wearing a kerchief tied under her chin like a peasant girl. She came with a retinue of four hulking male nurses in white coats and demanded of Issy, "Lie down please, mister." She kneaded his stomach, then asked him to sit up and stick out his tongue, which had a greenish tinge. "Gentleman," she said, "I want for you to come to the toilet with me and to make for me some samples right now, so I will see, yes or no, you go to hospital — by us you cannot go from Russia with catching germs."

The men in the white coats looked quite capable of carrying out these orders, but Issy managed eventually to charm the lady into returning the next afternoon after he promised to rest and drink the prescribed gallons of salt water. Late that night, with the help of the Canadian Consulate, we stole out of Russia and the threat of quarantine.

THE NEXT MILEPOST IN Isadore's business life was the Regent Hotel acquisition. Regent Hotels was a five-star brand operating mostly in Asia. With the collapse of the Japanese economy, Regent ran into trouble and came up for sale. So Issy flew over to Tokyo and negotiated a great deal. The deal signed in 1992 included 15 hotels. Tony Tsoi, a Toronto analyst, said: "It was a once in a lifetime deal . . . how often can you buy a major competitor at a reasonable price . . . that will fit your long-term expansion strategy."

Of the 15, we kept all the good hotels and sold off the lemons. Isadore explains the deal as follows: "We were competing against other companies but we had an idea of what the owners, the Japanese banks needed. I structured a proposal that paid the asking price of 104 million for the hotel management contracts, but also offered a partnership in some of our real estate holdings so they would not need to write down the book value of their assets. This appealed to the Japanese so we got the deal."

On our many business trips we would usually visit 10 hotels in 12 days. I think our record was 14 hotels in 16 days. So, in 1998 we began to travel by private plane. What a thrill. It's still a thrill.

I remember that first time, buckling my seat belt, my resident butterflies fluttering as I felt the surge and rattle of the Challenger 604 as it rocketed into the air, the Downsview skyline falling away beneath us.

Issy is sitting across from me; it's just the two of us and the crew. Our eyes lock as we exchange a small smile. Then the smile morphs into a grin and then we can't stop grinning — we're helpless. Because flying private is new to us. For the previous 30 years, travel had meant public transport, with me — "the wife of" — always in tow, because we are hinged together by habit. Also, I could be useful in the many social situations overseas, and act as a buffer in the seat beside him so Isadore could snore in privacy.

A private jet is ridiculously extravagant, but it makes good business sense for someone of Issy's acumen. In the same day, he can do a breakfast meeting in Budapest, a luncheon in Lisbon, and a dinner in Dublin. Meanwhile, back on that first July trip. It's Thursday on the plane and we've just awakened from the luxury of a flat bed to the scent of coffee and scrambled eggs served on a white tablecloth graced with one perfect black-purple iris. This is the longest leg of our tour, from Hawaii to Brunei, for hotel meetings and the birthday party of Sultan Hassanal Bolkiah. The plane taxis down the runway, and in the blinding desert sun we descend the few steps from the airplane and into the long black car that regularly awaits us on arrival. Once, I can't remember where, we had motorcycle escort, all the traffic lights green and traffic held up. In Brunei we are shepherded into the airport terminal, to an empty sitting room done up in gold damask. The room is cold and wet with too much air conditioning. Others have our passports stamped, and the luggage loaded while we sip a demitasse and watch the news in Arabic on TV. No doubt, somewhere in another part of the terminal, hordes of travellers even now are being corralled in queues from one pen to the next, as each access is locked behind them.

Issy is ushered to his meeting with the sultan and Prince Alwaleed of Saudi Arabia. They discuss a possible Four Seasons Hotel, Brunei, in a huge mixed-use tourist complex — liquor is prohibited. I always miss my glass of wine in Arab countries.

At 3 p.m. we show up at the stadium for the Sultan's Grand Military Parade. The soldiers are dressed in white cotton costumes.

So am I.

As we climb the stadium steps, I notice a sea of black silk dresses. Every woman is in black tunic and trousers, each differently styled and trimmed. In the evening, too, I am out of step in my black dinner dress. Every lady is dressed all in white, apparently the traditional evening colour.

I should have asked more questions.

The ballroom, like the ladies, is rigged out in white, and everything is gilded. Even, it seems, the golden light. Two hundred high-backed banquet chairs, like thrones, are carved in Jacobean style, and gilded. I'm ushered to one of these seats at a table covered in gold brocade, and in front of me are gilt-edged white porcelain plates framed by gold cutlery.

Dignitaries pay homage to the Sultan and his two wives, Anek Saleha and Mariam Abdul Aziz (Bruneian men are allowed four wives). Having presented his gift, each VIP backs away a few steps before turning to leave. A red carpet leads up to the three colossal gold chairs where the royals are seated — the Sultan raised on a dais in the centre, flanked by the two ladies resting their golden shoes, with upswept toes, on gilded footstools. One wife wears sumptuous bright green and gold silk, and the other is outfitted in red and gold. Tiaras float aloft on their black bouffant long hair. These two ladies — and I — are among the few women in the room with heads uncovered. After countless courses, more gift-bearing courtiers, and musical interludes, the festivities conclude, and we are escorted to the hotel for sleep and an early departure for Singapore — it's Friday — followed by Saturday in Bali.

In Bali, our jet plane pilot, Captain Holland, has a rollicking dinner in our hotel restaurant with the two other crew. A large man, the captain is dressed, surprisingly, in the full Balinese costume of long flowered skirt and headdress. When we fly on long trips, Issy always invites the crew to have a dinner on us — an extension of the way he treats his hotel staff. Four Seasons is the only company to allows its workforce to stay at any of the hotels gratis. This gives the staff an insight on how to treat a guest.

Finally, it's Sunday, and the last leg of this trip carries us 24 hours from Hong Kong home to Toronto. It feels good to snuggle under the familiar blankets of our own bed.

Occasionally Issy travels alone, and then I stay home and sleep with the Issy Bear.

The bear incident goes like this: Ty Warner, of Beanie Babies fame, brought out the Issy Beanie Baby, honouring our son Chris Sharp with proceeds to cancer — millions have been raised. One of these bears lives in our bedroom closet. One night when Issy was out of town, I brought the silky blue bear to bed with me, propping him up against the pillow — making a mental note to put him back in the closet before my assistant, Emie Buning, should find him in the morning. Of course, next day I forgot and left the toy bear in bed, but thank goodness Emie made no mention of it. However, the next time — and now every time my husband is away — guess who waits for me on Issy's pillow?

Most often, though, we travel together, and we can't help but wonder: how did it happen that two schleppers like us are now flying in a private jet when we were both raised in households where one bathroom sometimes served 12, and our parents came from a Polish shtetl with no indoor plumbing?

From horse and wagon on rural roads to paths across the sky.

Say It with Few Words, 2021, 54" x 60".

CHAPTER FOUR

Growing Up the Hard Way

I flash back and search my own early life for clues. How did my upbringing prepare me to be the "wife of"? What were the growing-up connections that kindled our attraction? It had been a long and more difficult road for me because my life in the Wise immigrant house was not as easy as growing up in the Sharp home.

In fact, God must have made a mistake when he assigned me to the Wise household. And he also went wrong in matching up my parents. If theirs was a match made in heaven, it had to have been made on a Friday before sundown because after putting these two together God needed a day of rest. Years later proximity proved to unite them and 50 years later when my mom was in the throes of dying and couldn't speak, she gestured to her wedding band indicating she wanted to be buried with it.

YDESSA BIRNBAUM AND JOSEPH Wise, lately from the shtetl of Ożarów, Poland, were married on May 26, 1935, in the rabbi's office in Montreal, with little ceremony: as my mother explained, "Who had money for a wedding party?" Right after the wedding, she and her new husband moved to Toronto, and three days short of nine months later I came along. Just the three of us till my brother arrived nine years later, when I was already a grown-up. Isadore and I both had the privilege of growing up in shtetl households. We are the last links to a life that spanned 20 generations: Jews who spoke Yiddish, read the Torah daily, and always endured anti-Semitism. Issy and I heard Yiddish spoken daily, enjoyed the time-honoured shtetl recipes, and were taught to lead an ascetic life. The word entitlement was not in the Yiddish dictionary, but foolishness (narrishkeit) was commonly applied to frivolous enterprises like sports and dancing. We the Wises were almost the only Jews living in North Toronto. We had moved when I was six months, in 1936, from 116 Grange Avenue, second floor — from the easy familiarity of the downtown ghetto where our friends and relatives lived, where kosher food and the Ożarów synagogue were only steps away. I admire my father for his courage in moving to the Christian, blue-collar neighbourhood — as it was then — of Yonge Street north of Lawrence Avenue, when he could barely speak English. He taught himself the language by reading the *Toronto Telegram* and later the *Star* every day, as he did until the day he died. My dad was a tailor turned entrepreneur. He opened Wise's Dry Goods at 3248 Yonge Street, an eight-foot-wide shop, and we lived in the back room, exactly eight feet by 12 feet — I measured it recently. The room was separated from the shop by a brown velvet curtain. And the next time I get my hair done after the pandemic, I will go to the hairdresser operating in that very store next to Kristapsons where I now buy my smoked salmon, and occasionally caviar.

I remember two incidents from 3248. It had to be September of 1938, judging by the gas bills my mother kept, and I was a two-year-old — sitting on her lap on a black Queen Anne chair beside the entrance of the store. The loose chair legs squeaked as my mother rocked me, singing softly. Because memory photographs in colour those moments when mistakes are made, I remember a customer came in wearing a moss-green bouclé dress.

My mother instantly stood up, rudely dropping me from her lap, and went behind the counter. I pulled at the lady's green dress for attention, and she looked down at me with an annoyed expression. I repeated the offence and was banished to the back room. Green remains a favourite among my tubes of oil paint, particularly "moss green light." Then there was the time, a couple of years later, I crossed Brookdale Avenue, having been warned never to cross a road unaccompanied. My father gave me a whack and put me down in the scary black cellar. He was not a good communicator and that was the only way he could impress on a four-year-old the mortal dangers of traffic. Mom taught me to approach any passerby on the street and ask, "Please, would you take me across Yonge Street?" I wondered why people were slightly taken aback but they rarely refused.

At 3228 Yonge, our next shop, there was a heavy trap door one of my parents had to open so I could use the toilet in the dark cellar with its one light bulb swinging on a wire. I remember the cellar as a *round* dark place because I was afraid to look into the corners in case a rat was lurking there. This cellar was the setting for a freakish scene. When I was about seven, I called my mother from the toilet when I found something, that I would now describe as a fettuccini noodle, swinging from my rectum. My mother took one look and gave a geschrei "oy gevalt," a shriek, for my father, who then attempted to pull it out. He pulled and pulled lengths of it until it broke off. This bizarre bathroom scene was to recur twice over the next 18 months, until the worm must have died a natural death. My parents ignorantly put the blame on me for eating too many junky sweets. Doctors we never called. In the shtetl there was no doctor, only the feltsher, the old-time barber-surgeon, who dispensed aspirin and Epsom salts and the like. Not until I was an adult did I work out that the "noodle" had been a tapeworm from the raw fish my mother chopped to make gefilte fish. She then used the same board for my peanut butter sandwich.

ON YONGE STREET, WE always lived in rooms behind our rented shops, three consecutive Wise's Dry Goods stores in the same block, at 3248, 3228, and 3230, between Cranbrooke and Brookdale. At 3230, which was the first store my dad bought, if you wanted some fresh air, you carried the one chair outside to the sidewalk in front. The chair was in Marcel Breuer style, chrome U-shaped legs, covered in peeling red leatherette — the same chair my mother would be sitting on when my dad came in from his piece-work tailoring and asked in Yiddish, "Nu, were there any customers?"

My mom would answer, "Not even a dog."

The concrete sidewalk outside our store was my front yard, good for skip-ping or chalk writing. If my dad was alone in the store and a woman came in, my dad would panic and yell, "Ydess!" because he was afraid the lady might ask to see a bra or some other feminine item. Dad rarely waited on customers. Mom was quick on her feet, like me. Ydessa was a crack saleswoman. I recall her in action, opening the shiny black box of Weldrest Hosiery (long before pantyhose) and slipping the back of her hand into the top of the stocking so the customer could see how the colour would look on the leg. When our old DeSoto wasn't working, the streetcar which stopped right in front of our store opened its doors to Dad who hobbled down the steps, schlepping huge cardboard boxes of dry goods for inventory.

Every Sunday Dad drove us slowly and deliberately the half-hour journey, always via Avenue Road, back downtown to the ghetto. We would lunch at Goldenberg's Kosher Restaurant on Spadina Avenue. It had a high ceil-ing, black bentwood chairs, and Yiddish-speaking waiters with long white aprons. My parents would order two meals and an empty plate on which they placed offerings for me, sometimes fatty brisket or stuffed miltz (cow's spleen). After lunch at the restaurant, we went weekly to Dad's sister's, the Weinbergs, at 325 College Street, next to Benjamin's funeral home where imaginable mysteries were performed. Later we would meander through nearby Kensington Market to stock up for the week on all things Jewish

— kosher meat and poultry; rye bread with caraway seeds; egg-white cookies known as nothings; cottage cheese, which would bear the pattern of the cheesecloth it was wrapped in; sour cream; smoked meat; schmaltz herring from one barrel and dill pickles from another. I ate none of the above. I preferred anything non-Jewish: sliced white bread, toasted, with peanut butter; cereal from boxes; Kraft Dinner; crackers with butter and jam; and Campbell's Cream of Mushroom Soup. This soup would ease out of the can whole, with a suction sound, and I learned to add the water gradually, to avoid a lumpy mess. Anything that came in a tin or a box and wasn't derived by killing — and especially didn't have a face — was safer. Although I admit I did not favour the ketchup sandwiches at my friend Lorna's house. When I ate my Nabisco Shredded Wheat, I would set the box in front of me, and while I munched, I studied the picture of Niagara Falls showing brown lumps where the water crashes down. I was certain these lumps were the shredded wheat, and I still can't shake the conviction. What other connection could Niagara Falls have with the cereal? The emphasis on food and the rituals of a kosher kitchen put me off eating, and I became emaciated. My clothes hung on me. Belts required an extra hole created with the ice pick. I still have a strong memory of *black dread*, like a stone in my stomach, when I sensed mealtime getting near — my mother watching my every mouthful, which sometimes just refused to go down. It was sickening to see, on the koshering tray, the blood drawn from meat being koshered with heavy salt. For an hour the blood ran in rivulets down the grooves in the white enamel tray and into the sink. The tray stood on a tilt, filled with all sorts of soft no-name offal, usually pinkish.

These and other animal parts I had to face every day at noon, for our main meal. The evening meal, according to tradition, was dairy, so every night my mom asked me the same question: "What would you like to eat? Cheese mit cream or benenes mit cream?" In all the years, she didn't seem to notice that I never chose either, and I have yet to eat a banana.

Because of this I catered to my boys' tastes, keeping one portion of lamb chops in the freezer for Greg on the days I served fish. A dish peculiar to our house and a favourite of my father's, was golkes, made from potatoes that were finely grated, wrung dry in a tea towel till they turned pink, then mixed with an egg and a little flour, formed into balls, and boiled. Mom served these chewy balls in soup or sometimes hot milk, which my father preferred. Golkes were dark grey and probably would have bounced if dropped, like the India rubber balls they resembled. In early days, my mom would save money by serving a burnt soup. She stir-fried flour into small balls in schmaltz, then added fried onions and hot water charmingly known in Yiddish as ugubrente zup. This was dinner for pennies a serving. Sometimes she added small pasta squares. Kashe soup was another watery menu. In our fridge there was often a bottle of buttermilk with black-green spinach pasted here and there on its sides: this was spinach borscht. And another bottle might have a creamy magenta-coloured beet borscht. Mom's kitchen was her truest realm.

One time at Mintz's Restaurant there were white maggots floating in the kashe soup. Unfortunately, I had already started eating it, because the grain and the maggots were the same colour. For the next fifty years, I skipped the soup course at home. It might have been the maggots or perhaps it was simply because, during the Depression, soup was sometimes all there was. I remember so well my mother in the kitchen, singing a Yiddish song while making pasta. She would pour the flour out of the bag into a tepee shape, take an egg, and, with a circular motion, make a well in the tepee, then crack two eggs into the well. With a knife she would fold the flour over into the eggs until the dough was formed. Now, in a rowing motion, she rolled the ball in an ever-increasing circle with the "valgerholtsz," Yiddish for a long, thin rolling pin, with no handles. When the circle reached about three feet in diameter, she picked it up, supporting it over her fingertips, and began to stretch it with rhythmic movements, as if she were conducting

Beethoven's Symphony No. 5. When it was stretched suitably thin, she hung the large circle of pastry over a chair to dry, later to be rolled up and cut into noodles. Today I could easily perform a demonstration of this ritual although the pastry would be rather lumpy. Mom was a consummate cook of all shtetl recipes. She made them exactly like her mother and probably her mother's mother — no deviation. Each piece of gefilte fish was encircled with the skin of the fish and had a carrot slice placed precisely in its centre. I was ornery as usual and have never tasted a piece. She was known for her veal patties — which I still serve as Ydessa's veal patties — made from veal ground in our silver meat grinder, an excess of garlic, dampened bread, onion, egg, and — my own touch — rosemary. I use that recipe not written but from watching her. My parents were serious about buying quality food at kosher stores. My dad went into Naftuly's Butcher Shop and pointed out the very piece of meat he wanted, and my mom would embarrass me in Perlmutter's Bakery, where she would designate a particular challah (egg bread): "Give me the brown one in the corner. No, not that one — the second loaf from the left. No, no, not that one, the one beside it. Yes, that's it." Everyone who entered our house was fed, and I still follow the same procedure, whether it's the plumber or a visiting sheik. I am reminded of Dr. Samuel Johnson, who once declined an invitation to a house where, on an earlier visit, no food had been offered. He said, "I don't go to a place where I come out the same as I went in."

At seven years old, however, it seemed to me that I was in the wrong house. I hated the un-Canadian food, the cut-down handmade clothes, the Jewish religion, and the constant warring. My parents spoke Yiddish to me, but I always stubbornly answered in English. I imagined life being quite different, if only I had been born in the "right" house — with the life I, as a Canadian, deserved. For example: parents who knew how to swim. Although it is written in the Torah that a father must teach his child to swim, my father could not. And besides, we spent only about two Sunday

75

afternoons a year at Belle Ewart Beach, where we would park at the end of a road on the lake and walk into the brown muddy shore. Dad would typically sink into the water up to his armpits and sigh in Yiddish, "what a pleasure," and do the breaststroke — his feet never leaving the bottom. I can't swim because there was seldom a body of water available. Nor can I skate. Ice skates and roller skates were not in the vocabulary of our house, so it was simply out of the question even to ask.

I daydreamed about a household like those in the books I read, where people spoke to one another in quiet tones, with friendship and interest. I remember walking past the houses near us, at dusk, when the windows were glowing with lamplight, and peering in, always wondering just what went on behind those windows. Were those shadowy moving figures loving and civil or were they quarrelling and troubled like us? Did all families have two personas — one within the home and one outside? Were they real or were they fake, like me? I felt like a fraud because my life was a pretence on so many fronts. I was masquerading as an eight-year-old, yet I was only seven, because my mom had enrolled me in school early. My parents didn't know about my other life as a Christian. My schoolmate Lorna Chisholm had invited me to the Sandys' house for a weekly Bible class. As we arrived, Mrs. Sandy was on the verandah of her red-brick bungalow, polishing the gleaming brass door handle and letter box. She was short, seemingly very old, her shiny white hair woven into a neat figure-eight braid on the back of her head. "Come right in, young ladies, you're early — just in time for tea and a wee slice of Christmas cake." She had a cockney accent I found new and appealing. We sat at the kitchen table with Sandy, as she called her husband. Newly retired from the Bell Telephone Company, he was wearing his flannel "combinations" — pinkish one-piece long johns with a trap door at the back. Mrs. Sandy brought down from the cupboard a pretty tin decorated with garden flowers, which she said her sister sent every year from England with the fruitcake. She meted out four very small squares of the holiday delicacy.

"How," I thought, "can a cake last a whole year when our family has little respect for yesterday's baking?"

The next week when the tin was brought out again, I said, "No thank you, Mrs. Sandy," like a good shtetl child — but also because I didn't want to be responsible for using up the stuff before the year was out. When a few other girls arrived, we all sat cross-legged on the oriental carpet in front of Mrs. S., who played the black upright piano, and we sang hymns like "Onward Christian Soldiers." Whenever we came to "Jesus," I mumbled, because it was a frightening word for a Jewish child. "Reboyne Shel Oylem — the King of the Universe" would come down on my head.

And then there were the glorious songs of Christmas. When I first heard Jussi Björling sing "O Holy Night," and the contralto voice of Marian Anderson performing "Ave Maria," I was enthralled. The words and music of Christmas carols are part of the nostalgia of my youth. Every Christmas at Bedford Park Public School, there was a holiday concert. Parents — not mine, of course — would be seated in the auditorium with the doors left open so they could hear the carols sung from all parts of the school. Students from each grade were stationed in the corridor outside their classrooms. Grade 1 always sang "Away in a Manger" from the main floor; Grade 2 sang "It Came Upon a Midnight Clear" from the second floor; Grade 3 "Bring a Torch Jeanette Isabella"; and so on. Every year I sang from a different location. Now, in winter, when my feet crunch on new-fallen snow, I recall "Good King Wenceslas" — "When the snow lay round about, deep and crisp and even." I can still hear in my mind's ear those carols echoing from far-off halls.

ONCE, IN THOSE ELEMENTARY school years, my mom sent me to Wilson's Fine Foods, a few doors down from our walk-up, for a bag of Five Roses Flour. Wilson's carried neat stacks of pickles, jams, spices, and brick-sized packages of tea leaves wrapped in foil with white labels — only packaged food, no fresh produce. The long, narrow shop was empty as usual, but I caught a glimpse of Mr. Wilson in the back room, sitting at his dressing table, applying rouge over the orange-coloured foundation he always wore. He was a tall, slim man with a peroxide-blond pompadour, and he seemed to take more interest in his makeup than in his merchandise. I asked him for a five-pound bag of mail, using the Yiddish word. For some reason Mr. Wilson could not understand me, and when he kept asking me to repeat "mail," I thought he was dim. Finally I pointed out a row of white bags, each decorated with five red roses. "Oh, I see," said the grocer, "you mean flour." I was embarrassed not to know the English word. "Flour" to me meant "flower" — like Five Roses. How can a rose and mail be the same word in English? For that moment, I felt like a foreigner.

In the '40s, Yonge Street saw many goods delivered by horse and wagon: bread, milk, and ice among them. The bread men would whoa the horse, then take a heavy round weight attached to a rope and drop it on the curb so the horse wouldn't wander off while he gave us our unsliced bread. Sometimes the horse would mindlessly drop its steaming mustard-yellow turds, which, when dry, looked like chopped hay. The street cleaner later swept these into a canvas folding receptacle that he emptied into his wheeled cart. Downtown, one still saw the occasional ornamental dark green cast-iron water trough on the edge of the sidewalk, for the horses. The milkman brought milk in a bottle with a double-gourd shape — the upper third was yellow cream. Homogenized milk was not available till the mid-'40s. The coal man, with blackened face and hands, would empty jute sacks of coal down a window that opened, from the street, into the cellar near the furnace. And on steamy summer days, we would run behind the ice delivery truck for handouts of slivered ice.

In the Wise household there was a marked absence of things — no clutter, only clean tables. No books, no magazines, no ashtrays, and few tchotchkes (trinkets). There was no liquor, wine, beer, or pop — except one bottle of the obligatory Crown Royal whisky in its purple and gold bag, and one bottle of Manischewitz sacramental wine: 33 percent sugar. To date I've never had a beer or liquor, except a very regular glass of red wine and even an annual jigger of 25-year-old Macallan scotch with its look and taste of caramel. Pop I find too sweet — which reminds me of my granddaughter, Dr. Julia, the award-winning paediatrician. When I offered her some toffee squares, she wrinkled her nose and said, "Too sweet." With a flash of recognition, I knew she was right, so I haven't had one since. We have kindred tastes as I do with my daughter-in-law, Jordy's wife, Carolyn, the entrepreneur, and a superb cook, who once served me a Japanese breakfast, which I've been looking for ever since, of rice, avocado, slivered fried egg, and vegetables from her own farm. I remember that moment talking to Jordy on the phone when he announced, "Carolyn is pregnant." I screamed so loud with happiness that the phone fell from Jordy's ear, and Carolyn heard me from across the room.

On the back of this photo is written: "Sept. 6th, 1960, our very happy fifth anniversary." I ran up the red dress on the Singer. The photo was taken by a stranger at the CNE, where we celebrated annually, touring the International Building to soak up foreign cultures. Little did I know that Riyadh and Langkawi would someday be regular stops.

On the French Riviera, when we were young and gorgeous, 1963.

In a Paris nightclub, 1963.

The hostess, Green Valley Road, 1965.

Okanagan with a dog's best friend, Jordy. This dog was one of the most decent persons I knew.

Why do they no longer have costume parties?

Okanagan at his Monday morning management meeting. Some of Four Seasons' best guests are dogs.

The Issy Bear, created in memory of Christopher Sharp. Ty Warner donated $2 million for cancer research from the sales of this Beanie Baby.

Sir Gerald Glover.

Nan Wilkins, Issy's loyal helpmate, whom he can't live without. Friends and associates have said, "The person you need to know at Four Seasons is not Issy; it's Nan."

Isadore, 1948.

And in 1980.

Officer of the Order
of Canada, 1992.

The intrepid powder skier in the
Monashees, British Columbia.

Issy pouring concrete for Motel 27,
1954 — the job that inspired him
to get into the hotel business.

With Jack Gould, centre, and Ciro Rappachietti, Motel 27.

Motel 27, 1954, where it all began for client Jack Gould.

The Four Seasons Motor Hotel opened
in 1961 and instantly became the
popular hangout for the literati
and glitterati. My brother Stan
the heartthrob lifeguard had
to keep the groupies at bay.

With John Sharpe, President of Hotel
Operations. John and Issy were the
first messengers to go on the road
with the "Golden Rule" dictum.

Ten and twenty Avoca cooperatives
Issy built in 1969.

Max Sharp in Israel, 1920, in a canoe he built. Max had come from the shtetl of Oshpitzim, Poland, and remained in Israel for five years. He worked on Israel's first kibbutz, Deganya, before coming to Canada.

Issy and his three sisters, 1934. Edie, Bea, and Nancy in front. They taught him to be tidy, to iron his own clothes, and to respect women above men.

Lillie Gotfried, 1926, soon to be Issy's mom.

Ryerson Rams basketball, 1952.

Ryerson Athlete of the Year, 1952.

Max Sharp & Son Construction.
Northview Terrace, Toronto, 1954.
Issy and I lived in apartment 1001,
his parents on the floor above.

Max and Lillie, 1938.

The Wises in front of our car on Cranbrooke Avenue.

From the press, 1960, working on a fundraiser for Mount Sinai Hospital.

The happiest kid in Grade 2.

Mom's family, the Birnbaums, Ożarów, 1939. Sarah, the older sister, missing. She was married with two young children. Her husband immigrated to La Paz, Bolivia, and never saw Sarah again. From left to right: Marmish, Yechil, Yochwed, Raisl, and Chaskel.

Ydessa Birnbaum and Joseph Wise, married in the rabbi's office in Montreal. Who had money for a party?

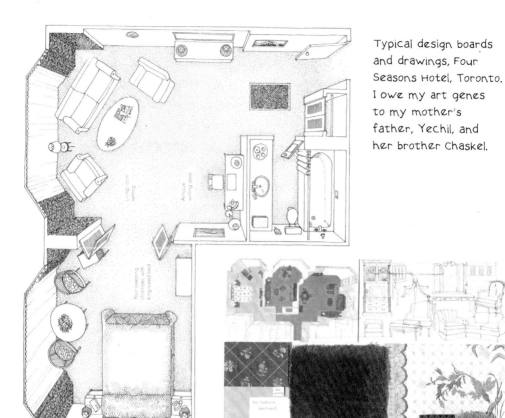

Typical design boards and drawings, Four Seasons Hotel, Toronto. I owe my art genes to my mother's father, Yechil, and her brother Chaskel.

Chaskel's artwork.

Mom's brother Chaskel, age 22, elegantly turned out, although showers and hot water were non-existent. He included this photo in his last letter, August 1939. I would have liked to meet him. Sadly, he was murdered by the Nazis.

Our store — before and after — designed by Dad, who made the children's wool coats, hats, and leggings (right) from his own patterns.

Our first house, 165 Cranbrooke Avenue — before and after. The upstairs window was fake. Dad was a self-taught designer. This house, the store, and a rear garage were the beginning of his career as a builder.

Chaskel's pencil sketch of my mom.

My mom's passport, 1930. She is wearing a shirt embroidered by her sister Marmish.

My dad, Joe, 1926. His younger sister Pearl, 1934. We didn't know she existed because she was banished from the family for 50 years, having married a Catholic.

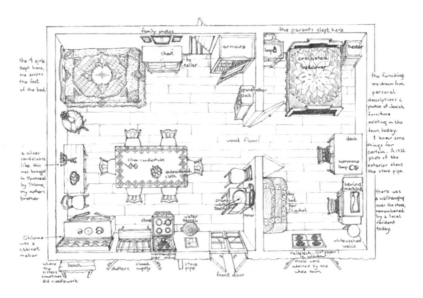

The drawing contains the following handwritten labels:

family photos — the parents slept here

the 4 girls slept here, me across the foot of the bed

chest — to cellar — armoire — lamp — crocheted bedcover — heater

the furnishings are drawn from personal descriptions & photos of Jewish furniture existing in the town today. I know some things for certain. A 1932 photo of the exterior shows the stove pipe.

a silver candelabra like this was brought to Montreal by Shlomo, my mother's brother

grandfather clock — silver candlesticks — embroidered cloth — wood floor — desk — kerosene lamp — sewing machine — there was a wallhanging over the stove, remembered by a local resident today.

enamel washing bowl — bed for Simchat

Shlomo was a cabinet maker

where the sisters sometimes did needlework — bench — shutters closed nightly — stove — water vessel — whitewashed walls — closed brick stove — stove pipe — railpolish (tar paper) in window — these were admired by the whole town. — front door

My guess, figured from a 1932 photo of the front of my grandfather's house in Ożarów, no. 1 Złote St.

Playing in the kitchen.

Tablescape for Passover.

Portrait of Aaron and Liza's One-eyed Cat, 2016, 31" x 31".

CHAPTER FIVE

None of the
World's Goods

At the early Wise household, we never bought any kind of paper — no writing paper, toilet paper, napkins, tissues. We never tore open a gift but rather carefully picked it apart. Then we reused the gift-wrapping paper by removing the creases with a warm iron. To this day, like my mother, I keep cardboard from shirts to write on, and the cardboard from pantyhose, with its rounded corners, makes an ideal bookmark for jotting down notes or splendid words. At our first store, we used old telephone books as toilet paper — logical, because we didn't have a telephone. I recall an alarming summons to the shop next door — a telephone call from Montreal that Mom's brother Shloime was dead at the age of 43 — in 1943, which makes it easier to remember. Phone calls came rarely, but when they did, they were scary.

In 1944, I attended the Borochov Jewish Academy on College Street, a walk-up just west of Brunswick. This was after school, which meant travelling for an hour on the Yonge streetcar in the winter when it was dark. The trolley stopped right outside our shop. Since my parents often needed my help after school, I went only about a dozen times. On one occasion, when I was almost nine, my mom asked me to pick up a chicken in nearby

Kensington Market on the way home. With instructions in Yiddish: "Be sure not to buy a capon."

Glicksman's Kosher Poultry was dark and smelly as I walked in. When my eyes grew accustomed to the gloom, I saw that the shop was completely empty, not a chicken in sight — just some distant shadowy cages and two people seated up front. The deck of the plate-glass shop window was bare but tarred and feathered with greyish-white glued-on feathers. I faced an old couple, short and dumpy, their clothes the colour of a sepia snapshot. They sat on two kitchen chairs, the man with a long grey beard and a skullcap and the woman wearing the sheitel (wig) decreed by Jewish law. They sat like twins, slumped, their knees loosely spread. I asked, trying to remember my mother's instructions. "I'd like a lady chicken if you have one." Mr. Glicksman, the chicken dealer, still seated, slapped his thigh and roared with laughter. This was apparently a new one on him. Still chuckling, he raised himself slightly by pushing his palms against the seat of the chair, fell back down, and tried again. This time the old man managed to pull himself up to his full height — not much taller than me. "Come," he said, and we waded together through the sawdust to the back of the shop where the chickens were housed in grungy wooden cages. The light was purposely dim so the birds would think it was night and be less active, therefore plumper. We selected a chicken with copper-coloured feathers, and the chicken-dealer carried the squawking bird under his arm out of the shop and disappeared across Baldwin Street into a laneway. A few minutes later he reappeared with the bird now featherless and missing its head. From the deck of the front window, he picked up a hose with a nozzle that became a Bunsen burner when he turned it on, and he sprayed the noisy blue flame over the chicken to remove any stray feathers. I carried the body, wrapped in pink butcher paper, to the streetcar and made my way home. It was rush hour and the trolley lurched and halted, lurched and halted. I didn't need to hold on because the rush-hour wall of people around me kept me from falling. The chicken in my arms, still warm and gamey, began to work its way out of the package. I could feel its bare, warm rump in my hands, and that and the odour, together with the lurching of the trolley, made me nauseous. Suddenly I had an irresistible urge to vomit, so I cried out, "Excuse me, but I think I'm going to bring up." At that, the wall of people opened like the Red Sea, and I gratefully plunged into the fresh air, and took the next trolley home.

I didn't bring any of my school chums home in case any gross blood ritual was going on in the kitchen. My friends' mothers didn't spend their days handling dead animals. They had bridge games, went shopping, played Debussy on the piano, listened to their daughters practise their music lessons, pored over crossword puzzles, and read the latest bestseller. My parents never read one book or went to one movie. My mom could not read English. Later I discovered she needed glasses and couldn't have read the small print of the newspaper anyway. She would never have spent money to have an eye examination, and magnifying glasses were not then available from the corner drugstore. She always needed me to thread her needles. "It's so dark in here, Rosie, please thread the needle for me." She wrote a phonetic Polish English in letters half an inch high so she could see them, and when older she got all her information by telephone or television. Since I could read and write English, my parents considered me a genius, a kind of prodigy. Dad's English was confined to reading. I therefore became the family scribe, writing business letters and all the cheques. Dad would pen his signature, *J. Wise*, very slowly and deliberately on each cheque — the pride was in his face that he had the money to cover it. It was the only writing I ever saw him do. When I produced his business letters, which always began, "This is an agreement between Joseph Wise and," my mom might say in Yiddish "A long life on your head."

I wanted to belong to a family where I could take lessons, like my friends. At least I should have had ballet lessons, like Marjorie Mackenzie, who could do the sword dance over crossed strings lain on her oriental carpet, or perhaps piano lessons, like Carol Welsh. I played on a piano keyboard I made from cardboard and sang along as I fingered Beethoven's Concerto in C Minor: "Da da dum — da dum dum dum — dadum — da-dum." Dad never sang a note, but Mom and I sang Yiddish tunes and popular songs like "The Isle of Capri," which she sang as "I Love Capri" since she couldn't read. She would stand me on a stool in front of company where I would sing "Put your arms around me honey, hold me tight." This 21-inch "square upholstered stool covered in a mushroom pink wool, with cabriole walnut knees" followed us from house to house to house. In our last home my mother would sit on it to watch wrestling, and one night when my boyfriend at the time, Steve B., came to pick me up for a date, I heard her say, from upstairs putting on my lipstick, "Sit there on the stool — that's where Issy always sits."

Ydessa loved to dance and sing and be with friends. Joe was solemn and slow-moving and preferred to be solitary. My dad walked with a limp, and only behind the wheel of a car did he feel equal to any man. A car to him was not a luxury or a status symbol. A car was his legs. To the end of his days, he drove a "Kedilek car," as he called the Cadillac. Dad was very sensitive about his limp. Mom would always walk two steps ahead of him because she was very quick on her shapely legs and had no patience for his slow gait. She would laugh and say Dad walked "arup un arof" — up and down. My dad's worst fear was that someone would call him a cripple — which apparently some guy once did, ending up with a fist in the jaw.

According to his two sisters, Dad always limped as a child. He gave out the story that he was in an elevator accident, but my guess is that he was born, like one of our sons, with one-third of a club foot. Our third son, Chris, had a corrective cast on his leg for two months when he was about 10 months old, and that solved the problem perfectly. We called him Thumper as he did his commando crawl along the floor with a big smile on his face, dragging the cast behind him. He was happily oblivious and not at all bothered by the extra weight, which he carried as if it had always been a part of him.

Music lessons were foolishness at the Wises, but book learning was paramount: "Jewish thieves steal only books." Dad would slowly examine every report card, and if he found one *B* among the *A*'s, there would be hell to pay. In his clumsy but caring way he would rant, "What's the meaning of this *B*? What do you want to do? Be a saleslady and work at Woolworths? Study harder —" he spoke in Yiddish, or "Get a Saturday job so you'll know the value of a dollar."

So, Saturdays I worked at the Ah Young Fruit Market, run by two brothers, just before I was 13 years old. The brothers never smiled but shuffled around the store resigned to their lot. Lunch for the brothers was always the same small bowl of rice. In concert, they would place the bowls against their chins and hurriedly shovel a continuous flow of rice into their mouths. The younger brother, Han, would paint the prices on cards with his calligraphic brush. Curiously he would never use the plural, so the signs read: "banana 20 c," "cherry 15 c" — maybe the Chinese plural is not at the end of a word. Even today, I notice the same practice in Chinese fruit markets. Working at Ah Young I was very cocky because I felt like the boss. The older brother, Li-Wei, once asked me, the Saturday clerk, "Where do we keep the Certo?" And charge account customers would wait on hold because I would steer them off the plums which were wrinkled and advocate the apricots instead, and one Saturday we had huge black strawberries such as I wish I had seen since.

Working Saturdays, I learned little about economy, since I would easily spend my $3.65 daily wage on a belt or some other frivolous item before I took the bus home. Once I was waiting at the bus stop in front of the window display of Lewis Howard Casuals, and I noticed a colour combination that made my heart quicken — a coppery dark chocolate velvet skirt topped by a shell-pink sweater. I bought the sweater on the spot, later found some brown velvet fabric, and fashioned my own skirt on our Singer sewing machine. Mom thought my boss, Mr. Young, was stingy and threatened to phone him and demand that he raise my salary to five dollars. I begged her, "Please, plea-ea-ease, Mom, please don't call — I'll never be able to face him again," but she called nevertheless, while I covered my ears in mortification. My wages were duly raised. My mother warned me never to go into the back of the store, even to use the bathroom. All the time I worked there, I waited till I got home to pee. I quit after two years when, on the one occasion I ventured into the back of the store, Mr. Young rubbed my nipples with his knuckles. And to add to the insult, he smirked as he did it, because my chest was still flat at age 13 — another cross to bear.

I can still name and enjoy the rare vegetables we sold at the Ah Young Fruit Market — kohlrabi, collard greens, rapini, and okra — and I learned that the avocado pear is a fruit, which I still find suspect. Not till the age of 78 did I taste one but haven't missed a day since. Every lunchtime I cut one in half, wrap and store the other half in the fridge leaving the pit in for freshness, and I'm convinced that I owe my longevity to this viridian green, textured like Moroccan leather, perfect oval, especially as I rarely eat fruit. Fruit and vegetables were as scarce at the Wises as an orange in a shtetl household. My father remembers he saw an orange only once.

The gap between my parents and me stemmed from our shtetl household. The food, the customs, the ethics, the dress, the asceticism — we were the only Jews for miles around, surrounded, in my mother's paranoia, by hostile gentiles. One of these "krists," as my mother called Christians, once brought me a gift of a Mother Goose book, which my mother dismissed as foolishness, dampening the joy of owning my first book. The damage ran deep, and I was married for 20 years before I saw any sense in buying books when they could be had free from the library.

Today, I look back with respect on the austerity of my upbringing. A lack of the world's goods, I now believe, fosters creativity. I have seldom bought ready-made toys for my own children, and they tell me they are grateful. The only doll I ever had was Susie, a homemade rag doll in a flowered fabric with a ruffle for hair and flat features embroidered by my mother. I longed for a real doll with a human face, with eyelids that opened and shut, and pink lips parted slightly to show pearly teeth. Marjorie, the girl next door, had a Baby Wettums that peed into her diaper after taking water from a bottle. My mother told me that I had once seized a doll's carriage from a strange child during a Sunday outing in Queen's Park. The closest I got to real dolls were the ones I drew on a shirt cardboard and cut out. I enjoyed making complete wardrobes for them, sketched out on paper, coloured, and attached to the doll with paper tabs that folded down over the shoulders. My husband says it's because I never had a proper doll that I now collect 18th-century porcelain ones.

Back then I made many more things out of cardboard — the piano keyboard, a sewing machine, 52 playing cards, all the signs for the store advertising specials like "Children's corduroy overalls — reg. $2.98 now $1.98." It wasn't only toys that were rare in our house: clothes we also had few of — just enough for three or four changes, and those we had were often made by my parents and later by me on the Singer treadle sewing machine, a central fixture in our house. That very Singer now has a place of honour in our son Tony's home, over which he has hung a photo of Wise's Dry Goods, which makes me smile at his tender-heartedness. Mom would pump away on the noisy treadle with her slim ankles. *Dad* was very vain about *her* shapely legs, formed likely by operating that treadle. She always wore high heeled shoes, claiming that low heels put her off balance — which she demonstrated by feigning a backwards fall. Dad sewed as deftly as if he were playing pizzicato on a violin. He would wrap the edge of the hem over his left forefinger, then pick three nimble stitches at a time before he drew the thread through. Once, Dad bought two huge bolts of red corduroy fabric to make children's overalls to sell in the shop. He cut through two layers at a time of the licorice-red velvet fabric, and he and Mom stitched up dozens of overalls. I sewed on the buttons and pinned on the price tags. To save fabric, my dad had cut the legs dovetailed, with the nap running in opposite directions, but that resulted in an unfortunate colour effect. When the overalls were made up, one leg appeared pink, the other red. The garments had to be marked down, a loss my mother never let my father forget: "Money down the drain."

It's true that all immigrants straddle two cultures, but in my case the culture of the Old World was to end with me, because of the Holocaust. Elvio Del Zotto tells me that when he returns to the small town of Cordenons, north of Venice, from which his parents emigrated in 1930, he can visit cousins whose lives have changed little since his grandfather's time. I've been back to Ożarów. Not a single Jew survives there or in any of the more than 2,000 shtetls in Europe. With the murder of the Eastern European Jews, a way of life intact for a thousand years has vanished in the space of one generation. My grandkids can have no connection to or race memory of that shtetl culture, other than through my stories.

In North Toronto we were occasionally called dirty Jews. Why was this, I wondered as I looked into the mirror, trying to fathom what was wrong with me. I searched my features for signs of dirt, or for some distinguishing feature like a long nose. Maybe we didn't wash as frequently as the gentiles. Mom had a habit of spitting on a hanky, and as she went to wipe my face, I would recoil and squirm out of her reach. I seem to remember bathing only once or twice a week in the bathroom we shared with the family of six who owned the house where we rented rooms. Anti-Semitism was a mystery to me, and I felt diminished by it. After all, I thought, there must be a reason to dislike Jews. I even became somewhat anti-Semitic myself — everything goyish looked better to me. How was it that anti-Semitism in Poland could evolve from persecution to pogroms, from the gradual denial of rights to expulsion and complicity in murder? Most countries in the Eastern hemisphere at some time banished their Jewish residents. I had always thought my mother was unfair in branding all gentiles as anti-Semites. I cringed when she used the word goyim, which sounded almost as demeaning as the N-word. During the war, I thought her tales about death camps were exaggerated, and I discounted her rantings that she would never see her family again. From the time I was six to the day I turned nine, I often heard my mom say, "Hitler has killed my parents, my sisters, and my brother. I know it! I'll never see them again."

The house reeked of fear. I went about the business of being a child and hid the spectres that haunted our home. And then in 1945 came the grisly news that the Birnbaum family in Ożarów had indeed been suffocated in the gas chambers. Ydessa was the last Birnbaum. She didn't have even one first or second cousin. Fifty-seven members of the Birnbaum family had evaporated as if a steamroller had crushed them. All this while my friends were taking tap-dancing lessons, and playing the flute, and swimming in sunny country lakes. There was an unreality about going to school with kids who belonged in the neighbourhood — whose grandmothers were not gassed, but took them to see the *Nutcracker* ballet at Christmas.

Luckily, I had the distraction of my beloved school.

On the way there one spring day in 1942, the first day we didn't need winter boots, my feet fairly flew off the pavement with such ease that with each step on Ranleigh Avenue, my shoes seemed to need weights to bring them back down. They rose up like leaves in the wind. The shoes were proper lace-up ankle-high boots, because Dad was careful that my feet would not be misshapen like his were, from the shtetl; the second toe of his right foot sat curiously on top of its neighbour. Not until I was almost six did I at long last have a pair of regular low oxfords like the rest of the kids. I had begged for these and remember the day. I skipped out of the store in my new shoes and pranced back and forth ahead of my mom on the sidewalk as she cautioned me, "Watch out, not so fast, you'll kill yourself."

Today I still wear new shoes out of the store.

In another frozen frame from my childhood film, I'm about seven, and I am folded at the waist over a pipe-railing balustrade, with my knees drawn in, holding on with palms up. An irresistible urge comes over me, to let my body freefall over the railing in a somersault, swinging on my hands. I grappled with the urge for a few days, trying to summon up the same kind of courage one might need to parachute out of a plane. After a struggle, I let go and swung headfirst over the bar and upside down. What a triumph! Another recurring frame finds me, at about five, on our apartment's fire escape, which was our balcony. I am sitting on the gravel roof and tearing bits of waxed paper into a pile. My friend Marjorie comes over from next door and asks me what I'm doing.

"I'm making Maple Leaf soap flakes to surprise my mom, so she won't need to buy them at the store," I reply.

"Don't be a silly goose," she says, laughing, "that's just waxed paper."

"No, it's not waxed paper," I argue, "because if you can't tell the difference and they look precisely the same, then these must be soap flakes." I felt like a fool to be so wrong.

In the next image I am in the schoolyard, the first to arrive. I swing mindlessly round a pole and wait for the others. After a while I wonder where the others are. And then it dawns on me — could it be that everyone is already inside? They were. School, to me, was the foolishness forbidden at home. School was my private Emerald City. There were stories and games and a tray with balls of Plasticine, a tongue depressor marked with our names stuck in each ball, each looking like a candy apple. We all had a turn striking the venerated triangle, while standing up front beside the piano. In the sunlight I saw the piano's shadow as chocolate on the seamless caramel-coloured flooring known as battleship linoleum, same colour as I would later find in the St. Clements library. It seemed to take forever until it was my turn on that precious silver triangle; if the names were called alphabetically, I was always last. At school, there was a boys' playground and a girls' playground safe from boys, "GIRLS" carved in stone over the door. I always felt privileged to be there, even if I feared that my membership could be cancelled at any moment because I was a Jew. And I knew enough not to mention to my parents just what went on at school, apart from reading and arithmetic — like art and other foolishness. I clearly recall one June day when school was let out, kids all around me pouring out of the school on the run, jumping and whooping because the summer holidays were beginning, and I trudged home with a funereal step to wait out the endless summer, until the fun would begin again. Summer seemed forever.

From age three to six, 1939 to 1941, I lived with my parents in two rented upstairs front rooms at 176 Bowood Avenue, a house we shared with the Kennedy family, who had four boys. The nine of us used one bathroom. Recently, I took a look at those rooms with the kind permission of the present owner — who I probably offended when I said, "It's so much smaller than I remember."

She asked if the house in the 1940s had been divided somehow, so that each apartment was private.

"No," I answered. "Every night we felt like intruders, as we tiptoed up the Kennedy family's staircase."

One November night when I was four, my dad and I walked the four blocks home to Bowood Avenue after working late at the store, and an almost full moon was up. It's my only memory of just the two of us out together, Dad protecting me against the dark and the unknown. He was walking with his uneven up-and-down gait, huffing with the effort. I was holding his forefinger. As we made our way along the street, which was so quiet we could hear our footfalls, I remarked, "Look, Daddy, the moon is following us." My dad did not say, "Don't be silly," but just murmured quietly and affectionately. He was a very dear and gentle man, except on those rare occasions when his dybbuk surfaced in a flare of rage.

Another night on Bowood, I woke for no apparent reason, climbed out of my brown metal crib — quietly so as not to disturb my sleeping parents — and walked to the window. It was almost first light, and there was an eerie bluish haze like the calm after a thunderstorm. As I turned to go back to bed, I noticed my father was sleeping naked, and in the blue half-light I noticed his genitals, which at first I thought couldn't possibly belong to him — of unimaginable design. Another night I woke to find my father on top of my mom under the greyish-purple blanket. I called out, "Daddy — stop! You're hurting Mommy!" I couldn't make any sense of the muffled laughter that came from under the blanket. I slept in that brown metal crib until I was six, even though I pleaded repeatedly that I needed a big bed because, "See, I can reach the end with my toes."

I have two other Bowood memories, both sexual: one where I am sitting in a tin bathtub on the white enamel kitchen table and resist when my mom, laughing, tries to wash my genitals. Another from when I was about four. I was in the shared bathroom with the youngest Kennedy, Bruce, where I was sitting on the toilet while he washed at the sink wearing only a T-shirt. I noticed that he had an interesting hook attached to the bottom of his stomach. "Brucie," I asked, "do you think you can you lift me off the toilet with your hook?" We worked on this until Mrs. Kennedy discovered us.

Soon the Wises moved up in the world, to a walk-up tenement. This was a step up from two rented rooms. In this luxury, I embarked on a fantasy life inspired by Hollywood. When I was four and a half, Mom would drop me off every Saturday at the Bedford Theatre — whether the movie was appropriate or not — to keep me occupied, because it was the busy day at Wise's Dry Goods. For the 11-cent show ticket, there was the Movietone News, a western serial, and a cartoon, perhaps a Tom and Jerry one, which I found wanting because only the feet of the Black housekeeper were shown. After the movie when you pushed out the heavy doors onto Yonge Street, the sunlight was blinding. Once I saw the romantic comedy where Ann Sheridan plays George Brent's witty secretary. So, I became one. I made a typewriter out of a Weldrest Hosiery box from our store. Then I arranged a red sweater on my head, just hiding my hairline, and tucked the sleeves in so it would fall like a shoulder-length 1940s pageboy. I would sit alone in the middle room of our dark walk-up and type on my box and talk to the boss — his girl Friday, like I was to my dad. My desk was Mom's transatlantic steamer trunk, always covered with the same diagonally placed embroidered tablecloth from Ożarów. I still enjoy going to the movies alone. At the Toronto Film Festival one year I saw 14 films, in empty theatres, masquerading as a member of the press, because Issy had a patron's pass for the previews. One critic asked me during intermission, "Who do you write for?" and when I answered, *"City and Country Home"* — I had written a piece for them on our cottage — he was stymied and made no comment.

Altogether we lived in six places in North Toronto from 1938 to 1948 — from one room behind the first shop to a five-room bungalow on Cranbrooke Avenue — all within a few city blocks. Whenever I stepped outside this domain, it was as foreign as a neighbouring town. I still live about six blocks north. The Yonge-Lawrence area has always been my realm. My present home, however, has more rooms than five, some even grand. Exactly 100 times larger than my first home, the room behind the store. From our living room you have a pleasing long view along the 98-foot gallery off three main rooms to the east garden, which is a valley hosting 18 black walnut trees a hundred years old. Ahhhh trees! These were planted in 1936 brought from the Mulock farm each at age 15. These stately trees are destined to live 300 years more. I'm envious. Last year our majestic three-trunked white pine keeled over from boredom at age about 450 years. We miss it but now we can see, as is said, the forest for the trees beyond. Our north garden is a 25-foot-wide window view of the Don River Valley — Rosedale golf course. The west garden has a life-sized white marble polar bear and the south courtyard a colossal Botero sculpture with a voluminous sensuality. Two lions of Judah, circa 1670, deliberate on the eastern wall, near the front door. And the address 180 is 10 times chai, the number 18 in Judaism for good luck, the same number of our walnut trees.

Rather different from my view through the windows of our 1941–45 walk-up apartment at 3267 Yonge Street, rear. Three tiny rooms gave off a slim hallway, each with a window closely overlooking the building next door, from which it was separated by a grey gravel alley less than three feet wide. The apartment was narrow — about 12 feet including the hall. This was our first private home, and I loved it. It seemed that every night when my mom and I came home from our store across the road, we would find a pool of water on the yellow and brown linoleum kitchen floor because the "shisel," the bowl under the icebox, had overflowed again. "Another pain in the neck," she would grumble in Yiddish as she rolled down her stockings, which sat above her knees over round elastic garters, and got down on all fours to mop up the puddle. The pattern on the linoleum was worn off in some places, and embossed with the shapes of the floorboards beneath. It was in that apartment that I begged for a party to celebrate my eighth birthday, in 1944. This was the only birthday party my mom had attended, ever. Birthday parties were unheard of in the shtetl; my mom herself didn't have even a birthdate. But she humoured her Canadian daughter, in a rare concession, and followed instructions. She bought a cake, and I invited two friends to our dark apartment. The cake, however, turned out to be standard-issue chocolate, about six inches in diameter, and plain — no Happy Birthday, no name — and when I said, "There ought to be candles," Mom brought out one fat Sabbath candle.

I slept in the middle room, which doubled as the sitting room during the day. I would be put to bed every night first in my parents' bedroom, and then later my dad, breathing heavily, would lift me, still asleep, over his shoulder, depositing me on the living room couch, which had now been folded out. This sofa was as firm as a table and would not lie flat, and I had to choose the upper or lower section, so as not to roll off the step in the middle. My mom carped about the defective couch because my dad had bought it from a cousin and paid too much. She said, "With relatives you should go to synagogue only." The couch was always covered in a pink plaid flannelette sheet. The day we moved, when I was nine, I remember sitting on that couch and tracing my finger repeatedly up, across, and down one of the darker pink squares of the blanket and vowing that I would remember that moment, that square of pink flannel, and that apartment forever.

It was not uncommon during the war for stores to be used as living quarters, and the shop below our walk-up apartment was occupied by a Mr. and Mrs. Burton. My mom would make snide remarks about Mrs. Burton, calling her in Yiddish a "kurve" (loose woman), because she reputedly had relations with Mr. Mason, the tailor in our block. I had also had relations with Mr. Mason — at the age of five. I visited the tailor shop, regularly, to play with the tailor's daughter, Daphne. The family lived in a larger room than ours behind their store. Mrs. Mason was grey-haired and grumpy, with a hard-done-by expression. On the shelf of their upright piano stood the sheet music of the Gershwin musical *Rosalie*. I remember Daphne singing this song to tease me especially as I covered my ears in annoyance. This is how I must have acquired my name, because my mother would always get spelling help from Mrs. Mason next door. My birth certificate reads "Rosaline." One day I came to visit when Daphne and her mom were out. We were in the back room when Mr. Mason invited me to sit on his lap on the maroon velour armchair and slowly began to slide his finger inside my panties; and then whether it was polite or not I slid off his lap and ran out the door. At five years old I don't know how I knew not to tell anyone, not even my mother. I lost touch with Daphne until recently when she told me that her father had gone into her bed every night when she was young. She used the term "full sex." When he was dying in a Montreal hospital, he had begged for her forgiveness, which she gave. Mr. Mason had also molested another young girl whose mother came to the tailor shop to complain.

Another friend on our block was Dorothy Worley whose father was the barber in the block. They had a bright green parrot who could sing the overture to *The Marriage of Figaro*. One day Dorothy and I, when I was about six, and she 11, walked downtown to Eaton's department store on College Street, maybe more than seven miles. I remember almost losing consciousness in my feet, the sidewalk walking me. Today Dorothy lives on Vancouver Island with her family and husband, Murray Lawrence, whose family, in the year 1795 had been granted 200 acres on what is today the east and west sides of Yonge Street from Lawrence Avenue to Eglinton.

During the war there was a housing shortage, so a few Yonge Street shops became homes with painted-out front windows. Yonge Street in those days was so much more like a village. Before malls and online shopping all goods were to be found in neighbourhood shops, and storekeepers did well. Today every block in that same Yonge-Lawrence area has a manicure shop, a restaurant, or a super-sized drug store — not clothes and shoes and dresses — and since the Covid pandemic one shop in every block has blanked-off windows with the sign "CLOSED."

My school chum Lorna Chisholm lived in a shop where the glass was painted light grey. I would sometimes stop by to collect her on the way to school. Her mom would be listening to the radio in her backless fur-trimmed mules, her hair in pink sponge curlers, a bowl of dry puffed-wheat cereal on the broad arm of the lounge chair. Lorna had an older sister who was soon to marry a police officer, but I never saw or heard about a dad. I preferred to pick up chums rather than have them come to my place. Sometimes I would collect Carol Welsh, whose father was principal of a public school, not ours. I would wait while she finished her piano practice. Carol had the goyish good looks I envied — platinum hair and green eyes. But apparently, I did look goyish, because my relatives nicknamed me "the little shiksele" (gentile girl). I read the subtext: think Yiddish and look goy-ish, but better not to have a goyishe kop (a gentile mind). Carol lived in a red-brick house with a central hall. The front room had an upright piano, golden lamplight on nice old furniture, and there were always flowers — in our house there were never flowers. Carol wore smocked dresses, and her parents met in the sitting room before dinner for a drink and quiet conver-sation. My parents' conversation was usually confrontational.

Curiously, my current driving route downtown takes me past this house and Bedford Park Public School. Recently, after a meal in a local restaurant, Tony and I wandered through the schoolyard and were surprised to find our family's name engraved on a boulder, which no one had mentioned, in honour of a donation, I guess.

Growing up it was always wartime. Some foods were rationed and there were coupons for tinned salmon. Somehow Mom made me use the issued coupons illegally to procure extra tins we were not entitled to. I recall being uncomfortable asking for these in Loblaws. And this gave me a mixed mes-sage about stealing and ethics. Once I stole a small paring knife from the five-and-dime as a gift for my mom. I thought she'd praise my ingenuity, but instead she made me return it. I did not give the knife back to the sales-clerk as I was bidden, but just secretly put it back in its bin. Mom sent me daily to Macdonald's Bakery a few doors away, for milk buns folded over and sprinkled with flour. Mrs. Macdonald, the plump proprietor, always wore a white short-sleeved uniform that revealed her dimpled, doughy elbows. In the window were trays of fragrant cinnamon Chelsea buns, two for a nickel. I used to love the corner ones that had a carbon caramel glaze. Margaret Macdonald, the daughter, would wait on me. I saw Margaret as a curiosity, because Mom said she was an old maid, which I understood to be a stigma. On the counter, the Macdonalds had a huge roll of aluminum foil to be donated to the war effort, peeled one piece at a time from the customers' gum wrappers and cigarette packs. Dad listened daily on the edge of his seat, to the newscasts of Gabriel Heater reporting on the war. During the broadcasts, no one could speak without Dad making a loud "shush." And every year the Buy Victory Bonds man came with his wooden silk-screen box that measured about three feet by four. At every block, he would put his box down on the sidewalk (sometimes even on the glass of a store window with permission) and pull his roller across. When he lifted the box, an image in blue paint would read "THIRD VICTORY BOND" or, the following year, "FOURTH." The paint would fade a little with each rain, until it disappeared. Also, during the war, the government issued tags to every shopkeeper, labelled "Wartime Prices and Trade Board," to be pinned on every item, price included. Before this, items were not priced individually. It fell to me to perform the tedious job of folding what seemed like thousands of the prickly, staple-like pins.

At school I was lucky to be chosen to sing in the choir. Miss Dorland, our coach, was as pretty and benevolent as Olivia de Havilland in *Gone with the Wind*. She was short, round, and, when she conducted, red cheeked with enthusiasm — as proud of us as a mother warbler is of her chicks. Miss Dorland would sing along, silently shaping tall round tones outlined by her shiny red lipstick, while her arms swelled and ebbed — first beckoning the altos and then drawing in the sopranos — tilting up and down on her toes with each upbeat. But Miss Dorland and the Bedford Park choir were to come into dishonour when we competed in the 1945 Annual Kiwanis Music Festival at Eaton Auditorium. Every school was to be judged on the same program of two songs: Offenbach's "Barcarolle" and the rousing tune "When Johnny Comes Marching Home."

When it came time for our school to sing, I was second in the lineup, waiting in the wings of the colossal stage with its black-and-gold-striped curtains framing the art deco proscenium. How did it happen that I came to be here on the stage of the grandest theatre I had ever seen? In front of me was the audience — two floors packed with doting parents. Not mine, of course. The adorable, bright-eyed Miss Dorland bounced backstage for a quick review of the troops. A white gardenia graced the collar of the navy and white polka-dot dress that swung above her curvy calves, each leg defined by a centre seam that rose from the heels of the silk hose above her platform shoes. When the signal came, we marched out to centre stage and formed a double line — I was in the front row, in the alto section with the boys. Miss Dorland raised her arms for the downbeat, and we were off:

"When Johnny comes marching home again, Hurrah! Hurrah! We'll give him a hearty welcome then, Hurrah! Hurrah! The men will cheer, and the boys will shout, the ladies, they will all turn out . . ." It was spring and the war was nearly over. People longed for their sons and lovers to come home from overseas, so the patriotic words rang out into the crowd, and everyone clapped along.

Now it was time for our second song, "Barcarolle." We waited for the cue from the piano intro, but something went wrong with Miss Dorland's downbeat and a few of us had a false start, so we had to begin again. The Bedford Park choir placed last in the festival.

If my parents had known I didn't spend the day at school, I can imagine the dialogue:

"Rosie, nu, where were you today?"

"I was at Eaton Auditorium."

"You mean you went shopping at Eaton's instead of going to school?"

"Well, no, on top of Eaton's there is a concert hall. You see, it was the Kiwanis Music Festival."

"Kiwanis — what means Kiwanis?"

Words like "festival" and "choir" simply did not translate into Yiddish. Soon after the concert, the war was over and "Johnny Came Marching Home." I was about nine then, and I became a different person — the one I am today. I remember the very moment. I was walking east along Cranbrooke Avenue, where we had just moved into the first house we owned, a small bungalow. I was on the north side of the street just passing number 40, half a block from Yonge Street, wearing white shorts and a form-fitting white T-shirt with narrow sky-blue stripes. For the first time I was very self-conscious and cocky about how I looked. It was as if I were two people and one of me was on the other side of the street appraising the new me.

At home my mother made it clear that she was not happy in the Wise household. She was always threatening to leave. "If I had any family here," she would say, "I would have left long ago — but I'm alone — I have no way out."

The first time I heard this, I trembled with fear, but after a while I knew she didn't have the guts. One minute she would be carping about her sad life and the next she would break into a Yiddish song. I think I once said, "If you want to leave, leave already."

I was often frightened in the night by my parents arguing in bed. Sometimes I worried that it was about me, but although I strained to hear, I could never make out a single word, only a rumble. Then the rumble got louder. My stomach would roll over with fear and my heart would pound and I would wait for my father's words to come to a crescendo and listen for the thud of his feet as he got out of bed. Then I worried that he might come into my room and hit me. He came into my room only once, and I think he only yelled at me, but for some reason I spent many nights afraid that he would do something to one of us. And now I cannot even remember what my crimes were. I know my mom kvetched about how little help I was around the house. Every complaint began with "You never" — "you never wash the kitchen floor like other kids, you never help with the dishes," and so on. It was true I should have helped more, but I became what she said. The house was a battleground, and I felt obliged to take sides. So, I sided with my father; everything became black and white, and I found fault with Mom on all counts — I was quite unfair. She would carp and complain about me, her sad lot in life, her separation from her family, and she maintained she would have been happier back in Ożarów with her "genteel" family. Mom would boast that her mother was a fine lady and her dad one of the respected elders in the town. In the social hierarchy, her family was a few notches above my dad's people.

Once upon a Time on Teddington, 2020, 36" x 36".

CHAPTER SIX

The Wind in the Willows

I never once saw my parents kiss, touch, embrace, or even place an arm around the other's shoulder or waist, although I found unexpressed warmth when I sat on my dad's lap as a youngster. It is no surprise, then, that I cringe when a couple in the movies kisses open-mouthed on their first date. And I'm not easy with public displays of affection, such as when the groom pledges his love over the microphone — I much prefer wit. Centuries of shtetl Jews have been very private about displaying affection. Maybe it's something written in the Torah.

We were living at 3267 Yonge Street, across from the store, when I was six, and it was then that I made a discovery of the most major importance — books, my great escape. Books were my world, my friends. It was easier to stay home than suffer the anxiety of making real friends, and at home it didn't matter that I wore funny clothes. And with books I could block out the noise of my parents arguing. Storybooks especially were my passion. The very first book was probably the most stupendous event in my life. It was Kenneth Grahame's *The Wind in the Willows*, read to the class a chapter a day by our Grade 1 teacher, Miss Sharpe, when I was five and a half. Without this book I would be someone else. I think books make the man.

I was in Miss Sharpe's thrall. I could hardly wait to get to school to hear the next episode in the adventures of Mole, Toad, and Water Rat — animals who spoke to each other like people, and helped each other out of jams.

Because I was younger than the others and unfamiliar with written English — there were no books at our place — I was bottom of the class in reading; but by the end of Grade 1 I was among the top readers. Miss Sharpe wrote on my report card: "alert, interested, talkative." Still an apt description.

Proudly I read some chapters of *The Wind in the Willows* to my granddaughter Erika when she was five — she fell asleep, and my great-grandchild Max had the same reaction to the archaic language. Another book I loved was *The Yearling*, which I gave to Tony to read at the same age. He thought it was a bore, but finally I had some luck with a title when the boys were in their preteens. I read them one chapter a day of *The Hound of the Baskervilles* by Sir Arthur Conan Doyle, and they were captivated. And tell me, what name has more ring to it than Sir Arthur Conan Doyle? As soon as possible after *The Wind in the Willows*, I joined the most important club — and the only club, besides a tennis club, to which I would ever belong — the library. I needed five cents to join, for which I begged more than once from my father. The St. Clements Library was a one-storey green and white cottage set well back from Yonge Street in a wide lawn — like an enchanting English storybook house. They demolished it maybe 10 years ago. The library was an almost two-mile walk from home, but for me it was a routine destination.

Reading was my refuge. One time I got a book early in the morning, read it, and returned later the same day for another. The librarian refused with these bone-chilling words: "See here, it is plainly stamped on the card pocket at the back of each volume, 'A book may not be returned on the day on which it is borrowed.'" The Doctor Dolittle books were favourites of mine. I remember exactly where they were in the library: on the second shelf up from the dark ochre sheet of linoleum, in the southwest corner. This series of narrow volumes, taking up a space on the shelf as long as my arm, was illustrated with simple pen-and-ink line drawings by the author, Hugh Lofting. When Doctor Dolittle was played on the screen by Rex Harrison, I refused to see the film, faithfully protecting the real Dolittle from the imposter.

Another book I loved was *The Princess and the Goblin*, by George MacDonald. The princess travels through subterranean caves on craggy ledges but is always safely guided by a magic gossamer thread she follows with her forefinger. The goblin community has some laughs at her expense when they discover that the ends of her feet are divided into five parts, called toes, while real feet like theirs have only two parts. I read like a mad fiend; my face often safely hidden by the book. I read at the dinner table, while walking to school, and late into the night. As a teenager, I stayed home to finish my book instead of going out on a date. Some unfading titles come to mind: *Nicholas and Alexandra*, *A Child's Garden of Verses*, *Huckleberry Finn*, *The Last Lion*, *The Thirty-Nine Steps*, *Kidnapped*, *Surely You're Joking, Mr. Feynman!*, *Down and Out in Paris*, *Working*, *The Great Railway Bazaar*, and if you asked me tomorrow the list might be different. In 1948, they began to build a new large library at Lawrence and Yonge a mile closer than my St. Clements one. I watched forever (a year) while stone masons slowly laid row after row of limestone blocks building the George H. Locke Library. Would it ever be finished? I missed the opening in January 1949 by a few days when we moved out of the district. Not until 1962 would I step into this grand library when my sons and I became card-carrying members.

WITH MY NOSE ALWAYS in a book, my mother would implore me to stop: "Rosie — please — put the book away already. You'll ruin your eyes." In fact, I did wear glasses, because I had one lazy eye that strayed and from time to time my nose would loom into view. My parents explained to friends in Yiddish that unfortunately I was shikldik (cross-eyed). My dad, who had little faith in doctors, tore off my glasses and said, "These glasses are doing no good. Your eyes will be stronger and straighten out better without them," and he proved to be right. I never again wore the ugly wire-rimmed glasses. I'm still a reader, and I always have a book on hand. Books are still comforts and friends — unlike people, who you are obliged to get to know too well.

When I was eight, I began to nag and beg my parents for two things: a bicycle and a baby brother. I got both. "But, Mom," I argued, "Dad rode a bicycle in Ożarów, so it's not foolishness, and I can ride to school like other kids." New bikes were expensive because it was wartime, so my dad bought me a rusty CCM second-hand bicycle that once must have been a maroon colour. He paid $35 for it, and for once I agreed with my mom that Dad had been taken. Of course, I didn't give her the credit. I bullheadedly maintained my censorious stand against her. My bike soon had a flat tire, and when the mechanic at Gerber's Gas Station uncovered the inner tube, it was so plastered with small rubber patches that it looked like Joseph's coat of many colours.

One day Mom wore a small guilty smile when I again brought up the subject of "Please, why can't I have a baby brother like other girls?" Although she loved pretty dresses, she now seemed to have lost all sense of fashion and had taken to wearing the same stained dress day after day — a shape-less wraparound affair in a faded teal grey. Then I caught her giggling on the phone that her daughter was teasing her about this dress. Later, when my brother was born, I figured it out — this was her version of a maternity dress. She also told her friends that she didn't need to tell her daughter anything about sex because the brilliant kid already knew everything. "Everything" had been explained to me by Florence Bongard, whose family rented the upstairs from my dad's sister. On one of our Sunday visits to 325 College Street, Florence told me, in her bedroom, about men and women, and which part of each body went where, a stunning and preposterous manoeuvre. But she also told me, probably I got it wrong, that men menstruated monthly like women, but that the stuff that came out was white. I held on to this misconception until I was 16 and almost gave away my ignorance in health class, which I quickly covered up when I caught on.

Stanley Barrie Wise was born when I was nine, and he was named after my mother's brother, Shloime. In the Jewish tradition you are named after the closest deceased relative, a person you therefore will never know, and the name recurs every few generations. The name Itzhak (Isadore) reverberated through centuries of rabbis. Mom recuperated from the birth, complainingly, in the first Mount Sinai Hospital on Yorkville Avenue, listed today as a heritage building. It was started by four Jewish ladies in 1920, named Cohn, Spiegel, Miller, and Adler, because few Jewish doctors were allowed in hospitals, and few accepted in university. None could rent an office in the prestigious Medical Arts Building. Whenever I visited my dentist there, I felt hostility in the marble lobby with its carved stone entablature over the door, "Entrance to Motors," which sounded excluding and haughty.

When my mother was in the Yorkville hospital, she stayed for two weeks, common in those days. When I visited, she was wearing her black "wrapper" with the bouquets of bright flowers and was walking very slowly, bent over, hand on her back and kvetching, complaining. Since then, I have always liked textiles with florals printed on a black background. Whenever my mom found my behaviour trying, she would remind me of the many torments I had caused her. She never tired of giving me the yarn that she had been in the hospital for "three days and three nights" giving birth to me, and that I was the only child in the city to have contracted chicken pox and measles simultaneously. She would often use standard Yiddish curses that made me laugh. They seemed harsh but were more benign than they sounded: "You should have the same troubles from your own children." Oh, gladly would I settle for the same troubles from my boys.

My new baby brother, Stan, arrived home with a greenish complexion from a touch of jaundice — not the pink doll-baby I had hoped for. But soon his colour improved, and he began to smile. Mom said it was just gas. Now my life changed forever as I took charge of the baby. There is a shtetl tradition that a sister should look out for a brother because women should always defer to brothers and husbands. Which recalls Isaac Bashevis Singer's shtetl short story where an elderly wife dutifully wants the best of everything for her Husband always with a capital *H* and buys only the best cut of meat for *Him*, and cooks the best soup for *Him*, and ultimately procures for *Him* a younger woman so *He* should have the sex that *He* deserves.

Stan should be grateful, because he owes me a lot: I saw to it that he had swimming lessons, he became a lifeguard as a teenager. I saw to it that Stan learned to roller skate and ice skate, that he has a middle name, that he's in this world at all, and that he has one single photo of himself before the age of nine. For this photo, I took him downtown on the streetcar to Starkman's Chemists, who had offered "a free baby photo with any small purchase." We waited in line half the day, with all the other mothers and babes. I was also charged with taking care of Stan from after school until bedtime, and on weekends. I was forbidden to stay after school. According to my dad, who had never attended school, only bad kids had to stay. One day the teacher kept the whole class in. I went up to her and pleaded that I was expected at home to take care of my brother — or else — but she refused to make an exception. My father was screamingly angry and would not accept my account. Another time the teacher asked that everyone buy a paperback 10-inch math workbook for 59 cents. My father said, "No, the school provides all the books." I was the only one in the class without one and had to read a book while the others entered sums in their enviable math books. Maybe this is why I could never do math.

Meanwhile, my brother and I became inseparable. We are still best friends — he and his wife, Martha, the world's best mother, are coming for dinner on Friday, the first Sabbath dinner in 18 months due to the pandemic.

As a baby, Stan was plump and cuddly, often wearing the same pair of soft, homemade threadbare blue flannel overalls, and I loved his trusting weight in my arms. What was he thinking, I wondered, when he stared with such an unblinking gaze at the wind rustling the leaves? He would sit, easygoing, in his carriage, with his dark melting chocolate eyes and brown curly hair, looking like an Arab prince. One Saturday a friend and I wanted to go to a movie in the early evening, but Stan didn't go to bed till about eight, so I hit upon a plan to make him sleepy. My friend had a bottle in her medicine cabinet with the label "Contains ether," and I had read the Nancy Drew mystery novel where ether figured in one of her crime cases. So, we opened the bottle and put it near Stan's nose. Well, he squirmed and refused to sniff, and as we followed his nose with the bottle, some of the liquid may have dribbled into his mouth and he began to scream. I called Webb's Pharmacy, as my mother always did for all medical advice, and Mr. Webb prescribed milk as an antidote. So, we plied Stan with milk while he continued to protest. That evening, Mom came home early from work and gave Stan a bath, during which he tried repeatedly to tell her the tale of his bad day. Luckily, I was the only one who could understand his baby talk. "What is he talking?" said my mother. "I can't understand a word."

On one of our long walks, Stan and I passed Loretto Abbey, a girls' boarding school. It looked to me like a fairy-tale stone castle, with its towers and crenellations — as Victorian as the one in *Wuthering Heights*. I boldly walked up to the door and rang the bell. A nun in full skirts answered the door. "Please," I asked, "may I come in and look around your beautiful mansion?" She graciously invited us in. I parked Stan and his carriage in the front hall, put on the brake, and followed the nun for an hour-long tour of the place. When she showed me the bedrooms for the boarders decorated with floral fabrics and white furniture, I gladly would have converted and moved right in. Even my own school, Bedford Park, was fascinating because it was palatial, with its Doric columns, broad staircases, and so much light from the six tall windows in each classroom. The ancient date of 1911 was carved into the stone lintel over the entrance.

I suppose gracious old buildings will continue to fascinate me. Once recently in Palm Springs, I was riding my bike to the market when I passed a handsome early-'30s house. Of course, I was curious to see the inside, so I rang the bell. The beautiful blond woman who answered was at first a little wary until I said, "We have a house of similar vintage and I'd love to have a look, and perhaps you would like to see our place just around the corner."

Perhaps my love for old buildings came from my dad — he had the mind of an architect-designer. In Ożarów he had settled for the profession of tailor because there were few opportunities open to Jews, but in Canada he reached his full potential. The man was gifted. He took our storefront on Yonge Street from the ordinary to the extraordinary. The existing store window was flush with the sidewalk, and my father redesigned it by pushing it back into a glamorous U-shape, so there was twice as much window display. The glass was curved, in three sections, with a dark grey bordered terrazzo entrance floor and a black sign in Vitrolite (a glass material) with silver letters. Business improved because there were now more items on display to entice passersby. My dad dressed the windows, and I made all the signs advertising the specials: LADIES' HOUSEDRESSES, MEN'S WORKING SOCKS, CHILDREN'S COATS, HATS & LEGGINGS, and BOYS' BRITCHES. Mom would look at my work and say, "She has goldene hent — golden hands." Customers often wanted only that item in the window, especially if it was the last one; then Dad would have to crawl, mutteringly, on all fours into his carefully arranged display. We had no full-sized mannequins, but we had plastic armless torsos to display bras and blouses.

It struck me as odd that Dad — super-tailor that he was — did not make his own suits but had them cut to measure (with two pair of pants) at Tip Top Tailors up the street. Of course, in the 1930s, a man didn't count for much without a nice suit, silk tie, and felt fedora. And then, each spring, a Jewish old-clothes peddler would come by and bargain for Dad's suit from the previous year. One day when my father was downtown buying inventory, two police officers came into the store while I was sitting on the lone chair reading. When I called Mom from the sewing machine in the back room, one of them told her, "Mrs. Wise, we're sorry to inform you, but there may be some bad news about Mr. Wise. An hour ago, we found a dead man below the bridge over the Bloor Viaduct, and he was wearing a suit jacket with the name 'Joseph Wise' printed on the lining."

Mom was hysterical: "Oh God, it can't be. It's not possible — he just went down to Matlow's on York Street to get socks and underwear for the store. It must be a mistake, God help us."

"Mrs. Wise, I hope you're right, but just to be sure, please come along with us to the morgue. We'll need you to identify the body."

The officers took her arm, and the three of them climbed into the curb-side cruiser, leaving me on the red leatherette chair to mind the store and to wonder. Maybe it was just a few minutes later when I heard the click of the back door, and who should it be but Dad, schlepping his brown paper packages by their rough string handles. When Mom returned, she gave us the lowdown. Apparently, a vagrant (i.e., "the body" — I regret I never did ask her what he looked like) had jumped or was pushed from the bridge to the road 200 feet below. When we remembered the peddler, the events began to come together.

My father graduated from tailor-shopkeeper to builder-landlord with the construction of a cement block one-car garage behind the store. It happened like this: A truck arrived and dropped about 200 10-inch cement blocks in the yard. Then Dad went off to the Selective Service, a government organization that provided pickup work for unskilled labourers. He recruited John Brennan, a new immigrant. Brennan was average height, young and muscular, with reddish curly hair, blue eyes, and an Irish brogue. He looked like the actor Albert Finney. He had some experience in building — we didn't know how much — but he knew more than Dad, so he became the adviser. "Well, to be sure now, Mr. Wise, first off, we'll be needing to dig us some footings four feet deep."

"Four feet, John? But the building is only seven feet high. Maybe two feet should be okay?"

"Well, to be sure now, Mr. Wise, 'tis the regulation, and if you don't dig a four-foot foundation, the building will be heaving, it will, come the first frost."

Dad reluctantly agreed to the unplanned-for extra cost, and Mr. Brennan soon finished the handsome block building. This one-car garage was not for our car, but to be rented out at $15 per month. Privately I thought, "Dad has a lot of chutzpah to ask such a high rent — who would pay that much for a garage?" When that cheque rolled in regularly, even Mom and I were impressed, and she made the $15 go a long way. And Dad thought, "What a simple way to make a living — no inventory." So, from that time on, 1944, when my dad was 33, he became a builder-landlord, although we kept the store another five years.

Business was brisk at Wise's Dry Goods, so we bought our first house when I was 10 and Stan was a year old. It was a five-room bungalow at 165 Cranbrooke Avenue. Steps ran up a steep hill to a path that led to the front door. Dad cut out the hill, jacked up the front of the house, and put a garage under the front porch, with flagstone steps curving from the driveway, which was now on grade, up to the front door. A piece of genius, although we were never sure if the jacked-up house was safe from collapse, because Dad knew nothing about engineering or building, and again relied on John to do the job. The neighbours next door, whose bungalow sat on the same hill, soon copied Dad's architectural design and made their house a mirror image of ours. I recall Dad and John Brennan at the kitchen table over coffee and a cheese Danish, poring over plans for the next project.

John continued as my dad's right-hand man for his next few buildings — one at a time — stores with one or two apartments above them. Then there were three stores in a row at Eglinton and Keele, and with the purchase of a 10-plex on Wilson Avenue, Dad's life on the third cushion of the living room sofa began in earnest. Ever since Dad had become a landlord, his routine never varied. He went out for coffee at six, came home, sat on the sofa all day, read the newspapers, and he never did five minutes of any physical exercise, even walking. He watched the news on TV, sometimes the wrestling program, a favourite of Mom's — waited for the mail to bring cheques from the tenants, and maybe went out to the bank or shopping for food with his wife. On these occasions, he always waited in the car — so no one would see his limp.

One time I was shopping on Eglinton Avenue near Oakwood, about 1950. Three red fire engines, each following the other, came screeching down the street, so loud I could feel it in my solar plexus. One of my dad's stores was located a few blocks in the direction the fire trucks were rushing. The thought came, "Could it be that Dad's store is on fire? No, it couldn't be — it's never the known evil that gets you." It *was* my father's store, rented to a sporting goods outfit. Luckily there was little damage and no casualties.

The Colours of a Day in the Desert, 2014, 36" x 36".

CHAPTER SEVEN

The Lost Genes

Even as a child, I had a bent for sketching and lettering and working with colours. I was surprised to discover that many members of my mother's family were also so inclined. I uncovered this connection in 1983, when, quite by accident, I first met my aunt Marmish, my uncle Chaskel, and all the other Birnbaums.

Well, the truth is, I didn't actually meet them in person, because they were no longer among the living. They were all murdered on either October 22, 1942, at the Treblinka death camp, or in the massacre in their shtetl of Ożarów on October 26. I wouldn't even know which date to mark with a candle or prayer.

I met the Birnbaum family while sifting through my parents' belongings after they had died. I remember that day. It was creepy walking up the five familiar steps to 606 Briar Hill Avenue and unlocking the door of the too-silent house to the stale air and everything in its place as if Mom and Dad had just stepped out for lunch. My mother had died of ovarian cancer in April 1983 and my dad four months later, the cause suspiciously absent. I walked into the dining room where the routine maroon and gold dinner plates were standing undisturbed in the china cabinet, as were the mock Louis XV green silk side chairs vacuum sealed in their clear plastic covers. I went through all the drawers and cabinets to ensure that their treasures were saved from the hands of strangers. So, what did we save?

An embroidered tablecloth from Ożarów, the trunk that travelled from Poland with my mother on the S.S. *Pulaski* from Gdańsk to Pier 21 in Halifax. Two pieces of the bedroom set my father had bought layaway — a wedding gift for my mother. He had taken the streetcar for two years to make the three-dollar payments we found on a stamped card. My mom kept every bill since her wedding. Sorting through the gas bills from the 1930s I could figure out the dates we moved from place to place.

And, in a top drawer, a worn paper box labelled "Weldrest Hosiery, silk, size 9." The box yielded not silk stockings but perhaps 100 brittle pages of closely written Yiddish script, in ink once black but now grey. These were letters from Poland, from my mom's three sisters and young brother, written between 1930 and August 1939 — when a New Year's card was returned, marked "Mail Suspended."

The Birnbaums were a family of five children. Shloime, the eldest, married Rachel Kestenbaum after immigrating to Montreal in 1926. Sadly, he died of heart failure at the age of 43. He had come home that night from his woodcarving work, had a hot cocoa, gone to bed, and died in his sleep. Shloime had work only in the synagogue. He had lost better-paying jobs as a cabinet maker because he was a pious Jew and refused to work on the Sabbath. He was never to find out that in 1943 the Germans would slaughter his close and extended family in Europe.

I last saw him in 1942, winding the black leather phylacteries round his arms for his morning prayers in his front parlour in Montreal. I asked him some idle question, which he answered with a stern look that taught me not to speak during prayers. Childhood memories often connect to mistakes made.

YDESSA WAS BORN IN Ożarów in 1914 — or so she told me. The truth is that she was born about 1912; she needed the extra two years to find a suitor before she was 21, the age of an old maid.

In 1930, Ydessa came to Montreal to live with her brother Shloime, his wife, Rachel, and their two young daughters, Goldie and Bella. A third daughter, Jeannie, came along later. Bella was said to resemble my mom, a comparison that never pleased the girl. Sadly, Bella was to contract cancer at the same age as Ydessa. They shared the same gene, which luckily, I lack. My mom worked in a sweatshop, chained to a sewing machine for five years as a factory drudge, not the elite "draper" she told me she had been, then married Joseph Wise, who came from the same shtetl. He was not her first choice, but she settled for him, as she was already, by her standards, an old maid at 23. In Ożarów she might have had an arranged marriage as young as 16, but her father had two other daughters for whom to provide dowries, so someone had to leave. Originally, it was decided that Marmish, the oldest unmarried sister, should go. According to Aunt Rachel, Shloime chose my mom instead — luckily for me — because Marmish was very bright and spelled trouble.

In a letter dated September 25, 1930, Marmish writes: "We'll see each other one of these days, when they re-open Canadian immigration. . . . closed to Jews by Prime Minister Mackenzie King." About Jews Mackenzie King had famously said: "None is too many."

To find out more about my disappeared relatives I hired a young school-girl living in Ożarów today — Anna Czajkowski. I asked her to speak to local townsfolk for any recollections of the Birnbaum family. Happily, I was to be given these precious gifts of memories: I found out that during the holiday of Shavuot, paper cut-outs, backlit with candlelight, glowed in the Birnbaum windows, and were said to be the best in town. And a local, who was once in their house, described a handmade embroidered wall-hanging over the stove and remembers the two sisters sitting on a bench beside the door embroidering tablecloths and other linens. Another resident, Mr. Pekalski, recalled that "when the Jews were driven out in 1942, there were plenty of tombstones left in the Birnbaums' yard, near the workshop behind the house, because Yechil was famous as a carver also in the neighbouring towns of Tarłów and Opatov." He also sculpted secular works — someone recalled a vase of flowers carved from local sandstone, the same material he used for the gravestones.

ONCE I SADISTICALLY CHALLENGED myself to a test: "the Gestapo Game." It goes like this: I imagine two Gestapo officers come to the door, wearing the hateful uniforms with gleaming black boots and silver swastikas. They click their heels and announce, "Madam, this house will be taken over by the neo-Nazis. You have one hour to collect your belongings. Your family will be relocated to a one-room apartment in the Jewish ghetto, and you will take only the following items in these three shopping bags: one for clothing, one for food, one for household items." "Good," I think. "This was bound to happen sooner or later — as it did to my family. Now I can simplify and get rid of this egregious accumulation and the guilt from having so much good fortune." I take the three bags and begin to move around our five principal rooms chockablock with china. Into one of the bags, I drop 12 items — most made in England in the mid-1740s: a Chelsea cup and tall milk jug; five sauceboats, from Limehouse, Lund's Bristol, Bow, Reid, and Worcester; one small Chelsea figurine of a crinoline lady; a vase from the St. Cloud factory; a pair of Worcester cream boats; and Chris's self-portrait. In my kitchen bag, I drop some Ceylon black tea, a loaf of Ace Bakery sunflower-seed sliced bread, some sweet butter, and the toaster. For clothing, I take my thinnest jeans, a John Smedley black cotton-knit turtleneck, a mahogany and persimmon chiffon scarf, and an ideal lichen-green fine pashmina shawl. When I return to the front door, the Gestapo has mysteriously vanished.

Two large portraits of my mother's parents, in oval Edwardian frames, hang in our rec room, now witnesses to a life they could never have imagined. Children emigrating from Poland to the New World customarily brought along such portraits so the elders could keep a watchful eye over their children. Before leaving, the émigrés would traditionally also visit the graves of their forbears to say their farewells. I have a photo of Lillie Sharp at her father's grave before she left Poland. The emigrants never expected to return, after their ocean voyage, especially by a jet plane.

The Birnbaums lived at No. 1 Zlote (Gold) Street, with the stone-carving workshop behind. Among other jobs, my grandfather was a tombstone carver. The house had two rooms, a kitchen and a bedroom, with beds in both. There was also an attic and a root cellar you reached by ladder. When potatoes were needed, the children drew lots for who would go down to the cellar and face the biting insects lurking there. You needed to be clever to make a living in Ożarów, so my grandfather had many trades and eked out a hardscrabble existence. Yechil was primarily a moneylender, but he also mended paper banknotes since the bank didn't replace torn ones. As well as carving the tombstones, he ground wheat at Passover and made matzos for sale.

Between 1933 and 1945, only 5,000 Jews were admitted to Canada. On June 14, 1939, Chaskel no longer writes about emigration. He appears to have given up and stoically puts up a good front. He writes: "There was a by-law passed that every shop had to have a signboard (to designate Jewish shops, as Poles were ordered not to patronize these). I know this kind of work, so I made quite a bit of money."

I would have been so happy to compare notes with Chaskel about my one-stroke sign painting, once making 50 signs for the restaurants and booths at the Hadassah Bazaar. We could have painted the signs together.

But how could Chaskel and my grandfather have imagined so outrageous a plan as the Nazis' systematic murder of every single Jew, to cleanse the whole world of us. Man's inhumanity to man on a scale never before or after perpetrated on one people. *Judenrein*, in Hitler's hateful word. The historian Hannah Arendt coined the phrase "the banality of evil," because the Nazi murderers had been from all walks of life, doctors and lawyers and postal workers, mechanics, storekeepers — all willing to carry out the grisly murders. Some were joiners like Adolf Eichmann, who was not very intelligent. Joiners are defined by the group they belong to, and characteristically don't think for themselves — like white supremacists.

I think people like Holocaust deniers and anti-Semites do not prosper, and they need hate to make up for their inadequacies. I wish that the profile of an anti-Semite could be universally preached on television — that haters are *their* own problem — that it should be a stigma to be anti-Semitic, that need to elevate themselves above their own envy and self-doubt. Anti-Semites are the personification of all that is warped and evil in humanity. Anti-Semites should be branded for the lesser men that they are, and they should be ashamed to admit it. I wish there was an ad on TV with a Dr. Fauci type cataloguing the profile of a hater and warning them that hating your fellow man is a mark of disgrace.

I measure all my troubles, large and small, against the terrifying accounts of my fellow Jews during the Holocaust. The Holocaust has indelibly invaded my consciousness and is always with me, like a dybbuk. It lurks around the fringes of my mind, a bizarre contrast to my good life. It's up to me to remember the Holocaust and make sure my kids never forget.

A survivor of the Holocaust says in one of the memory books that he would like to say to the Polish people, "You live in our homes, you sleep in our beds . . . you use our bedding, you wear our clothes." Every Jewish house in 1,000 Polish towns was simply seized by a Pole. Can you believe, according to Google, that today 48 percent of Polish people are anti-Semitic? Therefore, if four people are now sleeping in my grandfather's house and drinking his wine, two of them are anti-Semites.

And imagine Hitler needed all the fine art and valuables of the wealthy Jews to finance the war. The Swiss banks, silently and deceitfully, kept the money of Jews who had died until this was discovered in the mid 1990s, and in 1998 they returned $1.25 billion, but it is said that it should have been more.

Mom, when she was growing up, was afraid of the hatred some Polish Catholics harbour against Jews and remembered her brother was beaten on the road to Hebrew school. For centuries the Catholic Church had fuelled anti-Semitism in Poland. In 1936, the year I was born, Cardinal August Hlond stated that "three and a half million Jews in Poland are too many — half a million would suffice." Pope Pius XII was guilty by his silence during all the years of the extermination of the Jews. There was even an administrative connection between the Vatican's Curia and the Nazis during the war. For this the Pope was called "Hitler's deputy" — a history well told by Rolf Hochhuth in his play *The Deputy*, which I will always keep in my library. In my kitchen are two pairs of silver Torah finials from the mostly empty 2,500 synagogues of Europe. I like to think these were from my grandfather's synagogue, which was used as a warehouse for plumbing supplies by the locals.

Only 250,000 Polish Jews, out of 3.3 million, survived the Holocaust. Which gets me thinking. If CNN were around during the Holocaust, they would have been embedded beside the crematoriums; or if MSNBC had covered the Spanish Inquisition, history, I think, would have been very very different.

My people, the Birnbaums, were probably among those marched to the train station in Jasice and shipped to Treblinka although some of them may have been among the 120 who were shot and buried in the mass grave at the cemetery, including, it is reported, a mother holding a young child. Or they could have been with those who were killed in the street, as described by Polish residents living in Ożarów today. As a local poet put it, "the Jews were caught in the hot act of life." By October 26, 1942, the Birnbaums had all been slaughtered. I cannot stop remembering the horrors of the Holocaust.

MY RELATIVES ON MY father's side, the Weissfogels, fared much better than the Birnbaums. They had the good sense to leave Poland in 1927 and make their way to Toronto. The Weissfogels became Wises when they arrived in Halifax. In Ożarów, my father, Joe, had been apprenticed to a tailor at age 12. If he had been born in Warsaw, he might have become an architect, but through the ages Jews had been chased out of cities and had to regroup in small towns where they could practise their religion. Very few professions were available in the shtetl, and the best option for my dad was tailoring, a trade he continued successfully in Canada. He became a cutter — one of the elite members of the tailors' trade, making as much as $100 a week during the Depression — which my mother never let him forget, since when they were married, he had only $40: "He didn't have water to boil buckwheat," she said. Joe lived with his parents and his sister Helen and her husband. Helen recounts that when Joe first arrived from Poland, he was emaciated from hiding out in a basement, to avoid the military, and she couldn't make him enough of the johnnycake he craved. When his blond young sister Pearl arrived from Ożarów, Joe doted on her and spent much of his large salary either buying her fine clothes or paying the medical bills for his mother, Esther-Rifke, who was dying from diabetes.

Joe's father, Hillel, a baker, was born in 1884 and lived to be 100. Although he resided in Toronto more than 50 years, my grandad never drove a car or learned much English. We spoke together in Yiddish. After his wife died in 1934, Hillel was to have three more wives. I remember the three of them. The first was always in the kitchen, with doughy arms, often frying ponchkes (donuts); the last wife died in old age — I kissed her bright green forehead in her last days; and the middle one ran off to Montreal with a lover. I recall this lady wearing a wide-sleeved grey Persian lamb coat and heavy perfume. My grandfather had been suspicious of this wife, so he set a trap for her. He stationed his grandson in the closet and pretended to leave for work, but soon returned to find her "in flagrante." The grandson, Jake Weinberg, sprang out of the closet — the witness.

There was a scandal in the family in 1934, when Pearl ran off and married an Italian Catholic, Louis Natale, who converted to Judaism and underwent the prescribed ritual circumcision. The family hard-heartedly refused to accept the marriage, and poor Pearl had to seek refuge with her in-laws. She made every effort to maintain her religion. She carried her circumcised infant son to her sister for approval. The family stonily sat shiva for a week, a mourning decreed by Hillel, and did not see Pearl until 50 years later. Esther-Rifke, Pearl's mother, died at age 56 — her death hastened, allegedly, by Pearl's marriage. I never knew Pearl existed until one day, when I was about 11, I found a 1930s photo of a slightly familiar young lady stylishly outfitted in a felt hat and fur collar. "Mom," I asked, "who is this? Is she a movie star?"

My mother's evasive answers and guilty smile provoked me to pry the truth out of her, that my father in fact had two sisters.

"Well," I thought, "the Wise family is not so boring after all."

No one knew where Pearl lived or had made any attempt to find her. My brother, Stan, did a search, found her, and we had a family reunion 50 years after she had been banished. Pearl and her sister, Chayele, would come to us and grace holiday dinners and tell us tales about their early life. Pearl has retained her Jewish heritage and buys kosher food, but she still holds bitterness in her heart for the hurt done to her.

My dad's sister, Helen, tells the tale of her mother's brother, Lazar, who lived in Ostrowietz and married the girl next door when he was 50 and she 20. After a year they produced triplets, two boys and a girl. Because Lazar was a poor shoemaker, a rich citizen offered to foot the bill for a festive ritual circumcision. After the party, the donor, who was childless, proposed that he himself take one of the boys, for whom he could provide a prosperous future.

"Where," said he, "do you have enough space in your one-room house for three children?"

Answered Lazar, "Where I'm going to put two, I can put three."

My father's father, Hillel Wise, worked at Sherman's bakery, his wife's relatives. I recall that in the early 1940s, the crust of the rye breads from

Sherman's bore a small paper stamp marked "Union Made," which I hoped no one had licked. My father said I would never find a husband because I held the bread awkwardly when I sliced it. My mom always held the loaf against her chest. I remember her once cutting into a round rye loaf and finding a rusty nail inside — for a time I was wary of finding something foreign whenever I cut into bread.

The Wise family all prospered in the New World. My dad went from cutter at Tip Top Tailors to shopkeeper and then builder-owner. When he died in 1983, my dad left Stan and me an estate of about $750,000. I was pleased that the will stated that the money be divided equally — which I took to indicate equal love. My needs, however, were not equal to my brother's, because Isadore was a rather good provider. I kept some and gave the rest to Stan. The legacy was important to my parents, who had proudly denied themselves luxuries to leave more to us. With my share I bought a pearl and diamond necklace. Whenever anyone admired it, I gladly told them it was a gift from my parents.

The Weinberg family — my dad's sister Helen and her husband, Sam — also prospered in Canada. They moved to a derelict three-storey attached house at 325 College, which Helen renovated with her own hands and where Sam plied his trade of shoemaker in the bay-windowed room facing the street.

Every Sunday when we made the expedition downtown to visit the Weinberg house, we would congregate around the kitchen table next to the huge yellow enamel stove with the oven door at eye level beside the burners. Everyone would have tea in a glass with honey cake. Except me. I was told always to say "No thank you" to any food offered. I read the subtext: saying no is socially correct.

Eventually the market for shoe repairs went the way of the fashion for felt fedoras, so the Weinbergs moved to a more modern life in Los Angeles. My cousins Norman and Stanley chose well from the gene pool. Stan is an electrical engineer with a dozen inventions to his name, including a dimmer switch for lights, a device for recognizing ice on aircraft wings, and a personal "ionic" air purifier, which in these Covid days is very successful. Norman, a Ph.D. in chemistry, has published 24 technical books, holds 34 patents, and lectures widely. Norman and I were buddies. We were the same age and were both school bright and resourceful shtetl children. At nine years old, he wanted a camera, which he got the only way he could — he made one out of cardboard — the film was light-sensitive paper he bought from the drugstore with his precious 10-cents savings.

I cannot imagine, only wonder, what my Birnbaum relatives, their children, and their children's children might have achieved had they survived. Norman Weinberg also has a great interest in his Ożarów heritage. He headed up a successful cemetery restoration program and rescued the sacred ground from 60 years of garbage and neglect; it is now a park enjoyed by the locals, albeit half of them anti-Semitic, although their worldly goods have been enriched by their former neighbours. How much happier these Polish people would be if Jews still lived in their town. It's been proved that countries which expel their Jews do not prosper, because they are diminished by their hatred and the loss of a more buoyant economy.

The oldest Ożarów gravestone found so far is dated 1700, but we know there may be others still buried that are older. Someone once sighted a headstone with Hebrew and Ladino letters, which means the Jews came there from Spain. European Jewish cemeteries typically were built in layers. Every 100 years, new graves were piled on old ones because Jews were allowed only limited space. This is also why the headstones are sometimes so close together.

Jewish people have probably been living in Ożarów — named in 1568, for a man named Josef Ozerovski — since the early 1500s. The earliest record extant is an entry in the diary of a Hungarian traveller, Martin Csombor, dated 1616: "The majority of the inhabitants in Ożarów are Jewish. When we stopped there on Saturday, they were all calmly occupying themselves with their religious ceremonies."

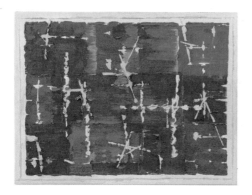

(left) Dragonflies in Concert, 2013, 16" x 12".
(right) Opposites Attractive, 2016, 18" x 12".

CHAPTER EIGHT

High School Capers

Back in high school I was almost a year younger than my classmates because my mom had needed me out of the way when I was little and had enrolled me in kindergarten early, at age four. Her last words as she had dropped me off at the Bedford Park School were, "Now remember, Rosie, your birthday is November 23, not February 23." Thankfully no one asked for my birthdate till Grade 3, though, and by then I forgot to lie. But I quickly recovered and told Miss Robinson, the teacher, "Sorry. I made a mistake. February 23 is my cousin Norman's birthday." God was on my side, and luckily my teacher did not challenge me further. Miss Robinson was small, narrow, with a mannish haircut from the '30s, and she never smiled. I remember she was sometimes preoccupied with blowing her long nose into her hanky, closely examining the deposit, folding the hanky fastidiously to a clean spot, and repeating the process.

Well, with my two dates of birth, in Grade 9 I was younger on average than the rest of the class, and also the smallest. Needing an explanation, I gave out that I had "skipped." I got along well with the boys in high school, but I wasn't a great social success with my crowd of girls. One of them called me a "kook," which I didn't even know how to spell, and I could spell everything. In high school, being an outsider is a disadvantage at first, but soon it becomes a distinction; to be named a true eccentric is praise indeed. Thereafter I didn't feel the need to fit in, to be like everyone else, as I had so longed to as a child.

The girls in my class had more belongings than I did. Once I was visiting a classmate, Elaine Levine, and she showed me all her "cashmeres," which sounded like a species of goat, and I had to ask for an explanation. I felt no envy because I didn't want to change places with Elaine. I considered my meagre wardrobe only an inconvenience. I owned just a couple of skirts I had made on our treadle machine, and every morning I ironed one of my white cotton blouses, which I had washed by hand the night before. We had no washing machine — Mom washed the clothes on a washboard that sat inside the laundry tub down in the cement-floor cellar, where the 40-watt bulb gave little light. Just as I never helped her with the housework, Mom never washed my shirts. Each morning I would decorate my blouse with a scarf or a ribbon to try to compete with the other girls who wore a new outfit every day. Two years later, when I met my future husband at 16, my entire wardrobe consisted of about three homemade skirts and five blouses swinging freely in my closet. The skirts I sewed were wool plaid, box-pleated, the pleats stitched following the lines in the plaid. Even my formal dress for the high school prom was a homemade tulle evening skirt topped by a store-bought bustier, costing a total of $14. My boyfriend — Isadore — bought me a red cashmere skirt-and-sweater set for Valentine's Day, and the next day he sent the same outfit again, in a cognac colour, for "the day after Valentine's." This colour is the same as my oil paint labelled "yellow ochre deep." The skirts were a sexy pencil thin style, a first for me since I always wore flared or pleated. Before this, like my mother and her sisters in the shtetl, I had few store-bought clothes. But I did not feel deprived. I would not have traded places with someone who had a fancy wardrobe because I preferred the package that I was and felt resourceful enough to put myself together with flair.

My raw materials for the sewing machine were sale fabrics from Eaton's, where I sorted through the table of remnants folded in squares, each labelled with its price and yardage. Once I bought a one-yard remnant of chartreuse green chiffon printed with tiny brightly coloured flowers. The fabric was 36 inches wide, same as my hips. I ran up a sleeveless sheath-style dress for the price of one dollar and wore it that same evening. And — early signs of my interior design flair — I also found a length of pink fabric printed with a small black-and-white figure to cover my armless bedroom lounge chair. There was not enough material for the back, and one side of the chair was also missing some covering. The chair had to be stationed in a corner with its back against the wall, and I was always conscious of this fault. I protected the chair by standing on its weak side — nervous that visitors to my bedroom would discover the deception, rather like Dr. Samuel Johnson in 1750s London who had a three-legged chair; he protected its defect in the same way. Although I might have occasionally carped about my few clothes and the many other limitations of our shtetl household, there is a value in privation. I used to tell my kids that I was sorry the one thing I could never provide for them was deprivation. I might have been a social flop with the girls at school, but the boys nominated me for Prom Queen. I lost. Issy's sister Neddy won. She had the Sharp family good nature and was popular.

Truer to my interests, I took the initiative to direct the decorations for the dances. For the prom, I conceived a tipping champagne glass 15 feet high, fashioned from chicken wire. I wanted to try out for cheerleader, but didn't because I couldn't do a cartwheel — I'm a congenital physical coward unlike my 10-year-old granddaughter Erika, the gymnast. On my high school debating team, I was a show-off, brashly making my case centre stage instead of from behind the lectern. This was bravado because in truth I'm nervous getting up in front of a crowd. Finally, there was some status from being the third member of a singing trio that included Carol Weinstein, our music coach and pianist, and lead singer Dorothy Goldhar. As I write this Dorothy and her husband, David, are coming here for dinner tonight, the first get-together since the pandemic began. And I've just trod through the early morning dewy grass to cut white conical hydrangeas for the table.

Back in high school we named our trio the Three Graces, and for the school's variety show we dressed in matching tight white sweaters and flared black quilted skirts, with a tight elastic belt around our then so slim waists. I recall standing in the wings just itching to go onstage to sing "Chattanooga Choo-choo." These days I tremble whenever I speak in public — although no one has detected this so far. Our trio even had an audition for television's *The Denny Vaughan Show*, with a repertoire that was mainly Cole Porter's "Just One of Those Things," punctuated with a lot of doo-ahs. We never heard from Mr. Vaughan. I also had an interest in languages. On the first day of French class, from the moment Mr. Mckewen entered the classroom, I was fixated on his fly, and it was a year-long struggle to keep my eyes on his face. A fly struck me as too obvious a device to hide something functional yet so secret and mysterious. Mr. Mckewen introduced French by giving us a short dictation in this language completely foreign. The dictations were marked and returned the next day. I noticed I had three mistakes, which didn't look good until he announced, "Miss Wise had the top mark by quite a margin." And so it went through high school that I was top of the class in languages. This was a boon because when we acquired the Four Seasons George V, I could talk to the chambermaid and was always good at ordering dinner though I was never able to transmit abstract ideas. And the summer I took the boys to Sanary-sur-Mer I ordered déjeuner at la plage, but I could never think in French. Monsieur Casaubon, my final-year French teacher, suggested I try for the scholarship in French. I declined because I had no interest in becoming a translator or a teacher. He was disappointed. Nevertheless, I decided to take four languages in Grade 13 so I wouldn't need to study, and so I could avoid math. But I was missing two subjects, Latin and German. I borrowed the

Grade 10, 11, and 12 textbooks and taught myself three years of Latin, studying one lesson every lunch hour. I had never attended a single Latin class before writing the Grade 12 Easter exam, and I got an 82, a mystery because I was just trying for a pass. Mr. Tough, the principal, congratulated me over the school P.A. system, which I heard while walking down the hall to class. I was surprised he even knew my name.

German was another language I taught myself, again writing the exam without going to classes. Here I only had to make up two years, and German was simple because it was related to Yiddish. My facility for languages was more a matter of photographing in my mind the vocabulary and spelling than of speaking. I've never been adept at speaking French, or any other second language, for that matter. To my parents I owe the determination and work ethic it took to learn two languages on my own. But math was another matter. I had no mind for it at all. Higher math is still a mystery to me. Trigonometry I can only spell, and for long division answers I email one of my sons, even for short division.

Spelling and calligraphy are still my two best skills, but both have become archaic arts, having been capably mastered by the computer. It would have been more useful to know how to swim. Back at Bedford Park in the 1940s handwriting was considered an art — important enough to be marked by the principal of the school. Somewhere among my papers I have my penmanship workbook signed by R.C. Cameron. I could hardly wait for Grade 3, when the empty inkwells in each desk were filled with the risky blue-black ink that could not be erased. We were taught just how to hold the wooden pen, and each stroke was to be evenly parallel at an angle of one o'clock. One day in high school, Monsieur Casaubon announced that there would be an opportunity to live with a French family for the summer in Trois-Pistoles, Québec. I wanted to go more than anyone in the class; it sounded so exotic, as wonderfully strange as one of Margaret Mead's field trips to New Guinea. I would have been willing to suffer any privation to go. But I never even mentioned it to my parents because, as with skates, they would not have understood. My parents would not even let me sleep at a friend's house, or babysit, so how would they let me go to Québec? They never knew about the trip.

Another trip came up the next summer, when my friends Merle Shain and Carol Weinstein were going to Europe for two months. I would have killed to go with them, but of course I made no mention to my parents of this trip either. Merle, I remember, bought an entire wardrobe of drip-dry clothes in black and white, so they would mix and match. These unresolved yearnings to travel somewhat dampened my eventual first trip to Europe, because the reality could never compete with the dream — a concept I later found a name for in V.S. Naipaul's book *The Enigma of Arrival*. Naipaul describes making the trip of his dreams to India, the land of his forbears, only to find garbage floating in the harbour. If I had gone to Trois-Pistoles, my expectations would probably have been dashed then by the "enigma of arrival." As I recall, Sandy Title, one of the girls who did go, got bitten by a dog and had to return home.

Recently, I discovered a truth about my yearning for summer camp. Ezekiel Emanuel, brother of Rahm, explained in his memoir that when he went to camp, he discovered that he wasn't a "group" person and camp was not for him. With a flash, I recognized that I would have felt the same. The summer that Merle and Carol went to Europe, when I was 14, I went to work in a sweatshop that looked like a Hollywood set for a Lower East Side factory before unions. Mom had found me the job at her cousin Meyer Riba's sweatshop, Reliable Embroidery, on Adelaide Street West. He was a third cousin, her closest relative. On the Monday morning, I arrived at 7:30 and walked down the steps to the factory, which was below ground. Steam issued from six pressers as the operators opened and closed them, and a dozen or so women were bent over sewing machines, embroidering "His" and "Hers" on guest towels. No one looked up. Uncle Meyer showed me how to punch the clock and ushered me to my summer station — cutting a roll of men's handkerchiefs one at a time, with a huge pair of scissors. The hankies were pulled along a table from a bolt on a roller. After the first hour, I was ready to leave. "How," I thought, "can I possibly last till lunch? Well, I'll definitely quit at the end of the day." But I came back the next day with my blistered hand bandaged, and I stubbornly worked that mind-numbing job for eight endless weeks before school resumed. When once I forgot to punch the clock till noon, I lost the morning's wages. My summer's earnings would later finance two dental bridges to replace baby teeth that should have been pulled. No doctors and dentists for our family (except for those I paid for myself).

Back at school in September, my friend Merle, home from her summer in Europe, sat in front of me in class. She wanted to be a writer, but I doubted she could achieve this, given that she couldn't spell. Disdainfully I watched her write uphill with her left hand, a wavy indecipherable scrawl, smearing the ink with her arm as she went. *Some Men Are More Perfect than Others*, the first of her three books, written when she was in her 30s, was a bestseller. But as fine a writer as she was, Merle was very unlucky in love, with many failed relationships. I tried to pick up the pieces, but eventually she became emotionally fragile.

When she was about 40, I took her to New York for a weekend to distract her from yet another lost love. Like most women, including me, the love of a man was more important to Merle than any vocation or prestige. As has been said, "love is to a man but a thing apart." But back in school, she was a very strong character, imitating the father she had lost at age 14. She was quite overweight, so she went on an apple diet and lost 25 pounds, which she kept off for the rest of her life. We were the same age, but she was much wiser, and she became my mentor. Once when I was plotting my revenge against someone who had wronged me, Merle taught me to "heap coals of fire on his head" — a concept I have continued to value. The phrase, from

Romans 12:20, translates: disarm your enemy by kindness — feed him if he's hungry and give him a drink if he's thirsty. In so doing, the guilt will be on his head. Shockingly, Merle Shain died when she was 53, of unexpected heart failure.

WHEN HIGH SCHOOL ENDED, I had to decide what I wanted to be — apart from married — which was the first thing on my parents' agenda. Was it art school to be a window dresser, sign painter, or fashion designer — or English to be a journalist? I decided against art school because I was in the academic stream, and it was a badge of honour to have letters following your name, so I followed Merle and my brainy friends to university. At the University of Toronto, the "ologies" appealed because they sounded so esoteric — particularly sociology and anthropology. I had read Margaret Mead and fantasized about fieldwork on some undeveloped South Pacific Island. But the truth is, I knew I couldn't handle the mosquitoes, the risky food, and the celibate life. I had reached the age when romance was everything. Ever since Mr. Rochester had cantered down the road on horseback and swept Charlotte Brontë's Jane Eyre off her feet, I was on the lookout for just such a man. Or even Heathcliff from Emily Brontë's *Wuthering Heights*, played by Laurence Olivier, my movie heartthrob for years. I had that strong prerequisite for romantic love, my love for my father — which is quite a mystery, because he did, after all, give me a whack once in a while. But nevertheless, we loved each other deeply.

In Grade 7, I had a serious crush on my English teacher, Mr. Vyvian, even the three V-shapes of his name. He was dark, reserved, and formal. I'm sorry I didn't question why he had asked Miss Wise, the only Jew in the class, to read the part of Shylock. Finally, when I was nearly 15, Morley Markson asked me out on a date and came to collect me on his motorcycle. On the spot, my father said, "Don't let me see him here now or ever again."

Dad screened each boyfriend carefully. He had to be Jewish and studious, with good prospects, and he had to bring me home, in the same condition in which I had left, by 11 p.m. I was not to wear lipstick or makeup, bare-necked dresses, or high-heeled shoes.

I'm surprised I had any offers at all, because at 14 my arms and legs were like sticks, and I was the only girl in my class with a flat chest — the bane of my existence. I would say to my mom, "How can you be so sure that I'll get any? Maybe God will skip me."

My mom refused to let me buy a bra. "You're so mazeldik — lucky — to be small," she said. "What do you need them for? They just pull you down."

Well, there I was in high school, still wearing an undershirt. Finally, I bought a size 30A bra and stuffed it with hankies. I was mortified one day when my dad came into my room and spied a hanky sticking out of my bra. He just scowled and said nothing. But Dad was pleased with my boyfriend Ray who was studying to be a doctor. My dad also okayed Howard Levin, a dental student, who came to collect me in his Hudson car. My friend was a bit miffed that I was not impressed with this rare vehicle — today I still classify cars by colour only. Howie left me in the Hudson near Fran's Restaurant on Eglinton and soon returned with two hamburgers and French fries. This was my first-ever store-bought hamburger. Mom ground her own patties, claiming, "You never know what the butcher puts in ground meat." She would clamp the cast aluminum grinder onto the kitchen counter and push the bloody chunks through the top and wind the crank, issuing red meat worms through a disc in the side.

I unwrapped Howard's hamburger, took one bite of the pink non-kosher patty, and pleaded a late lunch.

ONCE, IN HIGH SCHOOL, with my Saturday-afternoon earnings from the Ah Young Fruit Market, I bought a pair of clunky, low-heeled, beige old-maid sandals. For no apparent good reason, my father's dybbuk rose up in him and he went ballistic. I guess he thought the shoes were too sexy. He opened the front door, stepped onto the verandah, wound up like a baseball pitcher, and threw those shoes so far that they landed in the middle of the road. I thought he had lost his senses.

My mom said, "Quick, go for a walk around the block till he cools off," our usual routine when Dad got his dander up. When I returned, there he was, sitting sheepishly on the sofa, as if the incident had never happened.

My father must have been afraid I would get pregnant like his sister Pearl had at age 15, but he didn't have the skills to communicate this fear. He needn't have worried; even in high school I innocently believed that no one had sex before marriage. And I had a mistaken idea of what sex was. I didn't know sperm was involved and had never heard the word "erection" or that such a condition was a prerequisite. My first real boyfriend, Isadore, would convince me that it was unnatural not to have sex, so of course my dad was right about his fears. And I did, in fact, become pregnant, which no one ever knew. This has always been my darkest secret. It all began when I was going on 17. My high school friend Pearl Lottman was getting married, and I was a bridesmaid. It so happened that the groom, Leonard Godfrey, was Issy's first cousin, so seated at one of the round banquet tables at the wedding was the Sharp family. After dinner, Isadore came to the bridesmaids' table and asked me for a dance. He was wearing blue suede shoes, he had copper coloured hair, and with his slim build, his clothes hung loosely like on a model. When he gave me one of his show-stopping smiles, I melted.

That first night we met we had a few dances, and I tried my best to keep up with his nimble jitterbug, but he was too quick on his feet and far too good for me. Besides, I like to claim that the boogie-woogie was before my time — he was four and a half years older. I'm still trying to get the hang of it. Otherwise, we are quite attuned to each other on the dance floor.

Invariably at parties people come up to Issy and say, "You move like Fred Astaire," and to this I should reply as Ginger did: "I do the same steps he does, but I do them backwards." When we waltz, I am transported, sometimes airborne, and devil-may-care about falling even at this age of 85. I fix my eyes on his nose to keep my balance — the fixed-point ballerinas need when spinning.

Once Isadore asked a guest for a dance and while they were executing a silver foxtrot he chatted politely.

"Please don't speak; I want just to enjoy this," she said.

I clearly remember my first date with Issy. It was a movie at the Imperial Theatre: Jerry Lewis in *Sailor Beware*. We took the two aisle seats about 10 rows from the front on the right side. The film had hardly begun when Issy slid down in his seat and promptly fell asleep, even snoring a little. In his construction days, he was on the job by 6:30. I was in awe that he could be so cool on a first date. What an accomplishment! I have yet to fall asleep in public, or take a nap at home, for that matter. Naps are a waste of time. Sleep for me is at night, in bed, in pajamas, in a running position, with blankets to my chin.

Well, after that night Issy and I became an item, a questionable union because we were not at all alike. My previous dates had been more the nerdy type, while Issy seemed to be a sports person, and sports was a subject about which I knew nothing. I rarely attended any ball games in high school. From a young age, Isadore participated in every athletic activity of the season. Our son Tony also played football and was a star basketball player. We have a photograph of him from the neighbourhood newspaper dunking a basket. When Issy played sports, he didn't mind bodychecks in hockey or broken ribs from football. He even played double dutch with the girls. At the same time as he played junior football, he was a cheerleader for senior football games. One day the coach approached him to skip cheerleading; "We can use you for the senior team," he said, but Issy declined and joined them later in Grade 12. When he came second in the half mile with no prior practice, the school genius, David Gauthier, remarked: "I've been training for this race for months and you just run for a lark and beat me." And I've witnessed grown men, not the athletic sort, thank Issy for picking them first in the high school lineup for the basketball team when he was captain.

Isadore was always a team player. He still is. I've heard him say in many speeches to his employees that sports taught him how to handle defeat and how to lead a team. I played no sports. Perhaps that's why I can be such a sore loser. As different as we were, we were magnetically drawn together. I loved his sweet nature — although I did think he was a risky choice for a husband, a likely philanderer. I was right, because Issy did have a few dalliances during the time we were courting and "knew" each other. But I had no choice. I was smitten. We enjoyed our differences. I introduced him to Chinese, Japanese, and Italian food and black-and-white movies with subtitles, and to read the book I had just finished, and he taught me how to ski and the benefits of physical culture, including sex. And, later, a lot more about wisdom and how to count to 10 before speaking my mind, which I rarely remember. Issy arrives just on time or a bit late for appointments, he doesn't waste time waiting. I have a problem with punctuality. I'm always at least 10 minutes early. At our weekly massage at home, my playlist includes 101 cello concertos, many by Yo-Yo Ma, Itzhak Perlman playing the haunting "Shoshanim Atzuvot," Richard Strauss's four last songs. All on low volume so the music seems to come from over a distant hill as if I'm having my massage under a tree. Isadore's massage playlist features Patsy Cline, Loretta Lynn, and Johnny Cash. He likes Dean Martin and Doris Day. I prefer Joni Mitchell, k.d. lang, Bob Marley, and Andrea Bocelli. But to be fair we're both fans of the incomparable Frank Sinatra, Lena Horne, and Sammy Davis Junior.

Curiously our son Greg is an opera buff and a bit of a snob in his preference for Mozart over Verdi. He even attends the rehearsals of Opera Atelier. Meanwhile Jordy prefers bluegrass, and Tony is up on Motown. Chris didn't have time to get beyond John Denver.

Great-grandson Max, 2019, 18" x 24".

CHAPTER NINE

Go Together like a Horse and Carriage

Lately Issy and I have audited with a smile just how we have benefited from our differences. I've brought Isadore kicking and screaming into the computer world. He's now a Zoom whiz, we play bridge online daily, he clicks the "like" button on photos of his great grandchildren, and, as obediently as his dad, listens to audible books on our daily walk. He's taught me that regular walks and workouts are de rigueur for folks in their 80s. How did it happen that Issy will soon be 90? Are we at the "brink of the tomb," as Wodehouse would say? Or like my mother said in Yiddish, "life is but a dream."

In those early days when we were courting, we remember that my dad was not at all pleased with our alliance. He didn't think Issy was such a bargain. A son-in-law in the building business was not his ideal. He was hoping for a doctor or a lawyer, or at least an accountant. One day, Dad and I came to an impasse when he decreed that I was no longer to go out with Isadore because one of Dad's cronies had seen Issy in a bar the night before with a shiksa, a gentile girl. I did, however, go out with Issy one more time after this command, and when I came home from school the next day, my father had locked me out of the house — yet another of Dad's communication problems.

So, I went to Issy's job site on Roselawn Avenue, where he was building the apartment house we later lived in, and said, "Issy, I don't know where to turn because my dad is angry at my disobedience, and I'm locked out."

"Well, don't worry, it'll be all right. We'll go and talk to him," said my friend, who always faces a problem head-on.

I was embarrassed, but nevertheless I walked meekly behind Issy up the concrete path and the five steps to my front door, hoping my parents would let us in. I can still see, in front of me, Issy's rubber boots with the grey lining worn where the boots were folded. He looked very handsome. He wore an open shirt. His sun-bleached eyebrows and curly copper hair matched his rust suede sports jacket. The jacket, now demoted from evening attire, had come from Ed Provan, the upmarket Toronto tailor. Now dusted with plaster, it hung loosely on a lean, hard body — that boyish body he still has. As someone once said: "leanness goes a great way towards gentility."

We found my dad reading *The Telegram*, sitting woodenly on the third seat of the plastic sealed sofa, where he could always be found. Issy began making his case politely and quietly in his positive, winning way, and my father was obviously impressed. As Issy spoke, I saw my father's expression transform from haughty self-righteousness to the subdued demeanour of a humbled child. From that time, my father fell in my eyes. At that moment when Issy took charge, I transferred my allegiance from my father to my lover. Checking out the seminal events in our past, I now credit this incident as a milestone in our lives.

ISADORE HAS ALWAYS FELT that sex is as natural and vital in a relationship as any other form of communication. He still does. He persuaded me that premarital sex was the norm. This was a big surprise to me. I was certain that all good girls were chaste until the marriage bed — and that virginity was the gift a girl saved for her husband. At school there was gossip about the one bad girl, Barbara of the big breasts. It was rumoured she was easy and had known Jim and John and had done the lot with Henry. But Issy told me that my Victorian attitude about sex was outdated, and after all, he was 25 percent older than me and seriously persuasive. We then took to driving to romantic lanes after the movies, and he showed me how it was done. The steering wheel, I remember, was always in the way. But, although I admit I was a promiscuous teenager, I have only ever known one man, which makes me what — a virgin, once removed?

Now I was 19, and my parents and I were invited to the Sharps' house for Shabbat dinner. During dessert Issy surprised me with a magnificent diamond ring, platinum, with a large round stone. I was thrilled, although at some level I would have preferred a ring he had made by hand out of some humble material like copper wire, because I was a declared snob about material clichés like diamond rings and mink coats. Nevertheless, I remember sitting on our stairway landing later that night under the chandelier and marvelling at the prismatic colours in the stone. It was spring and we were to be married in the fall on a Tuesday. We decided on a Tuesday because on that day, according to the Book of Genesis, God was particularly pleased with his creation. Not once, but twice, he smugly "saw that it was good." (On the Monday, he had not given his new-made world even a mention.)

Issy's mom, Lil, was very pleased with me. I was Jewish, and her boy loved me, and that was all she needed to know. But now disaster struck in the Issy-Rosie romance. Our worst fear. Somehow, I was pregnant, despite precautions. For kids today, this would be no problem, but it was the '50s. Jewish children were expected to bring only naches — joy and gratification — to the family. We didn't belong to ourselves, after all. We were our parents' children. There was no question — we simply could not do this to them. My father might have killed himself. I tried some pills that made me ill. I recall that as I got out of bed that day, the floor turned upside down and hit me on the head. I remember feeling nauseous at dinner facing a bowl of my mother's dense green soup. So, at 19 years old and three months pregnant, I had an abortion at a stranger's apartment in Rosedale. It was an irresponsible act — at the time I believed there was a risk I might not be able to conceive later. Giving birth hurt like hell, but an hour after the soap-and-water douche on a kitchen table, and wobbly on my feet, I took the bus home. A few weeks later I anxiously went to see a Dr. Doris Bartley in the Medical Arts Building. Dr. Bartley, wide with the face of an owl, was miscast as a gynecologist, more like a spinster schoolteacher who had never known a man. When I told her what I had done, she said, "You have committed murder," and she was right. We have always felt that guilt, but at the time there was certainly no other way.

THE WEDDING WAS SCHEDULED for the prescribed mazeldik (lucky) Tuesday, September 6, 1955. So, my parents took me to Buffalo to buy a trousseau — largesse I had never seen from them before. I bought a bouffant cotton organdy dress that wasn't meant to be a wedding gown. I have never followed the rights and wrongs of fashion, trusting my own sense of style. I also bought 56 towels in grey and peach to match the tiles I had selected for the bathroom in our new apartment — early signs of the decorator. Dad was disdainful of my gift registry for Jensen Pyramid pattern silver, handmade pottery dishes, and modern crystal glasses with cubes instead of stems. He would have preferred conventional gilt-edged dishes that looked the price.

Later I found Dad's cache of invoices:

Wedding cake — 16 lbs., 8 pedestals, and vase — $27; Rental of silver cake stand — $1.50.

Menu: appetizer, tomato stuffed with chopped liver, main course, half spring chicken with kishke, knishes, and peas. Music by Ellis McLintock and His Orchestra — two songs by Manford Steer $15 — Gratuity for limousine driver — $1.

ISSY AND I HAD a nine-day honeymoon in New York, Miami, and Cuba. My first plane ride, my first stay in a hotel. Married! I was ecstatic! I couldn't believe my luck. A completely new life — I was newborn. An unknown adventure, a change of address. My heart was light, knowing I was now on a winning team — just how winning I would find out much later. On our wedding night, we stayed at the Skyline Motel in Toronto. Mysteriously, I was frightened in the middle of the night by the click of someone's heels in our bathroom. Apparently, we had a connecting room with a shared bath. In the morning, Issy carefully filmed the building's mediocre exterior with his dad's 16mm movie camera. About half of our honeymoon movies pan tediously up, down, and across hotel buildings, including a long stretch of dark footage of the gaudy interior of the Fontainebleau Hotel, which had just been built in Miami Beach. Even then Issy was dreaming about the hotel business.

The next morning, we were having breakfast in bed in our New York bedroom on the 38th floor of the Hotel Taft when Issy suggested we should call home. Max Sharp answered, and we said our hellos. Then he asked me, "So tell me, Rosie, how do you like New York?"

"Great," I answered.

"And nu, so tell me, Rosie, how do you like married life?"

"Well," I answered, "it's better than New York."

At the time I was wearing my short yellow cotton nightie from Buffalo, with the matching bloomers, and my new curly hair. My poker-straight hair had been permed before the wedding because I would never want my husband to see me in curlers, and he never has.

What surprises me, though, is the way my marriage turned out. I expected that Issy would continue his Casanova capers. After all he did lose half our wedding-gift money on our honeymoon — but he's never gambled since, and to all appearances he's remained faithful.

HOME FROM OUR HONEYMOON, it was late afternoon when we opened the door to find the apartment completely empty except for a mattress and box springs leaning against the bedroom wall, still wrapped in brown paper. It was a one-bedroom home at 130 Eglinton Avenue West, in a building Issy had helped his dad build. Our shoes left light footprints on a dark sooty floor that hadn't been cleaned since the last tenant left. Thanks to Lil Sharp, there were two brown bags of groceries on the kitchen counter. But the counter was also covered with a layer of grime, and the fridge needed wiping out. I slowly realized that for the first time it fell to me as designated housekeeper, and not to my mother, to do the cleanup.

A month later I magnanimously invited the whole family for a Shabbat dinner, as I thought a good wife should. I had no cooking experience because I had "never helped" my mom in the kitchen, as she was wont to complain. But by following recipes I thought I could do better, a more goyishe gentile meal. I got out my *Gourmet Cookbook* and planned an ambitious and pretentious menu, including some dishes I had only seen in print: petit pois cream soup, smoked trout with guacamole, blanquette de veau, garlic green beans, fried brown rice, braided rolls, and for dessert, baked Alaska. And since it was nearly Halloween, a huge orange jelly mould filled with knotted black licorice ropes. For the table centrepiece, I had a carved pumpkin with a small candle inside, the top decorated with a crepe-paper Afro. I began preparing all this bright and early on the Friday morning. Little did I know that my four-course menu was a two-day job for three people. By 4 p.m. I was panicky and only halfway done, so I reduced the number of courses but refused to give up on the stiff egg whites needed for the baked Alaska's meringue. The guests arrived, dinner was served, and we were well into the dessert — the meringue at half-mast — when the pumpkin exploded in flames and the crepe-paper hairdo hit the ceiling with a boom. Days later, small black particles, like fruit flies, were still floating down.

I DIDN'T HAVE MUCH to do every day when Issy went off to work except throw out the apple core he had left on the bedside table. Why was this my job? I had quit university, which I should never have done, on the advice of my mother-in-law, who said, "Meshugas! Craziness! A wife doesn't go to school — a wife takes care of a husband."

So off I went to work for six months as a salesgirl at Creeds, Toronto's poshest ladies' clothing store, thanks to an offer from Eddie Creed, who was married to Issy's sister Edie. The pay was $25 a week, plus one percent commission. There was a big room downstairs at Creeds where we salesgirls would have coffee. The "girls" were a group of former society doyennes, divorcees. Each was the classic 1940s "little woman" who, with apron on, dinner ready, and candles lit, would hinge her day on that moment when the front door would open to: "Hi, honey, I'm home." But as the husbands aged, some of them experienced mid-life crises. Then these husbands would adopt the best defence they could find against complacency and old age: younger women. It was not that they didn't love their wives — they just wanted to have another turn at the same life. In the '50s, women didn't take the college courses that trained them for anything more than matrimony. The girls at Creeds were all cast-off spouses selling clothes in the shop in which they had formerly had charge accounts — except for my friend Mrs. Vandermeulen, who was working to supplant the income her husband had lost in the stock market. She was frail, elderly, and wrinkled from smoking.

She once confided, between coughs, in her raspy voice, drawing on the cigarette she carried in a long holder, that her mother-in-law blamed her for being childless, when in fact it was her husband who was sterile. Mrs. V. had taken the blame forever and never told her husband or his mother the truth. She didn't want to bruise her husband's ego. You'd think she'd been born in the shtetl.

The girls at Creeds often asked me to join them at the Fifth Avenue Restaurant where they had the Businessmen's Lunch for $1.10. No way would I spend 25 percent of my wages for food, so I stayed at the store with my hard-boiled egg from home. I was a crack saleslady at Creeds, one of those aggressive types that accost you on the way in, like my mother at Wise's Dry Goods. Hapless shoppers were no match for her. They would come in for a pair of stockings and go out with a housedress as well. But I remember something unethical I did at Creeds. A young girl came in looking for a sweater that was to be charged to her mother's account. She was wearing jeans, saddle shoes, and bobby socks, and no makeup to cover her blond, freckled complexion. I should have shown her a casual cardigan, but since I was working on commission, I talked her into buying an inappropriately expensive cashmere evening sweater. The mother was furious, and the garment was returned.

At last, our new apartment on Bathurst Street at Roselawn was ready, in an 11-storey tower Issy had built, and I quit Creeds because I had a new job — decorating and furnishing our home. It was a two-bedroom suite on the 10th floor, 1,500 square feet, with one wall of windows facing the hot western sun, and it was just below my in-laws, who lived in the penthouse, which Issy designed. I still have his pencil sketch of the vast apartment, which covered the whole 11th floor — 7,500 square feet with balconies on two sides and a view of downtown. The centre of the apartment was a square hall eight feet wide, the floor two-foot squares of black and white terrazzo, each square outlined with a brass strip. These were laid out diagonally. Off this gallery were the main rooms, each 35 feet long with floor-to-ceiling windows.

Our apartment, suite 1001, was just down a flight of stairs. I never took the elevator. Issy left the decoration of our suite to me, and the results were considered fresh and dramatic. I took out the nib wall that typically formed the entrance hall and instead left the column exposed. This gave an open diagonal view from the front door of the L-shaped main room, and our apartment looked larger than others of the same model. I did the same in our current house, leaving out all the nib walls which gives a clean view room to room. In that first apartment, I put a modern mural wallcovering with a black ground on the long wall. Otherwise, the curtains were white on white, and the walls were painted white, which in those days walls never were — dark colours like Wedgwood green were in vogue. My friend Marion commented that our too-white walls reminded her of a hospital. The carpet and soft goods were pearl grey, and the dining room set was a black wrought-iron-and-glass oval table and chairs, copied from a photo in *House Beautiful* magazine and made for a song, to suit our budget. One day a four-seater sofa arrived from Eaton's, a gift from my mother-in-law. I never let on that the sofa was a great disappointment — I would have preferred to keep the space empty until I could afford to choose my own couch. Our bedroom suite, rather awful in retrospect, was custom-made in oak, stained a pale turquoise, and the curtains were in the same palette. I kept this apartment spotless, quite unlike the sloppy teenager my mother always complained about. Once, in my teens, I had come home late and just stepped out of my stiff skirt and crinoline and left them standing in circles on the floor. Anna Pupulin, our cleaning woman, came the next morning and vacuumed all around the clothes and the bed while I pulled the covers over my head and slept till noon.

Life in our honeymoon apartment was idyllic. The 56 colour-coordinated towels were folded in exact stacks of pink and grey in the closet beside a hundred rolls of toilet paper, bought from Eaton's at a quantity discount and also neatly stacked. In my yellow kitchen with its white vinyl floor inlaid with small black diamonds, I produced Polynesian stir-fry dinners for two, presented on our arts-and-craftsy handmade pottery with unglazed bottoms. With dinner we had loganberry juice — we didn't drink wine until our first trip to Europe five years later. In Paris at that time, if you didn't order wine, the waiters ignored you.

In our cozy apartment we often watched Issy's favourite TV program, then as now, NFL football, on Lil's four-seater sofa, my husband lying down and me sitting at the end, always knitting. I knitted blankets and sweaters and dresses, making up my own patterns and forgetting to keep even one example. I knitted because I had no interest in, or understanding of, football. From time to time, without taking his eyes from the TV, Issy's hand would drop down into the potato-chip bowl on the floor. The bowl was striped black-and-white pottery to match the décor and did years of service. Beside the bowl stood the crystal candy dish, with its stale green and black jujubes — the rejected flavours. We no longer have the black bowl, nor do we eat chips. We're great snobs about any food that's "fast," and make a fuss about brown rice, green tea, golden flax seed, and anything organic. Should anyone suggest herring oil is better than cod liver oil or that psyllium husk cures constipation, we add yet another potion to our after-breakfast lineup. I can't swallow pills, so I make a vile cocktail by emptying all the vitamin capsules in water. My mom taught me how *not* to swallow pills, just like she did, crushing half an aspirin in water.

Back in our honeymoon days, I was happy to have Issy relaxing on the sofa, a necessary respite from his long work hours — up at six and out on the construction job; building twin apartment towers at Avenue Road and Heath Street, in a Corbusier style. Isadore was a gentleman landlord, and I loved to watch him in action, dealing in his courtly manner with the demands of the apartment tenants. In our own building, whenever we met anyone in the elevator, they would invariably mention a leaky faucet or some other defect. My husband would disarm them with his smile and assure them that the item would be fixed ASAP. Of course, the ladies all melted. They loved him.

When our honeymoon apartment was suitably decorated, I needed a new project, so I thought, "Why not learn to swim?" When Marilyn Bell swam across Lake Ontario in 1954, I was awed and inspired. She had stepped into the lake that day with three other veteran contenders who soon quit, put off by the strong winds. The intrepid teenager Miss Bell plunged on despite squalls which carried her so far off course that she ended up travelling twice the width of the lake when she finally stepped onto the far shore. Her swim coach, Gus Ryder, had pushed her the whole way from his boat, shouting, "Come on, Marilyn! You're almost there, Marilyn!" Later I looked him up in the book and called. Gus gave me a lesson a week for six months — just him and me in the small indoor pool at the nearby Glenview Terrace. But it would prove easier for Mr. Ryder to coach Marilyn across Lake Ontario than to coax me to swim across the pool. I lost six pounds, swallowed gallons of water, and never quite got the hang of it. Once Gus said, "Today I'd like you to jump in the deep end and you'll see you'll just float up." I didn't, so he thrust a long stick in the water to the rescue. Nevertheless, I water-skied once and took one canoe trip.

FOR MY NEXT PROJECT, I began begging for a baby, as I had formerly begged my parents for a bicycle and a brother. Even though we had decided earlier that we would wait two years, so we could enjoy the carefree life, Issy gave in. In my anxiety to have the first baby quickly, I consulted a fertility book, which advised keeping my hips high on a pillow after sex, so the egg and the sperm would have a better chance of colliding. It also said that the first sperm to arrive were the boys, because girls were slower swimmers.

It must have worked, because I got pregnant on the first try, and was to attract those fast swimmers, four times. I loved being pregnant. It made me feel slow and satisfied and complete.

Jordan Jeffery was born in September 1957, two years after the wedding. He emerged from the womb on the run, and he hasn't slowed down since. Now in his 60s he's super fit and plays pro-like tennis with legs Federer would envy. Jordy was always getting into trouble. He was fascinated by the box of liquid shoe polish with round felt tips that I kept a stock of in many colours, so I put it out of reach on the top shelf in the kitchen. One Sunday, I rose late to find his white furniture decorated with graffiti in indelible shoe polish. The enterprising Jordy had simply pushed a chair to the kitchen counter and nimbly reached his prize. I did not spank him, which was my first urge, but declared in my best mother's rendition of the child-rearing book's advice, "Shoe polish is for shoes, not furniture, so we'll have to take it away." Another time he was curious about my hair dryer, plugged it in, and left it on high, setting the nozzle down on his plastic-covered crib mattress. By the time I discovered what he'd done, there was a square hole in the mattress filled with flames. I quickly took the smoking mattress down in the elevator, hoping to reach the ground floor before it exploded. And 1958 was the year of the great car accident. The press that day reported, "A 16-month-old baby and his pregnant mother, 22, escaped serious injury in a head-on collision on Roselawn Avenue east of Bathurst. Glass from the windshield showered Mrs. Rosalie Sharp who was treated for head and face lacerations. . . . Their auto struck by the truck of William Basha. . . . A passenger in the Basha vehicle required 10 stitches when he was pitched through the windshield."

Jordy and I were "Basha'd" while returning from our daily visit to my parents a few blocks way, where routinely Mom and I would share a cup of coffee while Dad played with the baby. On our way home, Jordy in his child's car seat, we were parked in a line of cars waiting, just a few yards from our apartment-house driveway, for the traffic light to change at Bathurst. I always leave a space from the car ahead, so it was in this space that we were hit. The next I knew, there was a flash of lights, a crash, and the steering wheel hit my nose like a sledgehammer. In a split second, our car was on someone's lawn facing in the opposite direction. Jordy had fallen forward in his car seat, and his face had hit the dials of the radio (later he would be a disc jockey for a time). He was screaming, and I was afraid to look at his bleeding face for fear he had lost an eye. Thank God he was okay, so I stormed out of the car and started yelling at the idiot truck driver, who was drunk of course. The point of impact was nine feet from our side of the 30-foot road. I must have looked a sight, eight months pregnant with Greg, blood running from my nose down the front of my tight hooded bright red mohair jacket. I had to have the smashed cartilage in my nose repaired so I could breathe — my nose has been crooked ever since — and Jordy may still have a trace of the scar. In court some months later, William Basha — what an improbable name — was not charged with reckless driving, the story went, because he would have lost his livelihood. Besides, I looked beautiful after an operation to remove the smashed cartilage from my nose.

And another disaster came on the scene one autumn day in 1958 when our honeymoon apartment was all but destroyed. It was a grey day, but we needed milk, so before the rain came, I set out quickly with Jordy in the carriage. I always bought jug milk because you got one quart free, a welcome economy on my $35 weekly household budget. (Shtetl people always manage. I never asked for more.) We hurried, under black rain clouds, the six blocks to the supermarket, retrieved the 35 cents for the empty jug, and put the milk in the basket under the carriage. As we made our way back home, I noticed that the rain had come and gone. But when I opened the door to our apartment, I was stunned by a bizarre scene. There was broken glass on the carpet, but no glass in the thirty feet of windows. The curtains were mostly missing, the tops hanging in shreds. The place looked like Miss Havisham's room in *Great Expectations*.

My light grey carpet was soaked dark, and most of our wedding crystal — which my father didn't like — had been swept off the shelves and lay in shards on the floor. During the 20 minutes we had been in the market, a 100-mile-an-hour west wind like Hurricane Hazel had driven through our home. Disasters are so banal. I took Jordy up to Nanny Lil's, swept up the glass, mopped up the wet carpet, and cooked dinner, while the wind swept through the apartment through the floor to ceiling west wall glassless windows.

Gregory Jay was born in March 1959, 18 months after Jordy, and Chris Hugh another 18 months after that, and Anthony David in another 18 months. Since we had only two bedrooms, Greg bunked with us until Chris came along and took his place in our room. It seemed like there were always three kids in diapers, and one of them sleeping in our bedroom. At first, night feedings were a nightmare, because with breastfeeding you never knew how much food the baby was getting. To make matters worse, if the baby cried, Issy would invariably say, "He's hungry; go feed him." So, I took to weighing the baby before and after feedings. The difference indicated the number of ounces he drank. But if he peed while he was nursing, this threw off my calculations.

Breastfeeding is one of life's special offerings. My granddaughter Julia was here yesterday feeding Cody who is named after my mother Ydessa, ingeniously derived by the last two letters of his name. There is an earthy scent to a newborn baby that is like that of a new puppy. I loved the sexual sensation when my babies drew milk from my nipple, their silky heads resting against my bare arm. I recall the beads of sweat on their noses pressed against my breast. They would take gulps, like the Morse code: take three, pause for four, take five, rest for three, all with eyes shut, worn out from the exertion. Moist eyelashes would grace a damp cheek and one tiny hand would spread like a flower and hold on to my breast for balance.

Those were moments I cherished, and I think Issy felt somewhat impotent that he could not feed the kids.

But he was a wonderful dad. He always changed the kids' heavy early-morning diapers before he went to work, a joy he says he wouldn't have missed. He would open the door to find the baby standing in his crib, his pink face beaming with anticipation for the day to begin, oblivious to the urine-soaked triple diaper hanging down around his knees. Issy felt that changing diapers was important to share with his sons — it was the only dialogue available at that moment. And on weekends, Dad would make the boys porridge. In later years, I would hand out a pile of towels to five naked guys — Dad and his boys together in the big walk-in shower. Isadore responds to all kids and all dogs. He'll get down on the floor and romp with a strange dog and let him slobber all over his face, then rough-house and play a game of dodge. He'll toss the kids in the air or wrestle with them on the floor. He'll scratch the dog behind the ears just like he hugs me, rubs my head, and playfully musses my hair. When our old dog got frisky, Issy would often say, "She's still like a pup" — which I know is the way he thinks of me at 85. Isadore has regrets we can't talk him out of although the boys have tried. He feels that in his youthful inexperience he chose to spend too much time at work and his priorities were wrong. That it was his mistake.

BACK WHEN THE BOYS were still all in diapers, after five years of marriage, at Issy's suggestion, we took our first vacation. Vacations had never been part of my life or expectations. Our honeymoon had been my only holiday. Shtetl people did not take holidays, nor did they even know the word "enti-tled" — which is not in my Yiddish dictionary. For our first vacation, we drove to Niagara Falls and spent three days in the Midtown Motor Inn. We thought the place was soo-o glamorous; we raved ad nauseam to each other about everything. We opened the sliding glass doors and stepped out to the patio, a concrete square placed on the grass, just large enough to hold two webbed plastic chaise lounges on which we promptly stretched out, in the sunlight, as we thought all good vacationers should. That night we both had such wicked sunburns, we couldn't even touch.

In 1962, since Issy had made good, I took a holiday on my own, because I had missed backpacking as a teenager and still had never been on a train. Well, I resolved to take the overnight train to New York and stay at the YWCA. Issy wouldn't hear of the Y and browbeat me into staying at the Plaza Hotel. In retrospect, I should, of course, have stayed at the Y. The plan was that I would shop and go to galleries for two days, and then, at five o'clock on the Friday, we would meet up in the Palm Court Bar. I went to three museums and Bergdorf Goodman, my first shopping experience alone and as a grown-up, the first clothes I had bought in seven years — and the most ever at one time. I found a dramatic white chiffon skirt and black backless top and a shoulder-length Marilyn Monroe–style blond wig. Since I'm invariably early — I showed up in the bar 15 minutes ahead, rigged out in my new gear and platinum hair. I took a table near the string quartet that I hope was playing "Some Enchanted Evening." Issy arrived, looked around, and sat at a table for two across the room. He ordered a drink, probably a rye and ginger ale, which he has since changed to very old scotch. Our eyes met, and he gave me an appreciative flirty glance but no sign of recognition. I ordered a club soda. He made no move. I sipped my drink and waited. Still no move. He didn't know me. So, I finally got up and walked in his direction.

He jumped up, kissed me, and said, "Sweetheart — sorry, I didn't recognize you. Your hair looks great, and you look fantastic in that outfit. I didn't know it was you. Your hair looks great. So, sit down and tell me — how was your trip? Your hair looks great." And so on.

He, of course, thought I had dyed my hair blond. Meanwhile I must have bored him as I gave him a breathy minute-by-minute account of my time in New York: tedious descriptions of the paintings of Turner and Boucher at Henry Clay Frick's beautifully scaled museum home and still more about Picasso's horrifying 24-foot-long masterpiece mural, *Guernica*, painted in 1937 and stored at the Museum of Modern Art from then till 1981 when sadly it wasn't there that year when I visited. I was told that it had been reclaimed by Spain. I briefed Issy that the Germans' bombing of the ancient city of Guernica, as allies of the Spanish rightists during the Civil War, had been their test run for the Second World War.

While I went on and on — in a voice that reaches an unpleasant, off-putting pitch when I'm excited — I slowly raised my hands and reached up as if adjusting a hat that has slipped back and pulled my wig slightly forward. Issy fell back and collapsed in laughter. The Palm Court musicians played on while we caught up. An evening to remember.

Bird's-eye View, 2016, 40" x 40".

CHAPTER TEN

Our Dream House

Living in a two-bedroom apartment with three kids had its difficulties, but only in retrospect. In the winter I had to dress all three and myself and then summon the elevator, by which time we were all in a sweat. After six years at Bathurst and Roselawn, we moved to a spacious modern four-bedroom house in Hoggs Hollow in 1962. I was pregnant with Tony. Four boys in five years! Only the first one was planned — the others materialized despite all precautions, including the pill, a diaphragm, an intrauterine device. It seems we should have used two birth control methods simultaneously. But four kids were fine, because in my fantasy life I had planned to have six kids — two adopted, since I considered this a mitzvah, a virtuous deed. In fact, I was to have six pregnancies — the last one was a miscarriage, although I was wearing a birth control device. While I was at it, I had my tubes tied, to simplify.

Isadore was working on his second hotel, and we enjoyed a new measure of prosperity. Our Hoggs Hollow home was designed by Peter Dickinson. The plan he drew up for us featured wood and fieldstone accent walls both outside and in. It wasn't the style of house we had wanted at first. Before Peter sketched up the plans, we drove him around the corner and insisted he see our idea of a dream house. He was not impressed. After studying the building for a few moments, he sniffed, "Oh, I see you have a preference for mock Georgian."

Of course, we were chastened by this dismissive remark and gave Dickinson the go-ahead. Issy collaborated with Peter and the result was dynamic. These days on our daily Covid jaunt we walk past that "mock Georgian" house we had shown Peter and find it lacking. I rang the bell one day, and found the front hall is very pleasing with clerestory windows. A few months before we were about to move into our new house, though, Issy had cold feet and thought, since the place had exceeded our budget, that perhaps we should sell it and move into something more modest. I was game; I was up to the challenge to make any place look good. Every house we looked at was fine with me, but in the end Issy capitulated and we moved into 36 Green Valley Road after all, which by the way has become a listed house.

Peter died of cancer a month later. He was six feet five inches tall, 35 years old, and one of Canada's favourite architects, with many good buildings to his credit, notably the O'Keefe Centre, the Beth Tzedec Synagogue, and Issy's second hotel, the Inn on the Park. On a visit to Peter in the hospital Issy mentioned that Dickinson's office had presented him with a disappointing drawing of a routine high rise for the Inn. Issy explained that the 16-acre site called for a spread-out low-rise building with lots of room for expansion.

"This is a resort! We need architectural drama that will attract people to make the drive to an obscure corner in the northeast of Toronto."

So right then, Dickinson said, "Leave it with me," and a few days later, propped up in his hospital bed, not long before he died, Dickinson made the perspective sketch that became the unique Inn on the Park. We kept this plan made on a long yellow pad with a 2B pencil — but we can't find it. Peter D.'s drawing integrated a famous Frank Lloyd Wright principle of 30–60 angles that allowed for a building to have continuous seamless add-ons. And the Inn on the Park was to have many angled additions to become a polygon when viewed from the air: 200 more rooms, the Terrace Bar, the Trillium Room, and a ballroom called the Centennial were added in 1967, so named to commemorate Canada's hundredth year. The polygon encircled a huge courtyard, which contributed to the immense popularity of the Inn. Sadly, Peter Dickinson died long before the Inn was built, but he had left his acolyte Peter Webb in charge.

Webb came to Isadore to say, "We can't carry on — we're broke, disbanded, and we don't even have an office."

"Peter," said Issy, "just rent an office, and I'll pay you weekly because we need you to draw up the plans," which they did, and then were to become the well-known architectural group Webb Zerafa Menkes Housden. Some years later, the architects held a thank-you dinner for Isadore with the accolades he deserved. They went on to design many hotels for us: London, Vancouver, Cairo, and Luxor.

It was at the Inn on the Park's vast 10,000-square-foot Centennial Ballroom that Max Sharp celebrated his 90th birthday among hundreds of guests. I wrote his speech, which he read dutifully, not changing a word — even the last line "well, my wife, Lil, would probably say 'that's enough Max — sit down,' so I will."

For a lark I had a three-walled structure rolled onto the dance floor after dinner, with buckets of plaster and tools, so Max and his brother Louis could demonstrate the plastering technique of their early days as the Sharp Bros. Plastering Company. They took off their black-tie jackets, rolled up their sleeves, and spread the plaster with gusto. It was a merry moment.

We had by then, the opening of the Inn on the Park, moved into our Green Valley house, spaciously spread on one level, with stone floors, cathedral ceilings, and rich, oiled cedar panelling that Issy designed, with one-inch-square vertical strips covering the seams between two-inch boards. Floor-to-ceiling picture windows gave onto the grassy dunes of the Rosedale Golf Club, where there were no Jewish members. This house was on the third hole of the course. Implausibly, our next house was on the first green of Rosedale, and our current home is on the 15th tee-off. When we moved to Teddington, the golf club higher-ups asked us to become one of the few Jewish members. We declined on the grounds that we didn't play golf, but the truth is we are not belongers.

Back at our first house on Green Valley, ever the interior decorator, I covered the plaster walls with natural burlap, and on my mother's Singer sewing machine I ran up drapery for the floor-to-ceiling windows out of the same fabric. Seventy-five yards of burlap, a dollar a yard, prickly with splinters, but I was determined to have the windows covered, even though there was little money. We had no furniture, so that first New Year's we had a square-dance party for 75 friends, few of whom are alive today. I ordered in rectangular bales of hay for seating and hired a square-dance caller from the *Yellow Pages*, a source that rarely lets me down. We enjoy having people in for dinner — me fussing with the food and the flowers — which is curious because I'm not a social animal, not at all gregarious. And our next party caused some confusion among our friends because my invitation read: "Please come to dinner on Saturday April seventh and/or Saturday April fourteenth." This was my democratic way of handling so many guests without designating an *A* crowd and a *B* crowd. No one knew how to interpret it, but the numbers were about the same both evenings.

At this time, in 1963, we took our first real vacation, to Europe. How did we ever leave the kids for five weeks? When we returned, Tony, the baby, then 18 months old, wouldn't speak to me for two days — before the days of Skype. What a great trip we had driving our rented Fiat, "the Reluctant Fifi," who was something of a mule and had to be prodded to climb hills. At dusk we would begin our lookout for the closest hotel, usually the seedy kind where, in those days, you brought your own toilet paper and soap. We chose either fleabags or luxury hotels, following the star ratings in our faithful *Fodor's* guide, always philosophically avoiding the in-betweens. In Portofino we splurged and stayed at the Splendido Hotel. During the night we were awakened by the wall behind our bed shaking for an hour while we tried to sleep and, in the morning, again our headboard was vibrating. Next, we heard a voice clearly ordering le petit déjeuner continental avec beaucoup de confiture. We were very curious to see these Olympians and luckily we caught them in the corridor just outside their room. They were short, grim, overweight like middle-aged twins, both with the same wispy gingery hair. In Paris, it was again the night for luxury, so we chose the five-star George V Hotel. That night, we ordered caviar and pommes frites at 3 a.m. I recall we were wearing the white terrycloth hotel robes when the room service arrived. Who could have imagined that in 2002 the George V would become a Four Seasons? Our drive through the Italian countryside was magnificent. I still have the ashtray I took from the bedside table as a memento.

We've always preferred travelling in the off-season. In November 1967, we spent a glorious sunny week in Venice, after the hordes of tourists had left St. Mark's Square. I can still recall the hollow echo of my heels in the streets by the canals, where there was no noise of cars. In the off-season of 1970 we were the only guests at Il Pelicano, a limestone villa clinging to a cliff 90 miles north of Rome. The pink-clay tennis court was ours at any time, but the kitchen was closed, so there was no food available. At night we would leave the staff having a fine meal in the dining room as we headed out to look for a restaurant, where we were again the only guests. Adventurous, I chose the least recognizable item on the menu, which looked like some sort of fowl. When later I consulted my Italian dictionary, I found I had silenced a song thrush. Twice in the winter of 1968, we skied in Chamonix, France. Issy later regretted not heeding my request to ski once in Zakopane in Poland.

Isadore was always a big-time skier — "intrepid" is the best adjective to describe him. He has been dropped from helicopters onto Rocky Mountain peaks in British Columbia and skied down virgin slopes between the close trunks of tall trees in the Bugaboos and the Monashees. He describes his whoops of joy when, with each steep turn, he drops 30 feet with the powder snow in a cloud around his head — a thrill he says is as good as any orgasm.

Issy taught me to ski when I was 17, but as with the jitterbug, I never quite got the hang of it. I somehow learned just enough that I could pick the easiest way to the bottom, mainly across rather than down the mountain. My goal was a cappuccino in the warm chalet just as soon as possible. With each turn, could I risk lifting a leg to step around? I imagined being torn up the middle while doing the splits headlong down the hill. I also remember the moment at Mont Tremblant when I gave up while I was speeding down, doing a snowplough, and released my desperate grip on the hill — hanging on by my toenails through the ski boots. I broke my ankle.

Instead of skiing twice in France, as scheduled in 1968, I suggested that we go skiing once in Zakopane, in the Tatra Mountains, while we were in Poland. That was the time I schlepped Issy to Ożarów. I wanted to see who was living in my grandfather's house. We arrived in Warsaw in the frosts of February, the temperature 25 below zero. At the Hotel Europesci we were assigned a room with two cots lined up against the same wall. There was frost inside the windows and on the sill — my mom had described similar frosty windows in her youth. When we called down for help with the draft in our room, the engineer came up and took our bathroom towels and stuffed them along the windowsill.

We called the desk clerk and asked if he had a suite.

"A suite," said he. "By us that is much bigger the price — six dollars a night."

Our suite turned out to be 10 times larger than the five-dollar room. Across the road at the Hotel Bristol, we went to see Hitler's bedroom. The décor was fascist-style Art Deco with a dark mahogany bedroom suite, the blankets covered in a counterpane, the pale green colour of my oil paint tube marked "terre verde." This blanket cover had a see-through circular hole in the centre, the same as my mother's Polish one. From Warsaw, we took the train to Krakow and then a taxi to Ożarów, where I shot a few photos in a snowstorm. The Birnbaum house had been taken down, as had all the Jews. We set off for the journey back, and the car rattled along a rural country road bumpy with ice as hard as concrete. It began to snow more and more heavily, until we were floating in a whiteout with no horizon. We panicked in frantic English, and the driver answered in Polish as he kept bouncing along the invisible road. Issy and I were frightened half to death, and I thought how ridiculous it would be to die on a country road in Poland, leaving four kids at home — and it was my fault. Suddenly, one of the windshield wipers flew off, and the driver left us in the car as he went out to look for that needle in the snowdrifts. By now Issy and I were not speaking to each other, sitting well apart in stony silence, wondering how this unnecessary adventure would end. Miraculously, the driver returned, gleefully holding up the windshield wiper, and Issy said, "Maybe this is a good sign."

We came to a village, hoping to find a train to Kielce. At the post office, I made a fool of myself with sound effects imitating a train, to ask, "Where is the choo-choo?" Issy recounts this anecdote too often. Our good friend the cab driver then drove us to the safety of the train station, where Issy handed him a bundle of American money in an amount I'm sure astounded him later when he unrolled a year's wages.

SAFELY BACK FROM POLAND, we were living in luxury, at our idyllic home in the valley. The kids and our Samoyed dog had a garden that led out onto the golf greens. In winter they snurfed on the snowy hills. The boys complain of too much support and too little love. I had grown up in a house where there was no display of affection. My granddaughters Emily and Julia have taught me to say "love you" at the end of every phone call. I know I made a lot of mothering mistakes, but it was my first try. Unfortunately, you don't get a second. I'm hoping, as Arthur Miller did, "to end up with the right regrets." I wish I'd had lessons in parenting. We'd had lessons in bridge and tennis, but for our most important job — parenting — we had no training. I consulted many books, by Dr. Spock and Dr. Blatz, about understanding the young child. What I failed to comprehend is that children should be allowed to be obnoxious. I would say to Chris, "If you're going to be revolting, you can't stay here with us. Go to your room until you can behave." I'm now guessing that kids who are not permitted to be anti-social grow up with too strong a need to please. The best advice came from the book *Parent Effectiveness Training*, which taught you to say, "*I* need help with the garbage" rather than "*You* take out the garbage" or, as my mom would have said, "You *never* take out the garbage." It was a frenetic time, with four boys under the age of five, the hardest period in my life. I was frantic, going from one diaper to the next, because first it was the older three wearing diapers, then the younger three. Sometimes, when I had no help, I had to leave the kids safely in the playroom while I tidied the kitchen and threw in the laundry (two loads a day).

It was a zoo. When Tony started to walk, I was so harried I went numb. Four rambunctious boys were too much for me. Tony was very curious — he was to become a mechanical engineer — and took apart every clock and removed the springs from all ballpoint pens, especially because I complained about it, so there wasn't a working pen in the house. I had to be very vigilant because, although he was a picky eater — mainly apples and very old cheddar cheese — he seemed more interested in sampling the poisonous cleaning solutions under the sink. All of these had to be moved to high shelves. But the kids were too quick for me. Chris swallowed a whole bottle of baby aspirin. I found him lying in a stupor on his bed and immediately brilliantly checked the bottle of St. Joseph's pills, where I had hidden it on the top shelf of the closet. It was empty — another trip to the hospital emergency room. One time a friend, Wally Cohen, came over unannounced on an average hectic day on Green Valley Road. He was cheerful as usual, but I wasn't myself. I just couldn't fake it. It's the only time I can recall losing the power to smile and pretend all was well. Finally when Tony was three and Jordy became a young adult, I regained my equilibrium. I was a very teacherly mother — we had painting sessions on the kitchen floor, each bottle of paint with its own brush. Once Tony was painting "a very bad animal" and he accidentally dribbled some paint across his paper. "That's just the way I wanted it," he said with his father's penchant for positive thinking. I took the boys to the library regularly and enjoyed reading to them, very keen that they learn to read for pleasure and know the comfort and magic of literature. Greg has become an avid reader of the classics. Recently, he even tackled *Mein Kampf*.

When Tony was three, I borrowed a life-changing book by Betty Friedan, the most influential book I have ever read, *The Feminine Mystique*. Ms. Friedan challenges women to escape their "trapped lives" as housewives and go out into the workforce and be people, not just helpmates. She asks, "Where will you, the housewife, be, when your children leave home?"

At my husband's hotels, there are now many more women in the top cabinet. Whenever a man in a high position retires, he is often replaced by a woman.

But back in 1964 I was poised and armed with the edicts of Betty Friedan. I resolved to take action. I waited until Tony, the baby, was old enough for nursery school, and charged his older brother Chris to hold his hand the whole three blocks home from school. I once came upon the two of them walking hand in hand on the edge of the road — a heart-warming picture I have stored. With the boys in school, I applied to take some part-time courses at the Ontario College of Art (now known as OCADU), because I believed it was important for the "wife of" to have her own credentials. My plan was to do some interior design for Issy's hotels. Of course, my mate spurred me on as always.

Well, what a crash of disappointment when I found out that the school absolutely refused to take part-time students. I gave up because there was no way I would abrogate my responsibilities as a mother by attending school full-time. I wanted to be home when the kids came home in the afternoon and called out, "Mom, what's for lunch?" But Issy, in his inimitable way, talked me into it. I've never been able to resist his reasoning. He is very persuasive, as well as too supportive, as Jordy says. I remember the moment. We were at Angelini's restaurant at the third table by the window. Over a glass of wine I told him almost in tears about my disappointment and why I had to give up going to college.

"Why not make your own schedule," Issy asked, "and attend at your own pace? What's the worst that can happen? You'll fail attendance, but you'll succeed at what you're looking for — you have a talent for interior design — look at how you decorated our apartment and now our house." Issy, amid his current reflections, credits this advice as another turning point because I would not have attended OCA without his push.

For four years I dropped the kids off at the Toronto French School every morning and went to college, always home when they arrived back at four o'clock. I hardly missed a day of classes and was usually the first to arrive. During the first three months, there were many days when I almost quit, but I would make a deal with myself: "Just hold on for another week — maybe it will get easier." Between homework and homemaking, my days were frenetic and fractured. The worst moment was the day my colour studies were due. Here I was locked in the bathroom at home — the only room where I could work undisturbed. The boys were banging on the door: "Mommy, when are you coming out? What are you doing in there? Mommy-y-y-y!" My paints were spread all over the bathroom as I tediously painted 100 postage-stamp-size squares of colour, each a tint, tone, or value darker than its neighbour.

"Mommy will be out soon," I yelled back at the kids, thinking, "God help me, what do I do now? Should I simply pack up and quit or give it one more day?"

If I had quit, I would never have found out that after Christmas the work came almost to a halt, as if the first semester was simply some sort of test. By January, a lot was left up to the student's initiative. Never again would I need to do schoolwork at home. The following three and a half years were a breeze, sometimes a joke, with lots of time to spare. Typically, every project had a three-week due date. Unlike the other students, who would pass their days in the cafeteria socializing, then complete the project the night before it was due, I would stay alone in the classroom and work. In this way, I was able to complete all assignments within the school day.

I picked up many new ideas at art school: Helen Fitzgerald, who taught us lettering, had designed three Canadian postage stamps (she did the artwork at three times the size of the stamp). Miss Fitzgerald told me I had "a feeling for lettering." I didn't mention that I wasn't new to sign painting, having done a hundred "one brush-stroke" signs for a fundraiser, not to mention signs for Wise's Dry Goods and that I had my Uncle Chaskel's gene for drawing.

In 1969, I graduated from the Ontario College of Art with two medals — the Lieutenant Governor's Medal and the Art Gallery of Ontario Medal — plus various prizes, and out of 240 grads I stood second, outdone by Sister Mary Emmanuelle (who did not have four children).

And then in 2006, I became the first chancellor of that school, when it became a university — a title conferred on me for a few reasons: Since 1969 I have headed up many fundraising events, each of which took up almost a year of my time, like the CADA Antique Show, which in a good year brought the college $200,000. I also served on the school council for six years and was chair of the OCADU Foundation (the college's board of trustees), and we did give the school $5 million to help build the Rosalie Sharp Centre for Design — a dynamic leggy box of a building designed by Will Alsop, which opened in 2004 to rave reviews and ruffled the feathers of some traditionalists.

School over, I designed a line of fabrics for house furnishings, printed on a table 30 feet long by five feet wide, in a design studio — Green Valley Workshop — we built adjoining the house. It was satisfying to paint the designs, usually floral, in black ink on mylar, one 54-inch sheet per colour, photographically transferring each to a silkscreen. I would mix the coloured dyes and lift the 50-pound wooden screens onto the long table. The dyes would be squeegeed across each registered screen to print a four-colour repeat design on about 10 yards of white fabric, which was then cut up for samples. I cut and stapled small swatches of printed fabrics, each topped with a cardboard border bearing its description.

I made up sets of samples and sent about a dozen different designs, each available in many colours, to Eaton's department stores across Canada, then sat back and waited for the orders to roll in. I never received a single reply — from which I learned the value of salespeople, especially as I was married to a supersalesman. I never did any commercial promotion and ended up getting most of my orders through Issy's contacts. When a client ordered any substantial yardage, the goods were reproduced in a factory. I designed a few custom-printed curtain fabrics for Simpsons Contract Department. They would order thousands of yards for hotels (usually ours) and office buildings. Once, Green Valley Workshop received an order for 4,000 yards of floral fabric for curtains to be installed in the Royal York Hotel. After the drapes were installed, Simpsons asked that I send them the standard two clippings, a piece of the original and one that had been dry-cleaned four times, to prove that the colours were fast. The clipping came back from the cleaner's almost blank — the pattern had come off in the cleaning process. I never submitted these. For some years I fully expected to be sued by the Royal York, but thankfully I discovered that hotels never clean their curtains, they simply replace them.

We installed the printing table in the basement of our next house and here the boys went into the T-shirt printing business — shirts with slogans like Greg's "Save the Environment" and 1,000 shirts for the Toronto French School from my own alphabet that I drew up in india ink with ruling pen and compass. The school went on to use that design for 20 years. Meanwhile, Greg, our household mechanical engineer, came up with an ingenious solution to a production problem. The issue was that we had to wait for each table of shirts to dry before we could print the next batch. Greg laid a string under every row of blank shirts and, after printing, simply lifted the whole row above the table to dry. I can remember about a dozen of these rows swinging above their heads as the boys printed yet another batch. Recently he devised a variation of the same device — designing a sleek silver cable and pulley system to lift clothing to dry above the head in his laundry room.

We were a productive household. Jordy started his music career, playing the drums first thing after school. He later played the banjo and sang with perfect pitch — which he didn't inherit from the Sharp genes, because the Sharps don't sing. I knew Jordy had arrived home from school when I heard him drumming behind closed doors in his room to "Moon Dance" by Van Morrison. His four-piece band, After Dark, played at school dances. And we have the photo of him when he won best bluegrass banjo player in Western Canada, 1994–95. Since my two favourite instruments are the banjo and the cello, I'm hoping he'll play at my funeral. Jordy's Toronto restaurant, the Santa Fe Bar and Grill, became a local hangout as did the Brunswick Tavern he ran in partners with my brother Stan.

I marvelled at the boys' ingenuity. They devised contraptions that depended on an advanced knowledge of maths and physics that defied my comprehension. Greg was always rigging up something that would fly. At age seven, he sailed off the roof with umbrellas and his own flying devices. Meanwhile life for a coward like me raising four boys on Green Valley Road had its challenges. They were always speeding on bikes no hands and homemade flying contraptions. Greg completed many triathlons and tells two stories that reflect his kindness. While speeding through the bike detail he came across a cyclist on the road with a flat tire, so Greg stopped and handed him a pump. After the race the announcer asked, "would the good Samaritan missing his bicycle pump please step forward." As the crowd clapped, the beneficiary then gave Greg a big hug as he handed back the pump. Next was the swimming segment of the triathlon, and he arrived at the exit ladder at the same time as another fellow. "After you," said Greg.

My mom, like me, was a coward on many counts, and I still share some of her fears. She was afraid of dogs, cats, cars, lakes, showers, planes, sudden movements, and any occasion that required the removal of clothes.

With trepidation I once drove down Highway 401 to Centennial Park with Greg's hang-glider precariously strapped to the roof and attached to the hood ornament with string.

Today Greg flies through the city on his bike. He once flew over a car door suddenly opened in his path and went splat over the nose of the car. And in fair weather he flew his ultralight, while Jordy has his pilot's licence. Jordy's first passenger was his dad, and Greg also took his dad up in his ultralight, their feet dangling in the open air. Luckily for me these planes were two-seaters.

Tony was a renaissance boy. He could knit, hats his specialty. He learned arithmetic on the abacus and taught himself chess from Bobby Fischer's book. Tony got his scuba diving licence in the icy waters of Tobermory, a four-hour drive north on a cold day in late September. Tony was a fisherman although he didn't eat fish and threw his catch back in the water. Once on the dock at the cottage he had a small squirming fish on a line and he said, "Mom, just hold it, it's so soft, just like a baby." And he would stalk birds like a cat, creeping up on them so slowly and deliberately with his hands out to catch them. Tony was a teacher's assistant in finance at Yale, became a successful real estate maven, and is the family number-crunching whiz. His constant companion is Sam the Labradoodle, who he says is a hypochondriac. Last winter Tony and Sam flew to Palm Springs to visit us — they both had first-class seats. Halfway there Sam thought they should be arriving soon so left his seat and sniffed the crack in the exit door for a while until an announce-ment came to "please return to your seats," which he did.

Tony and I, when he was age nine through 11, took three train trips across Canada. The first was to Newfoundland where the landscape near St. John's featured moss-covered cliffs but hardly a tree — just as Samuel Johnson had found that a tree in Scotland was scarcer than a horse in Venice. On the second trip we went north to Moosonee, where the tracks end. There Tony caught a brook trout by the tail, just by luck. The third and longest trip was to Vancouver Island. Saskatchewan, I recall, from the train window, was astonishingly ruler-straight — a landscape I found more remarkable than the Rockies. On Vancouver Island Tony caught a 34.5 pound chinook salmon called a "tyee" because of the huge size, which we duly stuffed and hung on the boathouse wall. So he can boast to have caught a fish in the Atlantic, the Pacific, and near Hudson's Bay. While Tony and I train-travelled, Isadore manned the home front for the other three boys. His cooking skills, to the present day, are limited to porridge, toast, and yogurt with trail mix. When I returned, the 11-year-old Chris said, "Without you, Mom — Dad's a loser."

That train trip with Tony was my fourth — after the solo trip to New York — in my long love affair with locomotives. I can sit still for days watching the world gliding slowly past my window on a train. It's calming. The humourist Mark Twain in his autobiography tells the tale of his train ride from London to Burford where he is happily gazing out the window until he notices the man across from him is reading a Mark Twain book, and now he can no longer enjoy the view because he must watch each page the man turns to see if he laughs. He doesn't.

Sometimes on my hotel travels with Issy, I will take the train and meet him at the next stop, as I did from Singapore to Bangkok, a 35-hour trip. Trains are an escape into anonymity, and nothing is expected from me. When Issy and I were in Taormina, I noticed that from the small quaint train station there was a 12-hour trip to Rome. Gleefully, I said let's cancel our flight and take the train instead. Issy looked doleful resting on the bed with his hands behind his head. He said nothing, but I could tell he was looking for a way out. I guess he couldn't come up with an escape. I said he could fly, and I would meet him, but we both took the long journey together. The train crossed the straits of Messina on a narrow bridge. It flew through tunnels that spectacularly opened to cliffs down to the sea and up to remnants of ruined castles on hills. I am hoping to ride the 4,000-mile train trek from Moscow to Vladivostok. But I would never take the Orient Express from Paris to Istanbul. I would take the next train travelling the same route but carrying no tourists please.

With the boys on Green Valley Road, 1965.

Dancing, which we still like to do at every opportunity.

36 Green Valley Road, our first house.
The roof on the right is my studio with
northern light. The house is now listed.

With Jordy, 1960.

The boys in the dining room. From the left: Jordy, Tony, Chris, and Greg. The first time I served a buffet, Jordy said, "Mom it's just like a party," so we had buffets every night, which was a lot easier.

At the Inn on the Park, 1964, where we went Sundays to swim. We changed in Issy's office instead of taking a guestroom and always sat on the grass to leave the lounges for the guests.

The Inn on the Park — architect, Peter Dickinson, 1963.

Christopher Hugh Sharp, 1960–1978.

Greg and Joanne, 2016.

Issy and Greg, Terry Fox Run, 2001.

The first hang-glider, 1973, built by Greg from bamboo and plastic.

The Fort, Green Valley Road, 1970. Design and build by Greg with an ingenious system of pulleys to lift the four-by-eight-foot plywood up the 30-degree hill. Tony helped.

Greg flying the second hang-glider he built, 1973. Now he flies his ultralight.

No. 41: Tony, captain of the basketball team, St. Andrew's Junior High. Photo from York Mills Mirror.

Jordy wins Best Bluegrass Banjo in central Canada, 1994–95.

Chris needed no instruction on how to operate the boat — he just got in and drove off.

Issy and I with three of our grandkids, Emily, Julia,
and Aaron, at the Terry Fox Run, 1995.

Our grandchildren and daughter-in-law Ann. From left: Emily,
Aaron, and Julia. Ann is the consummate mother.

Stanley Barrie Wise marries Martha Kohn. Stan says he
and I were lucky in our choice of mates.

(top, left) Our grandson Jyah Flam at architecture grad school.
(top, right) Julia Sharp and husband Jay Lubinsky.
(centre) Vernon Shaw, Ann's husband.
(bottom, right) Emily Sharp and husband Gabriel King.
(bottom, left) Aaron Sharp and his wife, Liza Hoos.

THE GREAT-
GRANDKIDS
(clockwise
from top left)
Viera
Henry
Isaiah
Cody
Max
Charlie

Chris and me at the cottage
in Muskoka, 1977.

Tony and Emily, Palm Springs, 1986.

Jordy, Carolyn,
Jyah, and
Erika, 2015.

Anthony graduates from Yale in 1988.

Tony at chess with Papa Max Sharp.
Aaron and Issy looking on.

Tony and I took the train to
Newfoundland and to Vancouver
Island, then north to where the
tracks end in Moosonee.

The patio at 180, home of six cabinets of antique blue-and-white china.

Our home in Palm Springs since 1986. There we lead a rather village life. The house was built for the Wurlitzer family in 1936. The olive trees are ancient.

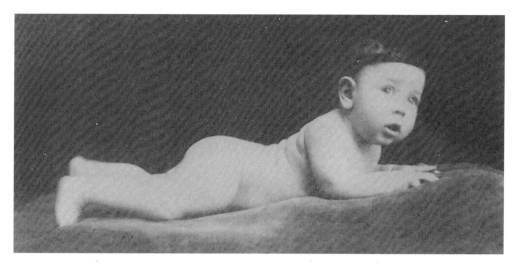

Isadore at six months. Rosalie below. He has the same build and canny demeanor. She has the same hips with an expression described in her kindergarten report as "alert, interested, talkative."

My Bonny Lies over the Hill, 2019, 33" x 33".

CHAPTER ELEVEN

What Flower Is That?

In 1973, I began seeing a psychiatrist for a year and a half. For two reasons: because my mother had terminal ovarian cancer and I feared I wouldn't cry at her funeral, and because Chris had been born with strange forces that formed him — perhaps an atavistic link to my father's dybbuk — some kind of no-name learning disability that made us all crazy. Ten years later, we would discover that the condition by then had a name — attention deficit disorder — and there were doctors who specialized in its treatment. In maturity, they said, the condition would fade, which it did. It would have saved a lot of heartache had we known this earlier.

Psychotherapy turned out to be a good exercise, though, like taking a course in understanding human behaviour. It made me more philosophical. My doctor very kindly shored me up, and we came to admire each other. In 1972, when Chris was preparing for his bar mitzvah, we moved from our unique, sprawling one-level house on Green Valley to a red-brick 1937 boxy house at 26 Forest Glen with four rooms upstairs and four down. Our son Tony was always nostalgic for the Green Valley house, so when it came on the market again in the '90s, he looked into buying it. I hoped the move to a conventional house would quiet the frenetic pace of living with four boys. Our previous house had such an open plan that from the front door you could see almost everything going on except who was in the bathrooms. The new house had the privacy of doors. And indeed, it did seem more civilized. Jordy immediately claimed the basement rec room as his territory, a private club off limits to adults. My daughter-in-law Ann tells me that I was duped, because there was pot smoking going on, and I didn't recognize the sweet scent.

I have never tried pot, ordinary life being heady enough. An art-school colleague once suggested Issy and I join her and her friend for an evening of indulgence, including pot. Issy said, "Nonsense. There's no reason to try drugs. How would we then have the collateral to convince our kids to be non-users?" He was right, of course. And except for a very rare aspirin, my consumption of drugs to date consists of one diet pill, given to me by a svelte beauty named Denise in the ladies' room of the Four Seasons. This pill speeded me up so much that I couldn't stop cleaning the kitchen and even found myself on all fours washing out the doghouse. I wouldn't take such punishment again.

We lived at Forest Glen for 35 years. The purchase of it, like many happenings in my life, was a chance event. I heard that the place was to be auctioned, so I brought Issy to see it. He didn't react to the house one way or another, which is like him, but he seemed to respond to the huge garden, which had its own forest. Either I forgot about it, or I didn't want to press him, I can't recall which, but about two weeks later, on the day of the auction, I remembered and phoned him at the office: "Issy, this is the day of that house sale, and I really liked that place and forgot to ask if you thought we should bid on it."

"Why didn't you say something?" he asked.

Well, we were lucky. We missed the auction, but the buyers had a change of heart, so the real estate agent called us because we had been listed as interested purchasers. We made an offer of $225,000 and became the owners.

True to its name, the Forest Glen house sat in a leafy glen, unfolding in three storeys down a hill and out to a back garden with almost three acres of sloping valley filled with rolling lawns, virgin pines, New Brunswick maples, chestnuts, and many other Canadian trees. Some of them have paired off in couples, so by the front door were Mr. and Mrs. Yew, he looking very trim although she had let herself go, and by the back door were pairs of pines and a couple of chestnuts, joined at the hip. Today in our Teddington Park house we have a pair of tall little linden trees, he strong and sturdy, she slender and standing a few paces behind.

The ancient trees were permitted, like us, to enjoy their old age undisturbed. Three of the pines may have been 250 years old. I miss Canadian trees in the winter when we go to the California desert, where the 25 varieties of palms are just an excuse for trees. My favourites in Canada are the flowering trees. One year, our flowering almond tree billowed like the pink tulle hoop skirt of an antebellum maiden, but unhappily, that year was its last. I wish I had taken a photo. And when the jolly yellow forsythia blooms, I'm sad, recalling how ephemeral life is: I know the flowers will die in a week.

When we acquired our first large garden, I applied my usual zeal to learning about plants. I made an exhaustive study of a book called *What Flower Is That?* and planted great drifts of rubrum lilies. Every year fewer survived, and then there were none. But that first year, when they grew to six feet, I had life-sized portraits of them painted on panels that now border the fireplace in our house in Palm Springs.

I think plants of a kind should collect in exclusive crowds, as they do in nature. I once saw a whole hill covered in snow-on-the-mountain; it brought a white light to an area darkened by a canopy of trees. So, we planted the same species under our own trees. On another slope, in clouds, I planted every gigantic-leafed ground cover I could find in the book. The colossal lacy white sprays of our Heracleum appeared unfailingly every July 15, resembling prehistoric Queen Anne's lace. Unfortunately, some of our chosen plants would have been more comfortable in the climate of South China, as the book suggests. Once, in Santa Barbara, I was stunned by a bank of electric-blue cinerarias seen in the magic hour, as Robert Louis Stevenson put it, "between the dark and the daylight, when the night is beginning to lower," that moment when colour is so strong it sings. I promptly planted a hundred feet of these across the front of our Palm Springs house, and we have planted them every year since 1987.

As well as flowers, I take equal pleasure in the shapes of leaves, particularly acanthopanox, ginkgo, and the chestnut, which resembles the acanthus leaf found in Greek, and later Georgian, art and architecture.

You might imagine from all this that I love nature, but I don't. I go for a walk in the garden hardly once every two weeks, preferring to survey, through the window, the long shapes of rolling lawns and the golf course beyond with its forty shades of green created by the dappled shadow from the tall trees. Mostly I go out for five minutes of sun on the front porch as we used to do outside our shop on Yonge Street.

As for real nature, I feel like a fish out of water. As outdoorsmen, Issy and I are a joke. In 1972, we took the boys on a canoe trip in Algonquin Park. The two of us slept in a rented pup tent, little more than a sleeping bag for two, which Issy pinned shut against snakes. I woke in a sweat in the middle of the night and had the most irresistible urge to escape, but I couldn't open the flap because we were pinned in. Well, I panicked and stood up, dragging my sleeping companion with me. He calmed me down and eventually induced me — I don't know how — to go back into the tent. But in the morning, instead of marvelling at the call of the loons skimming across the glassy water, I had a bout of real claustrophobia and could only think, "How will I ever ride back to the city in a car, with the roof so close to my head, when I'll be compelled to stand up?" I did get over this fear, but I'm not certain it won't happen again.

That was our first and last camping trip.

When Blossoms Mingle in the Spring, 2020, 57" x 63".

CHAPTER TWELVE

Disaster at Its Worst

In 1974, Chris called me into his room one day to look at a wart on the inside of his right calf. When I asked if it had changed in the last few months, he said yes. So, we went to see a skin specialist, who took a sample and a week later called to report that it was benign. But he had made a fatal error — Chris had an obvious lack of pigment in his skin, and the doctor should have given this vital information to the lab so they would know how to read the sample.

Disaster struck in November 1976, when Chris's school called me to say he had a growth in his groin the size of an egg. This was his first semester at St. Andrew's College in Aurora, where, for the first time since Grade 2, he was enjoying his studies and had brought home the best report card, since he had outgrown his ADD.

The doctor examined Chris's groin and ordered a biopsy. My first question was, "Will he miss any school?" I was not worried, because I could not imagine that it was serious. Why would the worst happen? As it turned out, it was mighty serious — melanoma. The cancer cells had multiplied madly in Chris's young, healthy body.

Before he became ill, Chris had been working out regularly, and he had a perfect lean body. He knew exactly the future he wanted. Of course, he would have a conventional Jewish home near us, an executive office at the Four Seasons, start the job right after high school, no need for a college degree.

And he was all set with his lovely red-haired girlfriend, Joanne Fogler. There was gossip that Chris had been seen climbing out of Joanne's bedroom window. Happily, Joanne is now the wife of our second son, Greg, and years ago she had confirmed my hopes that they "knew" each other. Chris and Joanne tooled around in his new red TR6 we bought him since we knew his time was short. Chris would be so happy to know that Joanne is now with his brother Greg, like stories of World War Two when a soldier would marry the widow of his slain brother. So Joanne is now Greg's "Yibbum," the Hebrew word for a brother's mate.

Issy's considerable business success gave us the trump card people of means hold — the power to pull strings. We found the best specialist available and arranged an emergency appointment. The specialist prescribed a most hideous, unnecessary operation for Chris, a so-called "exploratory," where they butchered him 10 inches up the middle of his chest looking for further cancer cells. The surgeon proclaimed him cancer-free. I thought to myself, "What's the point of the operation when cancer cells can be microscopic?" For this slaughter we had taken him to Boston. And after the operation I let him down by miscalculating what time he would be back in his room. Arriving late, we found him lying there quietly, tears running down his face.

THE SUMMER BEFORE, at our cottage, Chris had taken up golf and asked if we could join the Beaumaris Golf Club across the water from our island in Muskoka. We applied and were refused membership because we were Jews — a surprise because we Jews perennially believe that "it's different now." I recall that when we told Chris why we had been turned down, he was very sober for a few days. He was perplexed and felt diminished, like I had felt as a youngster. He thought there must be something wrong with us.

Now, at the cottage, the cancer returned, and chemotherapy was prescribed. For these treatments, Chris and I flew to the Memorial Sloan

Kettering Cancer Center in New York every few weeks. Our thinking was that if we travelled some distance and consulted the so-called best doctors, we'd maximize our chances. On one descent for landing, the plane careened dangerously close to the skyline — a view King Kong might have seen — but we just looked at each other and said, "What have we got to lose?"

On these trips we would go to the hospital, have the chemo, then make a mad dash by taxi to the Plaza Hotel, getting to our room just in time for Chris to drop down in front of the toilet bowl and pour his guts out. He endured about six of these sessions, but then he went on strike. He had asked the doctor, "Will the chemo cure me?" and when the doctor replied, "No," Chris said he'd rather take his chances than have another treatment.

In the 1970s, the treatments were so much more debilitating than they are now. We tried to talk Chris into more chemo, but he refused, and we respected his decision. Christopher and I became ceaseless companions. One time he and I were sitting at Sunnybrook Hospital, not far from our home, waiting once again for some doctor, and he said to me, "Mom, it's just you and me; you're always here." But Issy was always there for him too. He would spend every minute after work with Chris.

The grim time arrived when Christopher was hospitalized for what looked to be the last few months of his life in Sunnybrook's D wing (D for Death? I wondered). We asked could we take him home, and the reply was that the morphine he needed was illegal outside the hospital. But with our power to pull strings, we arranged to get a supply of the "Brompton Cocktail" — a combination of whisky, morphine, and other drugs.

We kept Chris at home instead of in the hospital, as if he had just the flu or a passing illness. At home he wasn't plagued with hospital routines and tubes of intravenous. Chris slept in our bed, and Issy and I took turns sleeping with him while the other slept in Chris's room. I remember the guilt I felt on those rare nights when we had sex in the other room while he was asleep. I gave Chris his shots myself, which I learned by practising on an orange.

While his body atrophied horribly, his face became more beautiful. He suffered the indignities of bedsores and relieving himself in bed, on paper, lying on his side. He said to me one night as I went into the bathroom, "You don't know how lucky you are that you can just get up and get out of bed." There came a time when I had to hold his penis while he peed into a bottle. He didn't seem to mind — there were worse things to mind.

Once, as I was fussing with the sheepskin he lay on because of the bedsores, he asked, "Am I going to die?"

I answered, "We hope you will recover, but it's possible you may not. No one knows for sure."

Once I said, "There can't be a God," and he answered, "Don't say that. There is a God."

Those were black days and black nights: I remember going up the stairs so heavily, with nothing but dread in each step. The night before Chris died, the rest of us ate a chicken dinner in his bedroom. We were chatting normally, hoping to make him feel included. He didn't speak. He just lay there quietly, very still, looking at the ceiling. I marvelled at that stillness that he had maintained during the three months he was bedridden — that last night he was wearing sunglasses, which he had asked for before dinner. He was removing himself; the way people do when they are ready to leave the world.

The next morning, Friday, March 10, 1978, the day he died, Chris said, "Dad, will you stay home today?" Issy stood by his bed, and I lay across the bed, and each of us held one of his big, beautiful hands. He was quiet and still, breathing heavily, and then he gasped, "Doctor — ambulance — hospital." A moment later, Issy gestured to me with his chin towards the slowly increasing wet circle on the sheet. It was almost 10 o'clock. Christopher's hand was still warm and I had to let go when the men arrived and put him on a gurney and took him down the stairs. I watched from the top as they had trouble making the turn on the landing because he was six-foot-two and, according to the doctor, not even fully grown.

I had been expecting him to die for weeks, and even at times had wished for an end to his suffering — yet I felt a shattering grief and emptiness. If you ask, would I wish this tragedy had happened to someone else, I can't say I would — I don't know why. Today we confer with Chris in our daily lives, and remember his kindnesses, his follies, his recipe for cheesecake — which we have on the wall, framed — and what his life might have been. We buried Chris in a bleak Jewish cemetery where it's unlawful to plant trees because the tradition, maybe in the Torah, is to pack graves as close together as possible thereby taking as little land as possible from the living. Well, two years ago Issy came up with the idea that we should move Chris to Mount Pleasant Cemetery because it's a beautiful park. Isadore bought a piece of land there, the most paramount and long-lasting real estate of his career. This square of land accommodates 20 graves, well 19, because Chris is buried there. News spread so we had requests for one of the 19 digs. Karina Bukanov, Tony's best buddy, and Vernon Shaw, Ann's husband, have asked to bunk in with us. Therefore, Chris will have the company of a nice crowd. And here he will have hosts of people pass by on daily walks among gardens and trees that reach the sky. A place of liveliness and beauty, which would suit him better. I designed a headstone in polished black granite five feet square, a Star of David engraved at the top. The inscription reads: "To Life and Joy." We've already heard from friends who have paid him a visit at his state-of-the art apartment.

And I have a rather good plan for Issy and me to join Chris. It is a plan not unlike King George IV's instructions to his peers — something like: "When I die leave one side of my coffin removeable and the same for Maria Fitzherbert's coffin so the sides can be opened and both of us can be together." (She was his secret wife for over 50 years, and could never be queen because she was both divorced and Catholic.) Since I have an imagined claustrophobia, I'm hoping for some similar arrangement.

On October 6, 2019, we buried Chris at his new digs at Mount Pleasant

Cemetery. Eighteen members of our immediate family stood around Chris as we welcomed him to his new home. By luck not one member of our greater family was missing because the out-of-towners were here for the high holidays. A table nearby held photos of Chris and squares of cheese-cake, made from Chris's own recipe. At first, we had planned the traditional ceremony. The coffin to be lowered into the ground and we each toss a shovel of earth into the grave, but at the last minute I thought it better to have him already buried and the whole 20-foot-square area around the cof-fin planted with Issy's choice of periwinkle. Isadore made this all happen, but it was a feat since there was hardly enough time.

The day of the ceremony was warm and sunny, and we all stood around to welcome Chris to his new home. Issy, Greg, and Tony spoke, and I gave a short eulogy. Here it is:

All the right people are here today, but the main person remains

Chris Hugh Sharp.

We can laugh at the irony that tragedy is random. Yes, it's unfathom-able that Chris died. When he was 17 and a half. And Isadore has said kaddish for Chris every day. I see Issy bend his head over a table with Chris's photo while he silently recites the prayer which he's said every day since Chris died Friday, March 10, 1978.

That was the day Chris had said to Issy, "Dad, don't go to work today," as he lay quietly in our bedroom where he had lain for three months, instead of the hospital and against doctor's orders . . . we thought if he was home he might be fooled into a hope of recovery. During those last months, I marvelled at his courage and acceptance. He was so graceful and quiet in his body — never a twitch of anxiety. He was still growing; the doctor said he would've been six foot three.

Before this, when Chris was well, he was the picture of beauty, with his blond good looks . . . peerless complexion and perfectly fit body, from daily workouts. He had no use for drugs, or cigarettes, even coffee. . . . God he was so wholesome. . . . His favourite songs were the sunny sentiments of John Denver. . . . Chris was masterful with dogs and with all moving machines — motorboats, motorcycles, and bicycles.

At four years old he persevered and after a few crashes taught himself to ride a small two-wheeler. At 15 he begged for a motorcycle. We said, "You're too young . . . wait a couple of years . . ." "No," he said, "by then I'll be too old for a motorcycle, I'll want a car." It was a good argument, so we bought him one. Once from the window I was alarmed to see him ride his motorcycle down a long flight of steep stone steps. At 17 he tooled around in his red TR6 and when a chum questioned his having a car so young, Chris replied, "Okay I'll trade you — you can have the car, but the cancer goes with it."

Chris put our dog, Snobo, through her paces — she looked up to him and minded his every command.

He was a take-charge person. Once a friend's collie got stuck in the ice and couldn't make it up the hill. Chris quickly came to the rescue, and without taking time to put on his gloves he held her collar and one step at a time they slowly climbed the steep hill in the freezing rain each footfall breaking the top layer of glassy ice as we all watched in the warmth by the window. When Chris was 11, he was invited to Val d'Isère to ski with the Creeds, Issy's sister Edie's family. One day there, he fell off the Poma lift as it turned a corner. Eddie Creed, Edie's husband, saw him fall but chose to continue skiing and left Chris on the hill to find his way back to the hotel, which somehow he managed to do, apparently arriving in tears. It's inconceivable that Eddie wouldn't have stopped to help him. We all remember.

Chris at his bar mitzvah — I can still see him as clear as a photograph suddenly standing up in the ballroom during dinner, his arms raised dramatically, calling for the great crowd's attention, and delivering his speech with such bearing and confidence that he had his audience in his thrall.

He was a chef who favoured Italian recipes and would sometimes take over the kitchen and serve a meal. And when guests arrived, he would be the greeter, and when they left, he would station himself at the door to shake hands. Christopher also had street smarts. He was the only one of the boys who wanted to go into the hotel business. His pragmatic plan was to quit school as soon as allowed by law and learn on the job. My guess is that, if things had turned out differently, he would still be working for Four Seasons Hotels.

Chris took up cooking and baking, especially a picture-perfect cheesecake he improved upon from a famous recipe. He had the consummate discipline never to eat this cheesecake himself.

Chris once rustled up a dinner for our friends, the Lipsons, who were just about to leave. "Don't go," he said, and he served up penne pasta with a cheesy marinara sauce. And when any guests left, he would always go to the door with them, shaking hands and saying all the right things, which made me smile. It was good to see him instinctively more personable than me.

Chris and I were very good friends, and when he was ill we were joined at the hip patiently waiting our turn for doctors' appointments and chemotherapy in New York — why New York? We fooled ourselves thinking our chances were better if we travelled some distance. One time, on our way into New York, our cab broke down and we stood in a heavy rain, hitchhiking on the highway. I was hysterical with laughter and tears — we were soaked, the water pouring down our faces. Was there a God, I asked, although I knew there was not.

The summer before he died, we were at the cottage, and he built a huge roofed brick barbecue with Tony and Greg's help. Recently, the owner of that cottage, Fiona Mccardle and her husband, called to say they are about to remove the barbecue and would we like a brick from it, which we did.

That summer Chris still thought he could beat the cancer with brute force. I saw him struggle mightily to pull himself up to the roof of the boathouse to dive into the water, a superhuman feat, weak as he was.

So that's it for now . . . just a few stories so you'll know Chris better. He would be pleased to reside in this beautiful park and so happy that you are all here, especially the families he never met.

I think Chris would have said about my refreshments here today: "What, you served no lunch — just cheesecake," and he would probably say to you all as you leave, "Please drop by this park anytime, and if you like, even leave me a stone from some far-off place."

This eulogy about Chris I hoped worked to bring him to life for my grandchildren, who had never met him. I remember Liza, our grandson Aaron's wife, in tears, perhaps because their oldest son is named Charlie, Katriel in Hebrew, after Chris.

Tony's Choice, 2016, 48" x 60".

CHAPTER THIRTEEN

Not a Decorator

M y life is divided into two periods: before Chris died (BC) and after (AC), when life sped up. The last 40 years have practically evaporated, probably because Issy and I buried ourselves in work. I think time passes more slowly when you're quiet and still.

I opened Rosalie Wise Design after Chris died. At breakfast one day on our stunning wraparound verandah at the cottage, my granddaughter Emily, age seven, asked me: "Safta (Hebrew for grandmother), what do you want to be when you grow up?"

"An interior designer," I answered.

"Well, that's what I'm going to be," and so she did, although currently she and her husband, Gabe, run an organic farm in Nelson, B.C.

Once when I was taking care of Granddaughter Erika when she was six, she turned to me and asked, "Safta, do you know how to knit? can you teach me?"

"Yes, but we'll need yarn and knitting needles."

"Would chopsticks work?" she asked, and with those the knitting began.

Once when she was visiting at the age of three and saw my stainless-steel toilet, she remarked, "We don't have one like that," which is what most people don't say.

Grandson Aaron's résumé describes him donating his summers to unpaid jobs like teaching English in Peru. But he's most proud of his online courses teaching tens of thousands of kids to create with technology, raising a small army of confident creative youngsters. But he turned down an offer to try for a Rhodes Scholarship, denying us the joy of boasting about him. When Aaron was seven, he was with us at a black-tie dinner honouring Isadore. A procession of waiters appeared, bearing trays of roast chickens. Aaron scrunched down on all fours and buried his head in the seat of the chair crying, "Oh no! I can't look — I'm so sad about all those poor chickens," and today he is a vegan. Aaron's wife, the lovely Liza of the long ballet legs, took her university degree on the environment, particularly oceans, so I picture her underwater stroking a fish.

Back in the days after Chris died, my fledgling design company's first project was for my patron, Issy, for the lobby and some model apartments at 120 Dale Avenue, and then I did the same when he opened Granite Place. Isadore made a trade with the Granite Club that his construction company would build their new premises on Bayview, and he would put up two apartment houses and an office building on their block-long St. Clair land. Along came the Canadian Jewish Congress and the B'nai B'rith and challenged Isadore to require the Granite Club to change their charter and allow Jewish members, which they did; and of course we were asked to become the first, the anointed Jewish members. This has now happened three times. After declining our first request to join, the Beaumaris Golf Club invited us to be the first Jewish members and so did Rosedale Golf Club. With satisfaction, however, we declined all three because we are not clubby people and we don't play golf.

When Granite Place was built, I so enjoyed decorating four model suites. I always had imaginary residents in mind and catered to their hobbies. The fictional occupants of model Apartment 203, Mr. and Mrs. Turcoman, collected carpets, so their den was wine coloured, draped with red madder and indigo blue rugs, and Apartment 303, in the west building, was decorated for the Italian aristocrats, the da Vincis, in grey-and-white Fortuny fabric and a silver monochromatic palette. A buyer came along and requested that condo, including the complete furnishings.

We also did some design work for a few of the apartment owners. Our first client, Mrs. Seagram, requested a beige wall-to-wall carpet that she felt would harmonize with floral sofas better than the oriental carpet which was a legacy from her mother-in-law. We showed her two samples, one a bonded carpet for $10 a yard and the other a woven carpet for double the price. She chose the lower quality because at her age, 75, she felt it would do the job. And I ended up buying her magnificent antique Sarouk carpet, which was a feature of our old house and now centred in our gallery at 180, and has been witness over the years to the goings-on of four wild boys.

I needed help in 1978, so I hired a partner, Stephen, who had always been so helpful to me in the Switzer fabric showroom where he worked. In proper socialist style, I always had partners — never proletarian workers. Stephen had impressed me when he said, "The first thing we'll need is a filing cabinet to keep track of billing and purchasing for our clients."

"Great," I thought. "Of course — a filing cabinet. Why didn't I think of that? Just what we need. Here is someone who will take charge of the details and make sure we're businesslike."

After a month, I came to understand that Stephen meant for *me* to do the filing. Each of us saw ourselves as the designer and the other as the filing clerk. So, I gave him a handsome settlement as my mother would not have done and sent him back to the showroom. Now I called up George Brown College and asked them to put this note on their bulletin board: "Wanted, bookkeeper for small interior design office. Must be willing to double as receptionist."

Enter Ruth Malitzky, a capable and honest Jewish lady five years my senior, with a Brooklyn accent and a rather bright green dress. She stayed for 17 years, until I closed the office in 1995 and moved home to work. At R.W.

Design, Ruth became the accountant, receptionist, purchaser, manager, and my protector. She gave the company credibility and locked away from the staff all paperwork germane to the finances. During her first week in the office, she was late because of a transit strike, so Ruth volunteered to deduct the two missing hours from her wages. She often cited afterward that I ruled against this, saying, "It was your intention to be on time."

Our office was a walk-up at 60 St. Clair West conveniently across from our Granite Place clients. The landlord, Mr. Lagussis, like the good landlord my mother had been, was always helpful and fair — especially during the cockroach incident. We had a lot of truck with cockroaches in this office and even at our next location. It seemed that Toronto's cockroach community had courageously migrated to North Toronto from the security of the downtown Jewish ghetto. What I hate about cockroaches is that they hide, unlike an ant, who will be friendly and tickle your hand as he ambles across. One day in the office kitchen, I was making coffee, which was my job, when out jumped an insect I didn't recognize, having never met a cockroach. Mr. Lagussis asked for a description of the bug, then said, "I will be over this afternoon to take care of it. Now tell me this, Mrs. Sharp — did it hurry?" Hurry it certainly did. But the bugs never reappeared after the landlord installed small roach hotels, which had welcoming entrances but no exits.

Our next office location, 3419A Yonge Street, eight blocks north of Lawrence, was a walk-up above Bill's City Restaurant, owned by the short-order cook, our landlord, Mr. Mintsopoulos. A stained cardboard sign in the window promised souvlaki was Bill's specialty. It was a tiny place with one booth, two tables and chairs, and very few diners. Steve and his wife, Mary, were the most annoying people, and as landlords they were abominable. He always wore a long filthy apron and she had bad feet and a high hairsprayed coiffure and was usually sitting down doing nothing. We put a lot of improvements into the premises — mirrored wall up the stairs, sanded floors, paint — and asked would he share the cost. Not a penny. The week we moved in,

Mr. Mintsopoulos ran up the steps, barged in, and had the temerity to accuse us of making our own coffee when we should be buying it from him.

One lunchtime, as I put a slice of Dimpflmeier rye in the toaster, because I can't abide untoasted bread, and pushed the lever down, out hopped an enraged cockroach. "Oh no, not again." This time I recognized the species — it hurried. I went down to Bill's for help. One customer was sitting in the booth having a cup of grey coffee in a thick mug and smoking a cigarette.

"A cockroach! It couldn't be, never! We've never seen absolutely not even one cockroach in this building, ever," said Mr. M., wiping his hands on his greasy grey apron.

"No, no, not even one," Mary backed him up, never leaving her chair.

"Ah, I see what you mean, Bill. Well, in that case, Bill," I answered, "let me assure you and put your mind at rest. Should you ever come across a cockroach in this restaurant, well you'll know for sure, where it's coming from — our office, upstairs."

At 3419A, at the peak of R.W. Design's success, we had a staff of seven. Eighty percent of our work was for Isadore and his hotels. Our advertising flyer read, "At Rosalie Wise Design we consider how materials meet." We had a wonderfully large, friendly front room, 30 feet wide, that doubled as our library and reception room, with a 10-foot-long antique pine table in the middle. The walls were lined with shelves of sample wallpapers and hundreds of fabrics, folded neatly in colourful stacks of prints and plains and stripes and velvets. There were four of us, on average, and lots of laughs at coffee break. I would tour the others' work at their drafting tables, and if I commented, "I see you're still doing your Bach exercises," this was a metaphor for "Go back to the drawing board."

To be alone, I hid in the back office, where I quietly phrased architectural interiors on a drafting table with an HB pencil, to the classical music on CBC-FM or tapes of some of my favourites — some would call them chestnuts. "Song to the Moon" by Dvořák; "Au fond du temple saint" by Bizet;

Symphony in G minor by Mozart; "Dôme épais" by Delibes, or his flower duet from the opera *Lakmé* sung by Mady Mesplé; all at high volume, of course. At home, Issy turns down the volume every time I turn it up.

I find the round nasal tones of opera sung in French have a particular appeal. Or give me an aria like "Der Hölle Rache" by Mozart, composed at the time my great-great-great-grandfather Shmarya Tyszler was singing in the synagogue in Ożarów. Like many people, I prefer the familiar over anything new. I first understood this prevailing taste when I came across Mary Delany chronicles of mid-18th-century English life. When she attends Handel's *Messiah* in 1740s London, she finds the "philistine" crowd unreceptive to the new music. As for my own modern music favourites, Jordy says, "Mom, you like any tune you can dance to." True. From a Scott Joplin Charleston to a Johann Strauss waltz, or give me a slinky Argentinian tango — I do them all by myself in the kitchen. And what about the counterpoint of Fred Astaire's phrasing when he sings Irving Berlin's "Let's Face the Music and Dance" or the Beatles' "I Want to Hold Your Hand."

In my back office, listening to CBC, my first big design job was the Four Seasons Houston in 1982: the guestrooms, corridors, and suites. Isadore reviewed all the architectural and interior design for all the hotels, and he was an easy-going and supportive boss, not just to me. I flew to Houston to direct the installation a few days before the hotel opened. At 9 a.m. on the day of the opening party, the Pavarotti Suite was empty but for the silver-grey carpet. Luciano P. was to arrive at four. We had to place all the furniture, plants, curtains, cushions, and bed linens in his sitting room and bedroom, as well as in the connecting bedroom, where the soprano would sleep. The decoration was a mixture of antiques, crystal, and modern glass tables and lamps in a silver-gilt and cream scheme. The opera star's bedroom had a high four-poster bed with a white eyelet canopy, and I wondered if he would sleep there or with the soprano. We were just placing the fruit and flowers on the dining room table as the elevator brought him to the 20th floor. Phew!

That evening I sat beside the master singer at the big banquet but hardly got a word in because of the continuous stream of ladies bending over between us to pay him homage. At one point, someone's long blond hair dangled dangerously close to my soup.

The next time I saw Pavarotti was when we opened our hotel in Milan in 1993. We were having dinner at the home of Riccardo Muti, director of La Scala, when he said, "We are rehearsing *Don Giovanni* tomorrow, and you are welcome to come." What an offer! At La Scala I was the only audience in the regal red velvet opera house, designed in 1778, the year my earliest known Birnbaum ancestor was born in Ożarów. I wish I'd attended La Scala in the time of Maestro Arturo Toscanini, ranked as the genius opera director of the 20th century. I sat up front near Mr. Muti and listened as he sang along with every aria, just as his predecessor Toscanini had done. Luciano Pavarotti was rehearsing the principal role wearing a ludicrously wide pair of jeans. It was an unforgettable afternoon of glorious music.

After we finished the Houston project, R.W. Design worked on many more Four Seasons Hotels: Washington, London, Vancouver, Toronto, and a new hotel in Paris that was cancelled after we had drawn up a complete set of specs, including a full-scale drawing for a custom hook on the back of the bathroom door. The French project paid us $80,000, which in the end hardly paid the bills for over a year's drawings and specs.

Over the years we designed thousands of hotel rooms, each featuring the identical layout: the ubiquitous bed flanked by two lamp tables, the artwork over the bed, the TV opposite in the armoire. At the time there were standards we had to obey. Issy insisted on three specs: wallpaper (I preferred paint); a quilted bedspread — this bedcover if rolled up and stood in a corner you might mistake in the night for your roommate; and a curtain valance, which I found redundant. When I featured a duvet in one of my model hotel rooms, Issy said: "We need the old quilted type. The duvet is too labour intensive — it won't work." Five years later the duvet was universally adopted. We also argued about the fussy curtain valance which I had campaigned to eliminate. Eventually, all my preferences have been adopted. In the Washington guestroom, in a black-and-white scheme we named "Magpie," we varied the typical layout by replacing the pair of lounge chairs with one chair and footstool and put the standard desk at right angles to the wall with two — instead of one — elbow chairs. When Issy reviewed the model room, he said (as my heart sank), "Let's see the desk against the wall," where desks had always been placed. Then, unexpectedly, he said, "Let's try it again angled." He was quiet for a moment, and then, thank goodness, he said, "Well, let's go with angled, that really looks good." For the next 30 years the angled desk became our standard and was copied widely throughout the hotel industry.

"Copied widely" was to become operative for so many of Isadore's innovations. He focused strongly on the customer. What would a guest away from office and home value and appreciate? Over the years Issy has originated many novel ideas that became Four Seasons standards and later, industry norms. In 1961, for example, he changed hotel bathrooms forever by installing telephones should there be an inconvenient call, as well as small shampoo sachets in showers and larger towels. The hotels had especially soft toilet tissue, as attested on CNN by Stanley Marcus of Neiman Marcus. And Isadore was the first to install super comfortable mattresses and offer them for sale. It would be 30 years later when other hotels climbed on the bandwagon and claimed they had the most comfortable beds. With his focus on fitness every hotel had a workout facility. In 1972, he came up with: non-smoking floors, the concierge, complimentary shoe shine, and — very dramatically — allowing employees to stay in any hotel gratis (which to date is still unique to our company). In 1976, Issy instituted 24-hour room service, overnight laundry, and fluffy white bathrobes. In 1980, with my nudging, light spa food on the menu, Kids for All Seasons daycare, TV on top of each fitness machine, and no housekeeping carts in the corridors.

To our satisfaction, Prime Minister Lee Hsien Loong of Singapore, with characteristic patience, instituted a 50-year plan to make their workforce the best in the world. They studied our company's hiring practices, employee benefits, etc. To this end they invited Isadore to speak to an audience of government people. I sat in, as I often do, with pride, or as we Jews say, "schepping naches."

To this day, innovations continue with, during the Covid pandemic, Christian Clerc's "Lead With Care" program, as per the advice of the Johns Hopkins doctors.

While Issy was innovating with his now 40,000 employees, I was working non-stop with my staff of four at Rosalie Wise Design. In 1984, we were offered a plum of a job in Nagasaki — a 400-room hotel with five restaurants for the Prince Hotel chain, a job which might have put the kids through college. We were the third interior design firm to be retained. The first two had been fired, and the hotel was due to open in a year, so there was a good chance they would keep us. Mr. Hashimoto, the project coordinator, asked me to present our fees, so we had an office huddle and came up with the number — $90,000 CDN. I wasn't certain this would be right in the long run, because we'd probably be worked to death as usual, so the next day I called him to say, "Mr. Hashimoto, I'm having trouble figuring out the fees on such short notice. Can you look at your budget and help me out?"

"Hei hei, Mrs. Wise, so sorry, no problem, so sorry, I will try to help out. Please may I call you back? Would it be okay if I get back to you tomorrow?"

When he called the following day, we said okay when he asked if we would accept $500,000 U.S. And soon we were off to Tokyo to present our design proposal for the new hotel to our client, Mr. Tadao Mitsui, at his 50-storey office tower emblazoned on top with MITSUI in 20-foot-high blue neon letters, or were they red? We rolled out our plans and I suggested a few design changes which didn't please the architect but were adopted nevertheless by the owner.

Over the next year, we had to ply our way to Nagasaki and back about five times — 24 hours each way, from door to door. I remember handing my boarding pass to the attendant when she said what sounded to me like,

"Have a good fright!" How did she know that when travelling on a plane I prefer to pretend I'm on a bus and rarely look out the window?

Whenever my colleague John Edison and I landed in Japan, Mr. Mitsui greeted us on the tarmac and immediately whisked us off to a restaurant for an expensive dinner, although we would have much preferred to go to sleep. John did not eat fish, and fish was all there was. Exotic platters of shellfish were offered along with a great golden whitefish, still blinking and quivering from head to tail. We were encouraged to try the signature dish, a large oval bowl of water teeming with tiny darting tadpoles. Our host showed us how it was done. He put his fist into the bowl and seized a few helpless tadpoles and threw them into his mouth. John, in the chair beside me, was making burping noises, as if he was about to throw up. I passed him a hunk of bread.

After dinner we continued to a karaoke bar. On the way, John whispered to me in the cab, "Remember now, whatever you do, don't ask me to sing. I don't sing."

"Tonight, John, you will sing."

"No, I never sing."

"For Mr. Mitsui, you must sing."

"I definitely will not . . . sing."

He sang.

We had a hectic 10 months, but Ruth managed to order and install all the custom white guestroom furniture and fittings in time for the opening. She steadfastly turned down offers of kickbacks, which in Japan are culturally correct as a means of augmenting the rather low wages.

The Prince Hotel opened to rave reviews, and Mr. Mitsui was very pleased. Isadore came and we all attended the opening-night banquet, and I was seated in a place of honour in the centre of one of the long tables. The principals spoke at great length, because in Japan it is considered impolite to make a short speech. No one, except me, turned their heads to look at the speakers. Looking at the speaker, it seems, is impolite. A few people in my line of vision nodded off, which is apparently quite polite. After dinner Mr. Mitsui pressed into my hand a note containing a customary bonus cheque of $10,000. He was especially happy with the change I had made to the solid second floor of the lobby elevation — now broken with an open balcony overlooking the entrance hall. Unfortunately, we also installed in the lobby a sunken black granite reflecting pool. We watched in horror as guests regularly stepped into the water by mistake, since it looked the same as the adjacent shiny floor.

The next day, before we left, Mr. Mitsui gave us a farewell luncheon.

After the meal, he brought the company to attention and, as if conferring some kind of award, magisterially announced, "I have decided to hire you, Ms. Wise, to design my new private home in Tokyo, and you would do me an honour if you accept."

Now I was in a spot. I had no interest in private homes, and besides, I'd had enough of flying back and forth to Japan. "Thank you so much, Mr. Mitsui," I answered, "I am very honoured. But let me get back to you after I know the scope and timing of the project."

In Japan it is considered bad form for one principal to say no to another. The usual practice is to send the answer later with one of the minions.

I diplomatically handed the design opportunity to John, who opened his own practice, did the house for the Mitsui family, and went on to do much more work in Japan.

R.W. Design, meanwhile, later used the Nagasaki half-million dollars to buy two houses in Toronto as a tax shelter, but these properties lost money in the next real estate recession. We ended up with close to $90,000.

Business was a bit slim in 1985 at R.W. Design, so I set out to drum up a project that was to become, in our office lingo, "the Yoo-Hoo Job." It came to me while I was idly gazing out the window at the construction of the Teddington Park Retirement Home next door. Two guys in hard hats were standing on the sidewalk looking at the building plans. I went out on the fire escape one floor above them and yelled down, "Yoo-hoo, excuse me, but we're in the interior design business. Is there anything we can do for you — maybe paint colours or can we get you some furniture or fixtures, whole-sale?" The taller gent, Tom Schwartz, invited me to descend the iron staircase and join them for a chat on the sidewalk. That was how R.W. Design came to design and install the lobby, the restaurant, and some work in the bedrooms of a home that, unfortunately for the tenants, had a rather quick turnover.

Our fees were $5,000 plus 10 percent on the purchasing — we gave them 40 percent of our buying discount. Tom was very pleased with the resulting cheap and cheery restaurant, and no doubt our low fees, of which my mother would have said, "Sell cheap and you'll have plenty of cli-ents." Tom invited us to do his next retirement home, but at past prices we couldn't afford the project. Upping the fees four times would never do, so we declined, pleading a full timetable, and handed off the work to another designer, who he ended up suing.

I had one more moneymaking scheme that didn't work out. The Avenue Road Church was for sale, and I had the urge to buy it and turn it into a permanent antique fair — I would call it the Avenue Road Antique Show. I imagined that shopping there would be like visiting a museum, but you could take the stuff home. I have a lot of respect for my antique-dealer friends, who I consider to be learned museum curators, and I envisioned being their appreciated patron.

I knew instantly, in my mind's eye, what the finished church would look like. From the door you would see five shops on the left, with five shops in a balcony directly above them. Wrought iron with brass trim would fringe the storefronts and balconies. A further 10 shops would be mirror-imaged along the far-right wall. Straight ahead, up the broad centre, on an inlaid black-and-white mosaic marble floor, you would see the Gallery Café, open to the huge height of the original church ceiling. The café would offer a menu of veal or cheese cannelloni, salads, and bitter chocolate biscotti. The restaurant furni-ture would be crashingly modern, made from acrylic, glass, polished nickel, and black leather. While you sipped your latte from a black and silver porcelain coffee can, you would have a clear view of both sides of the two levels of shops displaying antique one-of-a kind chairs, china, silver, treen, and more, all glittery in the golden halogen light. The whole place would be canopied by the grand scale of the existing gothic church ceiling and wall decoration.

The church was on the market for $2 million — twice what I could risk. I happened to mention this to Isadore's longtime real estate friend, the eponymous Francis Hilb, the "Have I got a deal for you!" negotiator. He went right to work and made a lowball offer of $1 million, which, incredibly, was accepted. You could have knocked me over with a feather. But, after a year, I chickened out — I didn't have the guts. Of course, I would have liked my fantasy church to happen, but I didn't need the risk, the nowhere to park problem, or the headache of collecting the rent. Thanks to me, the lucky inheritors of the Avenue Road Church were the Hare Krishna, who can still be seen around the building in their colourful regalia: henna-stained shaved heads, pigtails, and saffron skirted robes.

Back to the drawing board. My next project was a ballroom in London about the same scale and scope as the Avenue Road Church. Ballrooms and restaurants have always been my favourite projects — especially restaurants because they can be theatrical, whimsical, or capricious, and I could have a meal there later and enjoy the ambience.

At R.W. Design, our restaurants always incorporated three types of seating, so that from the door you didn't see a sea of 70 chairs all the same model. Instead, you might see an island of black leather and chrome chairs, a heavier version for variety, and some velour settees (with the dimensions refigured so they would sit like chairs). Our restaurant in Montreal in 1988 featured swivel office chairs on five wheels and room dividers made of fine silver chains hanging floor to ceiling in two-inch waves — chains that I sourced from the *Yellow Pages*, under Novelty Jewellery. The rough white plaster walls were painted by one of my OCA artist instructors, Dainis

Miezajs, in abstract sunsets. I would have had the floors made of polished cement, but couldn't get the approval from our client (Issy).

Another restaurant I had planned was a simulated outdoor setting — as if you were outside on the terrace off the drawing room of a stately home with walls of cut limestone. Tall French doors would have painted views of lamp-lit interiors featuring period furniture, Venetian glass chandeliers, and shadowy images of 1910 people in dinner dress drinking champagne while a Cole-Porter-type played the piano.

The restaurant we designed in Washington featured dining tables as art. Curious found items were embedded in transparent clear resin, and the wooden pedestal bases had a metallic automotive finish. Every table featured a different embedded item: one with rusty old handmade nails, one with peacock feathers, another with old watch parts, one with pennies and nickels, another with butterflies, and I've forgotten the rest. We did different designs of unique tables in three other hotels, and in each of those cities the manager gave me grief by covering them with tablecloths, which he claimed had always been the Four Seasons standard.

Every project for me was a chance to use colours that sing. With me, colour is a sensory necessity — like velvety dark chocolate. I paint oil on canvas every day to find the rush from colours that combine dynamically, like burnt umber added to scarlet lake. I try, but fail to improve on the colours found in nature; if you get them correct on canvas, they're too good to be credible — the reds of sumac leaves in October, the spring green of the willows outlined against the black purple of beech trees, or the peculiar reds of Japanese maples. These rare reds I achieve by adding a small quantity of cadmium yellow light. And blue flowers, particularly scylla in early spring and hydrangea, cornflowers, and cinerarias in summer. Colour schemes in my restaurant projects were always the driving force. Also our dining rooms in London and Toronto have showcased the work of Canadian craftsmen in glass and pottery, featured in open individual cabinets each with the artist's name and phone number in plain sight. The waiters were encouraged to sell the works on display, and we asked each artist to replace any work they sold with a new piece of their choice. One of the glass artists, Toan Klein, sent me a box of flowers every time he sold a piece.

I must confess I have made a few foolish mistakes in judgement. While designing the restaurant in Vancouver which I called Chartwell after Churchill's country house (you will remember his friends paid for it since he was always strapped for cash), I had to source the décor. I planned vignette oil on canvas landscape views from Chartwell with dark panelling surrounds and on one wall a group of blue-and-white English ceramic chargers. I hired an artist and set out to Bradford to buy one of the chargers from a dealer. It was pouring rain on the highway, but I carried on with stubborn stick-to-itiveness. I remember passing 16-wheelers when the water was so thick on my windshield it was blinding. I should have pulled over and waited for the storm to abate. When I reached Bradford, I found I had made a mistake — the shop was in Brantford. Undaunted, I sped perilously through the storm to Brantford, 130 miles from Bradford. I bought the dish and returned home — a total driving distance of 260 miles. Later the restaurant became a banquet room and who knows what happened to the chargers. My second most foolish mistake was in selling our Gerhard Richter painting for $2 million — it is million — it is now selling for $30 million.

IN 1983, WHILE WE were designing Washington suites to CBC music at full blast and going about other business as usual, disaster struck on the home front. Misfortune made another of its inevitable proclamations, this time with the news that my mom had only three months to live. Ten years earlier she had beaten the ovarian cancer that hit her, but now she suffered from leukemia, probably resulting from the cancer drugs. As she aptly said in Yiddish, "A healthy person has many worries, a sick person has only one."

The grim vigil began with daily drives to Mount Sinai Hospital, bringing something from home — sometimes food on a pretty china plate, and always words of hope. We all pretended this was just another setback because the truth was baleful and boring, and a waste of time. I never missed a day, partly because of the guilt I felt for judging her so unfairly. However, some years before, I had finally succeeded in forgiving my mom's shortcomings, which, after all, she herself had inherited. Only after forgiving her, had I been able to pardon my own sins. Ten days before she died, I made the Passover Seder and invited my whole family. After dinner my mom came into the kitchen, and, although she was usually shy and embarrassed by any display of affection, she hugged me freely and said thank you, and with that rare hug we declared love and peace.

Stan and I recently reminisced over lunch about our early days in the Wise household. We met at Harry's Charcoaled Broiled (this store was formerly Wise's Dry Goods), now run by a Korean couple. Digging into our omelettes, we Wise children recalled Dad's temper and Mom's discipline methods.

Which went like this: Mom never laid a hand on us but would incite Dad's wrath by listing her grievances against us.

"Stanley stayed out too late every night this week, and he won't listen to me."

"Where is that boy?" said Dad. "I'll fix him, so he'll know to stay home and study."

Then Mom would shield my brother with her body, her arms outstretched. "No, no, don't hit him — you'll kill him. Hit me — hit me!"

Dad would lunge to the left and right of her, flailing his arms and yelling, "Ydess, get out of the way or you'll be sorry."

She, like a matador, would dodge and parry, and somehow Dad just kept missing his target.

The truth was, as both of us clearly recall, Dad missed because he didn't want to catch us. Stan and I recounted all the scenarios we could remember and laughed till we cried, because not one of Dad's blows ever met its target.

In the hospital, Mom kept her teeth in a glass by her bed, which made conversation difficult. She could have saved some teeth, but in the shtetl they didn't visit dentists. Bad teeth were simply extracted. I went to see a dentist for the first time, spending my own money, when I was 16, and they found 25 cavities. Both my parents had false teeth: I believe my father had his remaining few teeth pulled because he thought dentures would improve his smile.

The doctor called me on April 25 to say I had better come down early because the end was near. I found Mom as usual with her dentures out, which made her look like her own grandmother. She struggled to tell me something in Yiddish. She motioned me to lean in closer, but I still couldn't make out her words. All I heard was something like "meshugas mit meshu-gooim — life and people are craziness."

Similarly, my mother-in-law's last words were inaudible — I had never even known she wore dentures. I hope that when Issy and I are in our last throes, we will have something amusing to say, since with modern dentistry fortunately we will still have most of our teeth.

In her last days, Mom had reverted exclusively to Yiddish. Sometimes, in her hospital room, when my mom had to pee, she would tell me, "Ich darf geyn mit di vasser," which meant literally "I have to go with the water," and I would wheel the intravenous bottle into the tiny bathroom with her. Often now when I need to pee, that Yiddish phrase comes into my head. Which is what happened one day when I was scheduled for an 11 a.m. ultrasound. I drank the required 32 ounces of water but didn't bother to measure. On the way I dropped into a sports shop to buy Issy six pair of tennis socks, but while driving to the doctor's office I met with a problem. I had to "go with the water" desperately. I scanned shops as I whizzed by looking for a restaurant — none in sight. Finally, there was no alternative. I pulled over, grabbed the package on the seat, and peed into Issy's socks.

ON APRIL 26, THE day she died, my mother's eyes were shut, but when I gave her some soup, she licked the spoon. Mom was always grateful for my offerings, especially the time I brought her an orange, which was precisely what she had been in the mood for at that minute. She said to my dad, who could never do right, "See, why don't you bring what I want, like Rosie?"

She was either 69 or 72 when she died. Dad put 72 on her gravestone. I cried at her funeral. I miss her. There are so many times when I need to call her up and say, "Guess what?"

At the funeral they asked, in what I suppose is a Jewish custom, that if I would like to see her one last time, they would open the coffin for a private viewing. I did not want to see her, but I said okay, in case it was right, but when I saw her, I was frightened out of my skull — her head on a pillow, her hair done up in a different too-bouffant style, looking surreally alive, but not quite like herself. One of those haunting, indelible memories.

EVEN THOUGH MY PARENTS had seemingly not been in love, the truth is that they did love one another, but not in any New World way. Their love was evident in their last days together. After she died, Dad seemed lost. Stan and I persistently tried to rouse him from his grief and pry him out of the house, but he preferred to sit alone on the sofa and nurse his wounds. We pleaded with him: "Please, Daddy, come for dinner — the kids love to be with you." He was so dear and quiet (when he wasn't ballistic).

When the bad news came, Issy and I had just arrived in San Francisco to review my colour schemes for the guestrooms. As we were deliberating whether the rather too gaudy cornflower-blue bedskirt should be flounced or pleated, the phone rang. It was my brother. Not a good sign.

"Hi, Stan, what's up?"

"I have bad news — it's Daddy."

"Oh no, what happened?"

236

"I called him this morning to go to Stubby's for lunch, but there was no answer, so I went to the house. All the lights were on, and he didn't answer the doorbell. I had my key, but the screen door was locked from the inside, so I had to break in. I called out from the front hall and then walked up the staircase. Daddy was in bed, wearing his best blue pajamas."

This was unusual because we knew he usually slept in the nude. "He was lying on his back and his eyes were open and he didn't look right. I touched him and he was cold, and then I realized he was dead. I was so angry. How could Daddy leave us? We loved him so much. I punched him in the shoulder. Rosie, it was so sad, because any day now I felt he would have rallied and come back from his gloom."

It was September 1, 1983, just four months and a few days after Ydessa had died. We didn't investigate the cause of death, but we should have because now we'll always wonder. It was creepy, though, to find out that before he died, he had tidied up the house, given away all my mother's garments, and paid all the bills, even tying up the loose ends in his real estate holdings. Dad was always considerate and never wished to be a burden to anyone. My kids will not have it so easy. Before the spring of 1983 no one in my greater family had died, but by September my grandfather had also died. He had been at Lincoln Place, an assisted living residence. I upgraded him to a private room and visited him weekly when we chatted in Yiddish. He was close to 100 years old, yet he never made the mistake of asking how Chris was — only the other three boys, by name. Once I brought him a new sports jacket for the Shabbat services. Before this one day when I was visiting him in his apartment and admired a small glass 1930s nappy, he took it from me, saying in Yiddish, "Leave it — all in good time," which I found curious and a reflection of his hard-won goods.

Aaron and Liza's, 2014, 57" x 63".

CHAPTER FOURTEEN

A Train across India

In 1985, I go on my own to India for two weeks. I pack one small carry-on bag with black and white clothes, like the monochromatic wardrobe my friend Merle had taken on that long-ago high school trip I envied so much. The airport in Mumbai is pandemonium. I am herded through the baggage claim by a crush of people towards what I hope is the exit. It's frightening. Somehow, I find a three-wheeled taxi, all the while wondering what a mother of four is doing here in this strange and distant place. A warm bath and a pot of palak paneer — I respectfully eat vegetarian — cheers me, and I'm back ready to go.

I remember it as if it's yesterday: I travel by train across the middle of India from Agra to Jaipur. The train rolls slowly from village to village in the dusty sunlight, past farms and people squatting in the fields to relieve themselves, sometimes sitting in circles. As the train slows down at each station, small boys offer us tea with milk in round clay cups without handles. A boy hands me a cup through the open train window, where I can feel the sun warming my forearm resting on the sill.

The train ride is slow, as soothing as a massage, rocking from side to side with a pretty clicking sound, as pleasing to the ear as the local English spoken with a Peter Sellers lilt. I prefer this slow ride, to the unpleasant speed of the hermetically sealed Bullet Train I once took to Kyoto, where hills of tea plants rushed by in a blurred film on fast-forward. Here in India the villagers get on and they get off, as they do every day, and I am the privileged observer for this one day only. I meet a young man, Yogesh Chaturvedi, on the train who invites me to lunch at his house in the next village. He assures me I could easily hop on a later train. I make my excuses, thanking him for the invitation. But when we all get off to stretch our legs at Bandikul, his hometown, I have an impulse to take him up on his offer, so we roar off on his motor scooter, me on the back, hanging on for dear life. It is a humble house indeed — two rooms, no water or power, with people sleeping on beds in the kitchen, like my grandfather's house in Ożarów. (Isadore likes to tell this Bandikul story to dinner guests.)

The one-hour flight to Benares is delayed five hours but the locals are as calm and unruffled as Khalil Gibran. On Thursday I rise at four a.m. for a boat ride on the Ganges, past steps crowded with people. The broad steps lead down to the muddy yellow river. Two boatmen pole us along the shoreline for a mile or so. A few bodies wrapped in coloured shrouds are burning on their wooden pyres, which takes three hours, and then the ashes are scattered on the river.

On Monday, October 14, according to my diary, I arrive in Delhi and drive through jammed streets: "donkeys with carts, burros, scooter-cars, elephants, rickshaws, motorbikes, cars, all converging like a kaleidoscope around a cow sitting imperturbably in the centre." Then, to "the Lake Palace Hotel in Udaipur, at the suggestion of John Kenneth Galbraith in his journal, when he was ambassador to India. The hotel, built in 1750, sits in its own reflection on a basil green lake of glass-like water. My room with its Persian arched doorways and faience tile borders around the window, is right on the water, a monkey loping on a nearby roof. Rajiv Gandhi appears on TV speaking to dignitaries at the airport, among them the 'Minister for Better Fertilizer.'"

Next is my visit to the Taj Mahal, which is a laugh: no water in the reflecting pool — just rusty pipes, while it is being cleaned, and I am surprised that there's no interior — it is just a solid white marble tomb. There were roughly two reasons I chose to travel to India. I delight in the colour, style, and sensual silks of the Indian dress. "Such a wild variety of turbans, dhotis, saris, bodices, skirts, shawls — the jangle of bright colour special to India. The Indian women dress exquisitely with a ring of ankle bells, gold jewellery circled on wrist and throat. All these wonderful costumes finished with the most curious footwear — adidas, thongs, rubber shoes, sandals." Also, I wanted to feel the serenity of the Indian psyche because I am rarely tranquil. . . . Always rushing in case time runs out. And later, when I am back home, I am calmer for a time, graciously ceding to others in lineups at the supermarket. Issy has recently remarked that it was very brave of me to set off to India on my own. And as I look back I wonder — was it courage or folly?

I made another trip on my own when Issy was off helicopter-skiing with our boys, in 1986. I flew to the island of St. Martin, on the French side, and stayed at a small, posh place. I felt a delicious sense of freedom — neither mother nor daughter nor wife. I took all my meals at a table for one on the terrace and noticed that I presented a curious figure, particularly to the married couples, since I was single and not friendly. The local cab driver who had brought me from the airport had said, "If you'd like to eat some real local fish and rice, I'd be happy to take you to a typical restaurant." So, I took him up on it and we had a fine evening, although as we were driving home along the dark roads, I'll admit I second-guessed my wisdom in accepting his invitation, wondering whether he thought I was looking for something more than dinner. But he brought me back safely to the hotel, and as we entered the lobby together, I noticed one of the male guests glaring at me with palpable disgust, bordering on hatred. Later I worked out that his disapproval must have stemmed from some repressed longing to have sex with a local girl, or perhaps he was simply a racist.

As new tennis players, Issy and I went a few times to Bermuda to the

Coral Beach and Tennis Club Hotel. What an idyllic spot with its four pink-clay tennis courts sunken in front of a thirty-foot hill of ancient dense green climbing ivy. There was a dining terrace high on a cliff overlooking the sea. Every night there was a 10-piece orchestra, and we swept across the terrazzo dance floor rendering a silver foxtrot to the rhythm of the rolling whitecaps far below. On our third visit there we noticed that the best rooms in the hotel were given to members, so we applied to join the club. We were refused. No Jews, please. That's the last time we saw Bermuda. Many years later an offer arrived to make the Coral Beach club a Four Seasons, but it didn't pan out.

Nowadays, Issy and I spend our winters in California, in the desert, where the sun sinks suddenly behind the mountain in midafternoon and the temperature falls from summer to autumn, so you sleep better. Copper cliffs make a jagged outline against a heart-stopping clean blue sky above our house in Palm Springs, over lands where, less than a century ago, only the Cahuilla (Hot Water) Indians padded around in their moccasins. In 1986, we bought a wonderful old 1936 house, originally built for the Wurlitzer family, who made organs, pianos, and the jukeboxes that made their name famous.

The Palm Springs house has a macabre past. Our gardener cum manager Charles Martinez is a mine of information about the old place. He remembers a grand piano in the bay window of the dining room. Charles's father, Pedro Martinez, was the Wurlitzers' gardener and built with his own hands — and the help of his seven sons — the four-foot-high fieldstone wall that surrounds the one-acre property. They collected these round rocks when the place was cleared. Charles recounts that Mrs. Wurlitzer was a severe, exacting woman who demanded that Pedro bend over while he was pulling out weeds — she forbade him to kneel on the ground.

The second owners (we are the third) were John and Josephine Hooker, San Francisco society people. Her family was in the gold business, and Admiral Hooker was an Annapolis man. When Josephine died of cancer on the horsehair mattress they left us in the master bedroom, the admiral was despondent. Dena the housekeeper told me that one day in April she put Mr. Hooker's regular gazpacho soup on the table and called him to have some lunch. "I'm not hungry just yet, Dena," he answered. "Perhaps a little later."

An hour later, Charles was working in the front yard when he heard a loud report from the back, which didn't sound like a gunshot, but when he searched the garden near the orange grove, he came upon a grisly scene. Mr. Hooker lay in a gory mess under the 100-year-old eucalyptus tree. The old soldier had shot himself under the chin with his double-barrelled 12-gauge shotgun — a queer choice since the man was described as a "neat freak." He lay stretched out on the ground; his face strangely wide — flattened like a deflated balloon. The back of his head was missing, and parts of his brain were dripping off the rough bark of the tree trunk. Whenever I walked past that tree, I was impressed by Admiral Hooker's courage. A soldier's death. The eucalyptus tree died a few years ago. But the curious lemon tree is still there, half of it producing limes.

The scent of orange blossoms is divine. I never wear scent, and I'm an insistent pest about using only unscented soaps and cleaners. Even my dental floss is unflavoured. Give me some rosemary or mint leaves from the garden to crush in my hand.

After we bought the Palm Springs house, the Hooker relatives came and removed the treasures but left all the rubbish for us to clear out. A lifetime of junk — a dozen pair of rubber boots, 50 saucepans, yard-sale dishes, and four greasy old ovens in the kitchen. Luckily, they also left a huge library of Everyman's Library Classics, titles from Austen and Dickens to de Tocqueville and Whitman. God knows I'd rather read Stevenson than Shakespeare. And I sampled de Staël and Bret Harte with little enthusiasm. Our first year there, I read across a whole shelf of Galsworthy, bound in linen in the "compose green" of my art supplies. It was clear these volumes had never been read because the unopened pages still needed to be slit, typical of 1920s book bindings. My recent reading includes few bestsellers or fiction. I prefer more obscure authors, such as those recommended in the *New York Times* book-listing section "Editor's Choice."

The Palm Springs house was big and grungy, so we were the perfect buyers. Issy had a gleam in his eye — here was another enticing project for the two of us mad renovators.

You enter "Casa de Sueños" directly into the living-dining room, which is about 55 feet long with a 10-foot ceiling. When we moved the sofa, we found a same-sized rectangle of rat droppings underneath, and under a lounge chair a square of yellowed newspapers 20 years old. We peeled everything back to the original — wood floors rescued from grimy green shag carpet; pink random flagstone replaced Mexican kitchen tiles; shiny white enamel paint rejuvenated the fine old panelled doors, fireplace, and cornices. Every room was newly painted in the palest possible ice cream colours, which gave the house a happy countenance.

We enjoy our time in our cherished California house same as Toronto, especially when our grandkids visit. Occasionally we go off from there, to a local bridge tournament. For a week we enjoy the happy challenge of duplicate bridge and stay in seedy hotels — which makes a nice change — like the one in San Bernardino with the rubber blankets. We first took up bridge in the '50s and would meet with couples from our old high school crowd. Sadly, many of them have died, or passed on, as some people prefer, or stepped into the next room. Last night we had an after-Covid reunion dinner party with eight of the old crowd, with lots of high school reminiscences.

We pass our days in California much as we do at home. Issy spends mornings from six to noon (nine to three in Toronto) on the telephone in the dining room, which is his office. When I wish to interrupt him, I "knock knock" in the air on a pretend door near his desk. After lunch we play bridge, so I walk part way and he picks me up. The problem is he sometimes drives right by me looking straight ahead so I endanger my life and run out in the middle of the road, waving wildly like the flag-wavers at airports directing a plane to park. After bridge Issy might hit with the pro at the historic tennis club a block away. In Palm Springs historic means 1936, the year of my historic birth. Then the highlight of the day, I don a dressy outfit and jewellery and we go out on a dinner date every single night, or maybe an artsy film at the Camelot Theatre and Café, where you are permitted to have your glass of wine and hotdog in the dark of the movie. At the end of the day, catching the late news on TV, Issy will say, "Well, I'm going up," the signal he's going to bed, although in Palm Springs, like our Toronto home, there are no stairs. Even if there's something good on TV, I will follow him up to bed out of habit. Wednesday nights we ballroom dance, part of my week's five hours of de rigueur exercise. At our age, working out is not an elective but an absolute necessity, to stem the inevitable stoop of old age. I remember when I turned 35, I was in my kitchen on Green Valley Road when Merle called to wish me happy birthday.

"Merle," I said, "this is it, I'm at the top of my form. I'm happy doing my solitary artwork in the northern light of my kitchen studio, and never will I feel or look better. It's a descending curve from now on — older can't be better."

This year in Palm Springs at Casa de Sueños the house is beginning, like us, to look its age. The decrepitudes are creeping in. When we arrived we soon called Goodman the plumber — no hot water — then Oistad the painter came to patch the peeling paint, and the terrace blinds seized up and finally we noticed the swimming pool was leaking. "Goodness," I said to Issy, "call the pool guy quick before the house floats off."

When Juan arrived, Issy asked, "Could we fill in the deep end and make it an all shallow pool?"

"Of course," said Juan, "we do it all the time. It costs less because when we chip off the old surface we use it to fill in the deep end and no need to cart off all the debris."

"Well, let me tell you, Juan, I may have invented the all-shallow pool, which I installed at the Inn on the Park Toronto in 1962 because I had noticed that most people stand around at the shallow end. (I wonder if that was the first such swimming pool?) For diving we had a dedicated diving pool."

Now, in Palm Springs, with our newly finished filled in swimming pool, painted eggplant to look like a pond, our 1936 Casa de Sueños has been restored to its former gracious splendour.

TODAY WHEN I BOUGHT a new piece of clothing for our nightly Palm Springs dinner date, I was compelled to remove one item from my now tightly packed closet to make room. I have rarely to this day bought a proper dress. In the early days I couldn't afford one. Later I learned that dresses are static and not nearly as much fun as mixing and matching separates. Today my closets burst with colour: lots of loud floral prints and vintage pieces and a vast collection of shirts, trousers, skirts, and belts, which offer me the fun and creativity of an endless variety of permutations. I still love to get myself together in some new way, playing with the balance of colour and design, perhaps too flamboyantly.

My daughter-in-law Joanne enjoys clothes as much as I do, and we have fun shopping, which we haven't done for a year and a half because of this pesky Covid-19. I shopped with my granddaughters Emily and Julia for most of their clothes all the while they were growing up, and they would tire before me. In the '60s, I would commit crimes against the dress etiquette by wearing hats and loud head scarves after five o'clock and velvet fabrics after February. When we opened the Four Seasons Centre, Maestro Richard Bradshaw, the opera director, murmured in my ear in his classy English accent, "I *like* your gear." Was my scarlet dress a bit too short?

Which reminds me of a recent epiphany while we were having our Thursday night pizza in a Palm Springs ristorante, Lucrezia's. If you get a chance — don't go there. Suddenly, in the quiet of the Covid-empty restaurant full of red-and-white checkered tables, Issy's global fame flashed across my consciousness. (My own fame resonated to the end of our block, maybe.) Like a floodgate it dawned on me that I was sitting beside a very famous person who had impacted the world. I hadn't noticed the extent of his acclaim because it had crept in casually, during life as usual. Such universal and lasting effects will surely continue long after Issy's governance is gone.

Because of Isadore, a hotel company was born; his Terry Fox Run made millions; a cancer complex was opened at the Mount Sinai Hospital in honour of our son Chris Hugh, thanks to a $20 million donation by Issy. A portrait of Chris hangs front and centre. And Richard Bradshaw had the opera house for which he'd been campaigning for 35 years, when Isadore gave him $20 million and eureka! The Four Seasons Centre for the Performing Arts happened. Issy explained that the association with the arts (like the Lincoln Center) would enhance the company brand. By our sons' reckoning, there are 30 other citations of how their dad helped others thrive, but rest easy, I won't bore you with the list. Well, maybe just a mention of the Toronto French School, which wouldn't have a building on Mildenhall. When our kids attended the TFS, it was housed in the basements of churches and synagogues. Issy, with his integrated thinking, developed a novel plan to build a school. He explained to headmaster Harry Giles that he should add a building fee to the tuition, which would allow Issy the ammunition to raise mortgage money. Issy called a meeting of three banks and persuaded them, in a business deal too complicated to explain, that their investment was safe. And one last compliment. I have been told by Four Seasons people that the "the Golden Rule" culture of the company changed how they raised their families. That's the end for the moment, of "in praise of Isadore."

To digress back to when we opened the arts centre, that night I dressed rather flamboyantly in that bright scarlet dress because I never seem to get too old to adore dressing up. And I do love a costume party. Issy and I have had a lot of luck winning prizes at costume parties. Once, for the Art Gallery Ball, with a Greek theme, we came as "The Midas Touch." I wore a gold bikini and gold body makeup and Issy was King Midas, with a red velvet cape. For the Venetian Ball, we came as "Venetian Blind" — Issy had sunglasses, white suit, and a cane, and I wore a transparent hoop skirt over narrow silver venetian blinds illuminated by small lights. And it was great fun waltzing together the time we dressed as twin bearded gentlemen fops, "A Pair of Pantalones," for the Gardiner Museum's Commedia dell'Arte Ball. Issy was always a perfect sport and graciously agreed to be the supporting actor for all these dress ups and wear whatever I asked. He always went along with all my meshugas (Yiddish for outlandish doings). Like his father he said yes — even to my revealing our secrets in print.

I RESENT THE AMOUNT of time I spend thinking about the amount of time I have left. Like Woody Allen, I'm neurotic in my fixation on death. About aging, I feel somewhat diminished now, because when I was young, I clearly recall feeling pity for the elderly because they had so little time left. Death is an insult — as if God screwed up and made a fatal flaw in his design of humans. Death is bizarre. We humans scurry around like a colony of ants till our last moment, amassing goods that formerly belonged to others and soon will belong to someone else. Issy and I have accumulated too much stuff, and I'm losing the battle to keep the influx in check. Here's why: when Issy comes home from the office, he is often carrying in some package given to him that he drops on the kitchen island. When he goes out every morning, he does not carry anything out. Over 60 years, these add up. He brings home framed awards and citations, as well as food samples, face creams, and body lotions from suppliers hoping to sell their products to the hotels. It's a constant scramble to give away enough items so the house doesn't sink, and the kids, probably Greg and Tony, won't have so much junk to sort through later.

We're healthy now, but how long can this last? The ailment I'm hoping to get is "hard of hearing." At our age, we're like ducks in a shooting gallery. The ranks are thinning. We're waiting for the unavoidable decrepitudes to set in. When I ride my bike, I try to be like that squirrel I watch from my window that swings perilously on the thinnest branch with no fear of falling. I'm still reckless. And certainly, the time has come to drink some of the good wine, use the good silver, and wear the good jewellery. But as Issy corrects me, we always drink the good wine and use the silver every night. The honest and trite truth is, I still feel middle-aged — I have not yet learned how to be old. Issy is now 90; so how many people do you know who are 95?

I think I don't believe in God. I am tone-deaf to words like "Messiah" and "redemption." I make my one appearance at synagogue for Yom Kippur. We go to the Shaarei Shomayim, a conservative shul, where the men and women sit separately. When I'm asked why such an orthodox temple, I invariably reply, "It's just as good a place *not* to go." I'm embarrassed to read the prayer books with their repetitious glories to our King of the Universe. At shul I'm conscious that I'm standing outside the circle — out of step with my crowd.

I attend synagogue because I'm awed by the certain knowledge that for thousands of years the ancient community of Jews has come together to pray on exactly this day with exactly these words. That's why I spend my one evening at shul — Yom Kippur. I feel a tribal link with the culture of my people, but not with their holy writ. I very much enjoy celebrating the holidays with the family, like Passover, Chanukah, the breaking of the fast after Yom Kippur, and the festival of the ingathering, Sukkot. Soon my family will gather here for Rosh Hashanah dinner — 26 of us. Two families will be absent due to Covid-related travel restrictions. I respect the time-honoured

249

rites of passage like the bar mitzvah and the wedding ceremony under the chuppah (marriage canopy), but I don't buy the dogma. I'm one of those who finds it difficult to reconcile science with religion. The Bible, to me, is a lot of tall tales, based on historical events that were exaggerated over long years of stories handed down. Especially the Catholic slavish, repetitious Hail Marys "fruit of thy womb" make me crazy. Why would God have impregnated only one woman? Is it right that Catholic Nazis could commit murder on a Saturday and make confession to God in church on the Sunday? How can any holy book — whether the Bible or the Koran — preach prejudice and violence? I wish there could be a secular law that forbids such scriptures. And revenge and reprisals simply do not work — the reverberation is endless, and the fighting foments generations of hatred and bitterness. To me, the greatest spiritual leaders of the 20th century were Martin Luther King and Mahatma Gandhi, not the Pope who was complicit both in the holocaust and the sexual abuse among his disciples.

God and I have a very uneasy relationship. We call on each other rarely. That doesn't mean I don't pray for help occasionally. Punishment and forgiveness are human concepts. Surely God would consider sin simply as the inherent and fallible behaviour of his merely human creatures.

Existentialism, when I first encountered it, made more sense to me than the Bible. At university, the works of Jean-Paul Sartre and Ayn Rand resonated, and I still believe that man makes his own fortunes, good and bad, give or take a little mazel — luck.

Every Friday I light the Sabbath candles, and we make the blessings over the challah and wine. I began to do this regularly when my children were grown, and I started to value Jewish tradition. I take pleasure in performing those same rites my people have done for centuries. We have the traditional Shabbat Friday dinner with our family, which is now into four generations. I enjoy the Jewish culture and the connection to the past: continuity transcends mortality. I have the greatest respect for Jewish ethics and integrity. Given the choice, I prefer working with Jews, because in my chauvinism I believe I can trust their word and their handshake. This is not to say that all Jews are honourable.

The contributions that Jews make to society are statistically stunning, per capita higher than any other people. In New York, in 1936, the year I was born, 65 percent of the lawyers and judges were Jewish, as were over half of the doctors, artists, and sculptors. Volumes have been written listing the contributions of Jews like Freud and Marx and Einstein to science and humanitarian causes. And take Irving Berlin, Gershwin, Jerome Kern, and Rodgers, Hart, and Hammerstein out of the 20th century, and what music is left? Although Jews number only one quarter of one percent of the world's population, 20 percent of Nobel Prize winners are Jewish. It surprises me that anti-Semites give no credence to how different our world would be without some of the great Jews of our time. If the six million Jews hadn't died in the Holocaust there would probably be a cure for cancer. It's difficult to imagine a deity who reviews his checklist regularly and draws lines through the names of people who don't please him.

How can this be?

Greg and Joanne's, 2017, 51" x 61".

CHAPTER FIFTEEN

Our Last House

The Wise household never had pets. But our four boys had many. When Tony was seven he had a pair of pet ducks that fit into his hand the day we bought them at the farmers market in Stouffville. Soon the large white birds, Donald and Lucy, grew to recognize their master's feet, which they followed. They even came when they were called. The pair had the run of the kitchen and playroom, but whenever they stopped, they left droppings. Every evening at dusk, at my prodding, Tony would round them up and put them in a fenced hatch in the garden, safe from the raccoons. But one night when I forgot to remind him, the raccoons got them, and Tony was devastated. It was a terrible moment — such anguish and distress. I hardly felt more wretched when my parents died. Here I was, a grown woman, wailing with my forehead pressed against the wall of the dining room, crying, "No, no-o-o-o! Please, God, I want to die!" I couldn't bear to see Tony's pain: my reaction was like that of my aunt Helen who threw herself on her son's coffin as it was being lowered into the ground.

But in the morning, I heard Issy's happy voice saying, "Tony, go outside. I think I hear Donald." It was true — one of the ducks had escaped. Tony decided to bring him to the duck pond at the Inn on the Park, the better to forget about Lucy.

Two other birds took up residence at our swimming pool, which I had painted an eggplant colour, giving the water an oceany hue. A pair of mating mallard ducks sat on the edge of the pool and looked at each other as if deliberating, "Is this a swimming pool or a pond?" They decided the pond would suit them and settled there for a few years. We named them Esther and Williams. Williams would arrive first to confirm that all was quiet for the missus. Whenever we saw him coming in for one of his clumsy cartoon landings, we were afraid to look. He would careen and touch down on one outstretched heel, like a float plane on a single pontoon. One year, when the ducks didn't return, we imagined they had set up housekeeping at a proper pond in the golf course.

After the mallards had left, I campaigned to fill in the pool and replace it with grass, since nobody swam in it, including me. I was outvoted for 18 years, until the day that Issy wanted to add a huge, 40-foot living room. I was against the project, but Issy pointed out, "To build the room we'll have to fill in the swimming pool." That guy knows how to negotiate.

When the kids grew up and moved out, we did not move to a condo. After spending my first five years of marriage in an apartment I resolved never again to live on a shelf. Therefore, instead of downsizing, in 1990 we upsized and added Issy's large room plus two more, just the right-sized house for two. "Suitable rooms for different hours and occupations," as Edith Wharton wrote in her 1897 book, *The Decoration of Houses*. The added-on rooms gave the house all the charm of a bulging Victorian mansion in which the windows are designed from the inside, placed willy-nilly to suit the furniture, with no regard for exterior harmony. The new library — entered by a door that was formerly a window — hung over a cliff, adding yet another tenuous protuberance. Issy and I are both cheerfully mad renovators. While the house was being remodelled, and the band of carpenters and plasterers whistled and hammered and chopped, we lived in a small room, just upstairs from the kitchen.

One night I heard a crash as Issy went down the narrow winding stair. "Are you okay?" I called from bed.

"No," he said, and I knew it was bad because with him it was always "I'm okay." He broke his toe.

Give us a wreck of a place and we'll light up with the intoxicating possibilities in a new project. We have converted two other places — a summer cottage on Kempenfelt Bay and our house in Palm Springs. Both were white elephants, with black soot on the ceilings, on the market for two years. We gleefully attacked the 1905 cottage — moved the staircase into the pantry and turned the sitting-room windows into three pairs of French doors opening onto a wraparound verandah. From this very verandah Lawren Harris painted a canvas titled *Sunset on Kempenfelt Bay*. I spotted the actual trees that were featured in the painting. When I researched the place, I found Harris's grandmother had lived there, unbeknownst to the people from whom we bought the property. Her name was not Harris. I've forgotten what it was. We Victorianized the place with wooden fretwork and trellises like the lacy collars and cuffs of an Elizabethan princess. The exteriors of four buildings on the property were painted in pastel colours of yellow, peach, rust, and turquoise, as beguiling as fairy-tale houses, with names to match — the Witch's House, Seaside, Rose Cottage, and Ann's Folly. Ann's Folly turned out to be Greg. The waterfront of our cottage was at the bottom of a cliff 40 feet high accessed by a steep narrow staircase. So, with the help of Franc Amsen we cut down the hill in a walk down curve with massive rocks and stepping stones, and a small sandy beach at the bottom for our grandchildren. Soon we noticed other cottages followed suit and cut down their hills.

IN 2009, I RESOLVED to move house, but unlike Issy I am not persuasive, and I take no for an answer. It all began exactly the way I had moved Issy to the Forest Glen house. I dropped hints. I took him to see a small house for sale that I could tear down and build a bungalow. He didn't respond. He was happy where he was. My fatalistic argument was that later when we could no longer climb stairs, we would be banished to a so-called retirement home. So, nothing more was said, and we went off to Palm Springs for the winter. On our return I started in again to sell the idea of building a one-storey house while we were still ambulatory. Issy always knows that moment to capitulate, not to disappoint me, so we bought the small house we had seen on Teddington Park Avenue.

I drew up a set of plans and elevations with peach-coloured Portuguese limestone walls inside and out, stone floors inside and out, and broad windows to the floor. We hired a firm to do the mechanical and electrical, and we had the wonderful construction company of Andrea Zuccarini build it for us. It was heaven watching the place rise out of the ground. For 20 glorious months we visited daily, walking over from our house. We admire good craftmanship and bonded with the admirable band of workers, bringing a buffet lunch every other Thursday, complete with flowers, wine, and floral tablecloth. The workmen prided themselves on making the house perfect. The Ontario flagstone floor looks like black-brown shiny leather thanks to my invention of waxing and polishing with Briwax. It gleams. I should have patented the process. And I have our son Greg to thank for this floor since I had given in to the builder who said it would be too difficult to install garden stone indoors.

Greg said, "Stand your ground, that's a great floor," and am I happy I did.

Later Issy changed the folding doors of the patio to one sheet of glass 26 feet wide which was hoisted over the roof from front to back on a day we purposely left town. The panoramic view of Rosedale Golf Club and the Don River Valley is astounding. When the house was built, our first party was for the men who built it who brought their families to show off their handiwork. About 300 people attended. We have spent this year in Covid solitude enjoying this house every day. The plan of the house, with no nib walls, is a joy, because you can see almost the whole floor with views of trees in every direction. Issy will often say, "Have I thanked you lately for this house that I enjoy so much."

Our sons have followed in this passion for creating architecturally pleasing homes, and our grandkids Liza Hoos and Aaron Sharp are at the moment enjoying building a handsome 1920s style house across from theirs in Durham, North Carolina. Jordy, Carolyn, and Erika live in a house they renovated in Maui. And Jordy designed and built their lake house on a hill on Salt Spring Island with the help of his son Jyah, who is now studying architecture. Greg and Joanne are improving their cottage, cheerfully incorporating some 35 of my oil-on-canvasses, including five wooden headboards in the magic realism genre of Joanne's commission.

The day we moved here to Teddington Park in 2010 was so smooth. A happy monster of efficiency, I wore my fancy black cocktail hat to unpack almost 2,000 pieces of our china collection. Previously I had photographed, cut out, and pasted every piece to a scale that fit one inch to a foot drawings of the new four-shelf cabinets built into the walls, and I had packed each piece according to its location. In hours everything was placed, and I had a glass of wine, still wearing my hat.

Our huge collection of 18th-century English and French ceramics was on display. Every room was chockablock with them — a cabinet of salt-glaze teapots and open shelves in every room featuring a hundred sauceboats, teapots, botanical plates, and porcelain figures five inches high. I started collecting all these ceramics in 1986, and this very morning I was up at five to answer the phone when Bonhams auctioneers called from London, and I bought the Bow mug made in 1756, always heeding Isadore's instructions never to be the underbidder.

It was colour that induced me to start collecting china, ceramic colours — molten glass really — brighter than the flowers in Flemish paintings or the blue of sapphires. Ceramic colours that never change through the ages. China can shatter, it's true, but my St. Cloud sugar bowl made in 1710 looks the same as the day it was made. As was once said, "Beauty may triumph on a china jar and bloom uninjured for a thousand years."

At first, we collected Regency floral plates, but now our passion is wares made in England between 1745 and 1755, the first decade after the English discovered the formula for porcelain. We still buy rare pieces, now perhaps only a dozen a year, but like a proper china maniac I still enjoy the chase — bidding in the middle of the night by phone to London or Amsterdam — for some very rare cup marked with an "A" that may have belonged to the Duke of Argyle, or for porcelain pots from a Chinese junk that sank off the coast of Vietnam in 1690 and was raised in 1990. Every June we would travel to London for the ceramics fair, sadly now no longer, because the now generation has no use for objects with a 'past' as they order up their goods online.

I love London like Dr. Johnson who once said, "when a man is tired of London, he is tired of life." Every trip I enjoy the royal parks of London, especially the voluptuous foxgloves and roses of Kensington Gardens.

In London, for 25 years, from 1986 to 2004 I would line up for hours before the 11 o'clock opening of the fair, rush in to Mr. Geoffrey Godden's booth, who had the best bargains, buy a Worcester teapot, pay for it, carry it back to the hotel, wrap it with extra bubble wrap, place it safely in my suitcase among my underwear, declare it at the Canadian border to humour Issy, unwrap it at home, wash it, and place it on the shelf next to a teacup in the same chinoiserie pattern. This process or similar would be repeated at least 1,500 times because most were bought one at a time. I knew I was in trouble the day I was lamenting my china mania to my close friend James Bisback on the telephone and he said, "Not to worry. At least you haven't started boarding up the windows yet."

At that very moment, a carpenter was hammering — making a cabinet out of a window.

Isadore and I enjoy rearranging the ceramics as if we were making a collage. Every time we get a new piece, compositions change. In the early '80s, when only a very few pieces were on display, a dinner guest remarked, "This place looks like a museum." It was a stab in my heart — the one remark I had hoped never to hear. So, with nothing to lose, I began to collect with a vengeance, ostentation be damned. So now there are 1,800 pieces. Why so many? Maybe it's because I don't have my grandmother's silver candlesticks, which my mother had to sell in 1935 to put food on the table.

Today some visitors, uncomfortable with the egregious presence of the china, simply ignore it and make a fuss over the few name brand paintings. Museum curators and serious collectors from abroad call every other month for a tour when they're in town. Busses filled with ladies and gents come on occasion for lunch from local as well as American cities, because we are often asked to host fundraisers or museum visits. Typically, after touring the china, the guests will congregate in the sitting room for a talk by the hostess and a Q&A. I say I will answer any question except one: "Who dusts all this?" and once someone asked, "Is there a catalogue?" Today I can offer three books: *China to Light Up a House*, volumes one and two, and *Ceramics, Ethics & Scandal*, which I wrote because the curious collector — which I am — cannot help but wonder about the world in which the china was made. I searched the secret cellars of museums in London, New York, and Boston to find pieces painted by the same hand, china painters who in 1750s England would be seated at long worktables bravely painting scenes on biscuit porcelain teapots and teacups. Mistakes could not be erased. I searched for the makers, and what were the ways of the wealthy and titled buyers? The lower classes ate from pottery plates not porcelain. The sleuthing was intriguing, working to unravel a whodunit and a whohadit. I wonder where my pair of Chelsea Chinese figures have been since 1749. There are a few pieces that have a handed-down history. I have a huge 13.5 inch blue and white scenic delft bowl, made in 1690, that belonged to Queen Mary, that I bought on the phone at 6 a.m. from a London auction. A red earthenware chocolate pot has a letter inside which states: "this pot belonged to my great-grandfather then given to my daughter who I hope will hand it down to her great-granddaughter." Also inside the pot there is a reference to an article in *Connoisseur* magazine where the pot was pictured in 1903, which surprisingly I pulled up in Google. I guess I now own the chocolate pot because it must have become too valuable for the Ayton family to keep. Chocolate, by the way, was a drink as popular as coffee and not produced as a solid chocolate bar until 1860s England by Fry and Cadbury. Very dark chocolate is a staple of my morning meal and afternoon pick-me-up.

Issy takes me to London every June for the ceramic fair. He arranges business meetings for that week. One day, I was in a taxi on my way to Bonhams to bid on lot 114, a slipware platter dated 1715. I had calculated what time this lot would come up based on the usual 80 lots per hour. The taxi came to a halt in a snarl of traffic, so I started to panic. When it got too close to the time I needed to be there, I paid the driver, jumped out of the taxi, and began to run. Ten blocks later I arrived in the auction room gasping for air as I heard the gavel come down on lot 113. So even before I sat down I began to raise my hand, and today that platter rests smugly on our sideboard. My math memory defies me as usual about the cost of some of these pieces. Was this platter 2,500 pounds or 2,500 dollars? I can't remember if the number I recall is the English price or the converted cost.

MATERIAL CULTURE CAN DEFINE an era. So, I escaped to 18th-century England with the journals and letters of chroniclers Samuel Johnson and Mary Delany, and to the 19th century of the great collector Lady Charlotte Schreiber. I've been likened to her — I don't know quite why. The lady amassed 12,000 pieces, never bought retail, had 10 children in 13 years, combed Europe for English china with her second husband Charles Schreiber, 12 years her junior, who had been her son's tutor. Often, I have visited her collection in the Victoria and Albert Museum. Five of Lady Charlotte's pieces reside now in our collection, including three small yellow Worcester vases, which had been a gift from her friend, about which she writes in her journal, "Mrs. Fortescue . . . did not like my sending the three little vases to the museum, so I must keep them back."

We have a magnificent service of brilliant claret-coloured Chelsea china in a whole floor-to-ceiling cabinet, in companion to two other such cabinets on the same wall of the dining room, one of a Sevres collection all in the same bright green, and the third display a Derby botanical collection in a border of butter yellow. The Chelsea pieces, which I bought in different lots, I can trace back to February 16, 1770, when they were offered by Christie's auctioneers, lot 86 and unsold. I found this entry by accident while reading 100 small early catalogues I once bought for $50. The next time these dishes surface is about 1800 in the home of Charles, the eighth Lord Kinnaird, born 1780, so I know more about the life of these dishes than about my great-great-great-great-great-grandmother Breindela Tishler who was born in the shtetl of Ożarów in 1784, my earliest ancestor, on my mother's side.

Composing my book, *Ceramics, Ethics & Scandal*, was a challenge I was almost not up to — I remember masses of notes spread all over the rec room floor. At times I was floundering, not clear on how to pull it all together, but as I wrote in the preface, "The best parts of this book happened accidentally, as I suspect is the case with most creative work. Writing it was, admittedly, a kind of conceit, rather presumptuous, but always an adventure."

To promote the book, I gave china talks: once at the ceramic fair in London and sometimes material arts groups in Toronto, usually not very well attended. One day I had to give a talk in the morning and had a date for a colonoscopy in the afternoon. I calculated that I could drink the prescribed quarts of liquid and get back from the talk in time for the ensuing diarrhea. I had a few stomach rumblings while I was speaking, but luckily finished in time. Now disaster struck when a young man, Martin (not his real name), approached with some ingratiating questions. He went on and on, telling me he wasn't quite right because his mother had dropped him on his head when he was an infant. Finally, I interrupted him saying, "Sorry but I really must go," and he walked off in high dudgeon. Now delayed, I drove off in a great panic but "oh no!" I could not hang on and defecated all over the leather seats of Isadore's fancy car. At home I parked in the driveway and took off my clothes in front of the kitchen sink, naked from the waist down. Luckily Issy was watching TV. Next, I took a pail of soap and water out to the car and washed the seat of the car again and again. Phew! When I went back in, luckily no one had witnessed this bizarre operation. And on top of this, Martin, who, as he had admitted, was definitely not right in the head, began to pester me and phoned to say I had snubbed and insulted him just because he was challenged. Finally, I asked Issy to meet him, and he did his magic, what else, and the man was suitably tranquilized.

Back in the early days, before I gave talks as a china maven, and there wasn't much money, I bought yard-sale china for both use and display, because I prefer things with a past — and besides, new pieces were more expensive. I bought my first piece of china in a Crystal Beach collectable shop. This dish now sits in a place of honour on my bedside table — a Mason's Ironstone plate with handles in a charming palette of green and terracotta. If I didn't have the means, today I would still have just as much fun collecting on the cheap. Prosperity has deprived me of the satisfaction of finding a treasure whilst sorting through junk. When I see a sign for a garage sale, my heart still quickens just for a moment.

At our summer cottage, every plate was different and bought from local antique shops. I love to eat from plates with a past — last night at dinner .

we ate from the plates which once belonged to Charles Darwin, made in the Flight Barr & Barr factory — with green border and the family crest. From the date, around the time of his marriage, likely they were a wedding gift or purchased by Charles himself. The Darwin crest is a griffin facing left over the motto "cave et aude" (beware and dare) and originated from Erasmus Darwin (1731–1802), a physician and poet lauded for his theory of evolution which his grandson Charles made universal with the 1839 publication of *On the Origin of Species*.

Ceramics are my passion — my cheerful madness. A precious teapot will sit snugly in the palm of my hand while paintings are more aloof on the wall. Of course, we never buy paintings anymore because I need all the walls I can get for my own oil canvasses. Twenty-seven of these are hanging in the kitchen and stairwell, not to mention about 100 in the rest of the house and the same number in the houses of my wider family.

Recently Isadore had a suggestion for me, and with his power of persuasion he usually gets his way. Since I had by then, 2019, amassed 1,800 pieces of antique ceramics, he said why not donate the 600 pieces of the blue and white collection to the Gardiner Museum. These were all made in England in the 1750s and '60s, and my plan had always been to have the lot put up for auction or handed back to the kindness of antique dealers so others like me could have the same joy of collecting. As Horace Walpole once said: "Philosophers make systems and we simpletons collections for we know in a few years our rarities will be dispersed at an auction."

When Isadore suggested I give away some china, I acted like Modestine on the subject and said flatly no. Modestine was the heroine of Robert Louis Stevenson's *Travels with a Donkey in the Cévennes*.

When I first met Modestine, I had that instant flash of recognition . . . this donkey and I were so much alike. As Stevenson relates: "she [the donkey] was patient, elegant in form, with a kindly eye, a determined under jaw and a sober daintiness of gait." Likewise, Isadore is rather vain about my nimble feet. . . . Modestine usually held doggedly to her pace but when there was a lull she would stop and "as was her invariable habit," she would munch her favourite food — and mine — dense black bread, although I prefer mine toasted. Stevenson and the donkey, much like Isadore and I, had a great affection for each other although sometimes Modestine would stubbornly come to a halt and each time Stevenson would prod her with a long stick and then she would move on, which is what Isadore manages to do with his prodding, at which he is relentless and usually successful. Although mostly he lets me go at my own pace, I will occasionally rear up. But not this time. Isadore did indeed persuade me to move on and give my coveted ceramics to the museum. He had a room built at the museum and stipulated that the six cabinets be constructed just the same size as ours and that each piece be displayed always exactly as they are in our house. It's up to me to decide just when I will part with these 600 dishes and teapots and platters and mugs. But not just yet, and who knows when, because like my counterpart Modestine, I remain a donkey on the matter.

My shtetl background makes me rather pragmatic about art. My strong preference is for useful crafts over tableaus. In foreign cities I always choose to visit the decorative arts museum over the art gallery. Paintings are signed, but an artisan's unmarked work is more mysterious, and it was that mystique that led me to write the book about our collection and about the 18th-century English lords and ladies who poured the tea or made the teapot.

Back in 1962 was when I first discovered auction houses and all the heart-stopping excitement that goes with bidding. At Ward-Price Auctioneers, I spotted a four-pedestal English mahogany dining room table, circa 1780. It was 10 feet long and extendable. An elegant table would have a civilizing effect, I hoped, on our rambunctious four boys. I wrote the sum $300 in my catalogue as the highest I would bid, but my arm went up involuntarily again and again, so I paid $600 for it. Twenty years later it was worth $20,000. When the kids were little, we sat at that table every night, in the dining room, waiting for Dad until 7:15. If he hadn't arrived by then, we would start eating without him. But just as we lifted our forks, we would hear the click of Issy's sleek shoes on the parquet, running his usual five minutes late. Today we're still dining at that table, 20 feet long, even last night at a dinner party and the site of a thousand family and business dinners.

That same year, 1962, I bought a John Chambers painting of a blond child, sitting in a field of poppies; the boy resembled our son Christopher. It cost $700, but I told Issy it was $500 (in retrospect, the cost wouldn't have bothered him). I paid the Isaacs Gallery the balance on time, from my housekeeping money. The painting's value soared to $30,000. Never, though, have I bought a carpet, painting, or piece of china as an investment.

Our first Forest Glen collection was antique oriental carpets, about which I made my usual intensive study — hit the books and joined a carpet club where we learned how to distinguish between vegetable and aniline dyes, how to identify the weaving area by type of knot, the number and colour of the wefts, and was it woven on a tribal wool warp or a city cotton warp? Every one of our rooms still features a large antique Persian or smaller Turcoman rug. These carpets are glorious to live with — they seem to harbour the soul of their makers. My favourites remain those made by the Qashqai nomads of southwest Persia, who, it is said, follow the grass with their flocks of sheep by day and sleep by night in their black tents, covering about 400 miles a year. Their only luxuries are the pile carpets, mats, and tent bags the families hand-knot with the spun wool of their own live sheep (wool from dead sheep has no lustre). Their tent's mud floor is typically covered with a main carpet, two runners, and a prayer mat — tent bags are used in lieu of chests of drawers. Along the way, the Qashqai trade these goods for staples like shoes, and tea, and sugar. The carpets are as supple as silk velvet and coloured in the unmistakable blues of the indigo plant, madder reds from roses, and golds from saffron crocuses.

Innovation has no place in the hearts of these weavers; in tribal tradition over centuries, they faithfully reproduce the same heraldic motifs. I believe I could identify the finely knotted texture of a Qashqai carpet — barefoot and blindfolded.

Around 1975, our acquisition budget upgraded from ordinary to extraordinary. We had been comfortable, but careful about luxuries. Before this when we went skiing to Devil's Glen on weekends, we all stayed in one room in the Grace Motel near Collingwood, with its cold, pink concrete floors, and very narrow plastic shower stall. It was a mom-and-pop concern, and the wife would cook breakfast in the small café. One morning when we came in to eat, the missus was missing. It seems she ran off.

I was a good manager, especially when we needed to save money, because my mother, the economist, had taught me well the lessons of the shtetl. In another life, Mom might have been a financial officer in a commercial company. When she married Dad, she sold the duvet and the silver candlesticks she had brought with her from Ożarów, to finance the inventory for the new dry-goods store. Mom became the banker, and with her business acumen, salesmanship, and economy meals such as burnt soup, she kept the family afloat. Mom changed the habit of saving into an art. I have inherited my mom's energy, and, as Isadore attests, I work every waking minute — painting, or writing, and auditing the world around me with never a nap.

In typical tribal tradition, we usually did not buy retail. Even today when I'm buying a piece of china I will usually ask, with my mother's savvy, whether there could be a better price. (Issy usually steps away while I do this.) Once Mom sent me to have my shoes resoled, and when I returned, she asked how much it would cost. When I replied that I hadn't asked, she sent me back to the shoemaker for the price. My mom trusted her own business savvy and felt that my dad and I were a couple of rubes who could be fooled easily. When I first went into the interior design business, Mom had the audacity to ask me, "Nu, Rosie. Tell me the truth — are you

266

charging the customers for your services?" In a way she was right, because sometimes I didn't really care if I got paid. She also advised, "Don't pay for goods up front. Money paid; work delayed." I've been royally swindled a few times — once I was out $100,000 by paying up front.

My dad paid all his bills immediately, always in cash and in person, from a bankroll in his hip pocket, no credit card for him. "Leverage" was not a word in my dad's vocabulary.

One day I pulled out my Visa to pay for Emily's shoes when she was six, and she said, "Good thing you have that card, Safta, so you don't need to pay."

To this day I pay my bills *also* the day they arrive and pay for all antiques on the spot.

The only item I've ever paid for in installments, other than a painting, was *The Encyclopaedia Britannica*. When the salesman came to the door, he found an easy target. Jordy was still in diapers — I wanted my kids to have a resource I never had. Remember there were no books in my house growing up. "Do I dare," I thought, "indulge in these regal maroon almost-leather volumes with gold letters on each spine? Can I forgive myself such extravagance?" The $15-per-month payments seemed to go on forever. Through the years, our encyclopedia set has sat regimentally undisturbed, though occasionally it's served to elevate the bed, between the box spring and mattress.

Hand Me That Wide Brush, 2014, 51" x 61".

CHAPTER SIXTEEN

260 Oil-on-Canvasses

In the 1980s, Issy's hotel business boomed, and all the world's pleasures were within our reach — no limits. We could have bought a yacht, or a plane, or an Aston Martin. I prefer to drive a generic car and spend my money on ceramics. In 1982, I still had my aging Mercedes, which I planned to replace with a Toyota, so Ruth, my office manager, put an ad in the paper.

Someone called and asked, "Does it have a sunroof and what colour is the car?"

"Rust and white," I answered.

"Oh, you mean it's a two-tone?"

"Well, not exactly. It has a bit of rust here and there."

The car didn't sell, so I let my colleague Harry drive it instead of taking the bus. After some months he came to work one day by public transport. I waited for him to offer some explanation because I didn't want to put him on the spot, but there was no further mention, that day or ever. He continued to come to work by bus. The car had simply vanished. My next and favourite car was a red Toyota station wagon — not a blue red, but the yellow red I preferred. It was great for transporting plants and flowers. One day as I was stepping into the car, I happened to look down at the chrome threshold of the open door and was confounded to see there the word . . .

"Volvo"? Seems I still catalogue cars by colour. At least I can find it in a parking lot with its licence plate: MRS HTL.

Eleven years ago, when I closed my interior design business, I began painting oil-on-canvasses in the felicity of my kitchen studio. I don't cook. To date I've done 260 works, some as large as eight feet, and in all the genres of realistic abstract or stylized landscape. Thankfully, my greater family have given a home to most of these works. My kitchen stairwell is covered with 25 paintings hanging three high. At first, I had none of my own paintings hanging in the main rooms, but slowly I inveigled first one, and then others began to creep in to replace Issy's name brands. Now only five of Lawren Harris's best works remain. Instead of the Paterson Ewen and Lawren Harris abstract in the dining room, two RSs perform.

A few weeks ago, I was in a hurry to put up my latest canvas in the living room to replace a Jack Reppen. Issy didn't mind as long as I didn't remove one of his precious Harrises. As I was struggling to hang my four foot painting, Issy Sir Galahad came to the rescue: "Leave it, I'll do it."

So, he climbed up the two steps of the step stool holding the painting and with his foot raised to step onto the buffet he lost his balance and fell backwards landing on his shoulders in a spectacular slow-motion freefall. I wish I had a video. During this slow fall I had great guilt and visions of wheelchairs. But instead of breaking his arm, Issy rolled, with style and grace, in an Olympian manoeuvre his gymnast granddaughter Erika might have applauded, and he promptly rose to his feet with a jump, still holding the painting.

Our sons seem to have also inherited the artist gene. Jordy, like my mom's brother Chaskel Birnbaum, is also a natural graphic designer — he made a wonderful three-dimensional sign for his restaurant, the Santa Fe Bar & Grill, and in his spare time performs and produces bluegrass music; Greg is an architect, software designer, and the family go-to person; Chris's favourite class at school was art, and of course he had plans to work for

Four Seasons; and Tony has a tender streak, an eye for art in the décor of his apartment while brilliantly choosing real estate, perhaps because he has his MBA from Yale, about which I can't help boasting. We admire our boys for their decency and are happy to share their successes.

PAINTING MAKES YOU VERY aware of shape and colour. This year as we take our daily Covid neighbourhood walk, I audit the negative shapes among the leaves of the trees and recently did three stylized landscapes inspired by the pastel spring blossoms and a local charming Queen Anne style cottage. This cottage has appeared in three of my latest paintings, so I dropped photos of these in the mail slot of the door. Bruce Herzog, a psychiatrist, answered, and next week we will exchange house tours and a glass of wine. I have never had a proper art gallery showing. I'm still waiting for my framer, Nic Rukaj, who has a gallery to suggest hosting such an exhibition. All my relatives have many of my grace and favour canvasses displayed on their walls. When someone needs a painting, I send them to the long downstairs hall where I hang the not-so-good ones. Many works have been donated to fundraisers and the highest price paid to date is $6,500, not so great because the framing can cost $700 or more.

Isadore makes a big fuss of my artwork, and in 2017 for our 62nd wedding anniversary, he hosted a huge party for us in the ballroom of the hotel just to showcase my art. Seventy-five of my paintings were on egregious display. I was suitably honoured. Everyone spoke.

Jordy, with his usual wit and humour, welcomed the crowd of 400. The big ballroom at the Four Seasons was dimly lit so that 75 of my oil-on-canvasses provided a jewelled glow around the perimeter. Greg and Joanne hired the band and spent many hours in the ballroom for two days ensuring that there were no hitches. Greg and Joanne wrote a tribute to us which Tony will now read.

Welcome to a celebration of an exceptional marriage full of love and colour. Sixty-two years and 75 paintings!

Friday night dinners at our parents' — if you wander into the kitchen, you'll find at least one painting underway. More times than not our dad appears, and as if standing in front of a Picasso, will tell you why this latest painting is one of her best.

She paints. He promotes. They are full-fledged partners in life.

Partners in bridge: she is the one who takes the risks and swings for the fences, and he plays more by the book and the percentages, yet rarely an argument, and they regularly place near the top.

Partners in design . . . not the least of which is their new bungalow, where our dad concerned himself with light, views, and land assembly, and our mom, the architecture, interior design, and getting rid of that second floor — which came to her in a dream. Partners in dance . . . and, can they dance! Partners in fitness — still following Jane Fonda's Advanced Workout from 1985.

Supportive partners — our mother — who can't swim — donning a life jacket to go on a family canoe trip and waterskiing to boot. Our dad driving the streets of Palm Springs in search of our mother, who has taken a two-hour head start, on foot, to the bridge club.

Partners in philanthropy. Including what our mother considers one of our father's best achievements: establishing the Terry Fox Run. Proposed in a telegram from our dad to Terry, the run is now the largest single-day fundraising event in the world, having raised $750 million for cancer research.

And of course, partners as parents. Sharing and living the values that have guided us as a family, and for which we are grateful.

Neither one will speak publicly without highlighting the other. Our mother, on her book tour a few years back, described our dad as "uxorious" . . . a perfect word for two reasons; it's uncommon, and it's true:

"excessively fond of one's wife." Our father, speaking to any audience on any topic, instantly softens as he declares our mother his unfailing helpmate of 62 years. Our mother is allergic to beige. She lives vividly — every endeavor infused with colour — most recently in her paintings, but all along in her designs, her textiles, her clothes, and the accessories she buys for our dad — like those bright socks and ties, which he wears with such aplomb. There's no lack of colour in her collection of 18th-century porcelain and pottery either. 1,800 pieces, which she has painstakingly collected over 32 years, and has now catalogued in two volumes — over 500 pages . . . In the prologue of volume two, she writes how she ". . . has so enjoyed each piece, from the buying, to the wrapping, shipping, unpacking, washing, and finding each one a home on the shelf closest to its relatives."

Not only can she tell you how and where she acquired each piece, but she knows its provenance, and at least one great story about its past.

Did you know . . . that behind every great woman, there's a great man?

Our dad founded the world's leading luxury hotel company, and a global brand synonymous with "being the best." One hundred and ten of the world's finest hotels. And they visit each one. During those visits our dad holds a town hall — an open Q & A for staff, with standing room only. Afterwards he'll hang around while employees form long lines waiting to get a selfie, a book signed, or have a chat.

Chats where he listens and speaks with his characteristic sincerity — with everyone from cooks to valets. A week later, our parents might find themselves at a dinner with leaders of industry, princes or presidents, where our dad listens and speaks with exactly the same sincerity. Our mom invariably enchants a prince or a pundit who she's sitting next to, by knowing his full history, or the obscure book he's written.

Our parents' remarkable achievements are very different in nature, but they share some crucial elements: unwavering belief in and support of each other, hard work, generosity, and honesty. Their mutual love and respect lasting and growing stronger over these 62 years is as extraordinary as it is beautiful.

As accomplished as each might be, I can tell you from first-hand experience that all of that takes second place to being a dad or a mom to us, or to their grandchildren, or great-grandchildren. Please join me in a toast to my parents, Issy and Rosalie.

THE TRUTH IS, ISSY and I wouldn't change one thing about our growing-up years. We look back on our youth with affection and nostalgia. Especially in this year of Covid. Well, maybe a trip to Trois-Pistoles would have been good. Life at the Wises' defined me and the deprivation armed me to face reversals later. I admit I was too harsh and critical of my parents, and the idyllic life I sought existed only in the books I read. My shtetl life gave me many gifts: I learned to enjoy my own company and to be satisfied with either a little or a lot, and that if you can't buy it, you can make it yourself.

From our parents Issy and I found the strength of mind to accept our son's death with equanimity.

It was a privileged childhood — not at all bland. Our parents treated us as adults. Our kids and grandkids have little connection to thousands of years of Jewish life — our children have been deprived of those connecting threads.

It is as Roger Cukierman, the French Jewish philanthropist once said, "that whoever cannot know his grandparents, nor the faces, places, and sounds of where they lived, is memory's orphan." I wish we had known our grandparents like our progeny know us.

This year of solitude has had its rewards. Fewer responsibilities, no travel to hotels, none of the business dinners hosting 20 people in our dining room every few weeks. This year there was lots of time for introspection.

Looking back at the traits and talents of our forebears, we both lucked out on which of those genes we inherited. I suppose the longevity gene is important and what about the "keep your wits" gene. Isadore was handed his big self-confidence from his "no self-doubt" mother. And he inherited the "imperturbable equanimity" gene from his father, illustrated by a small incident when he was at Ryerson. The names of the chosen football players were posted on the bulletin board, and Issy noticed he didn't make the team. With his "go-with-the-flow acceptance" he handed in his uniform. The coach laughed and said, "Of course you made the team." The gene for which I am most grateful is the "art skills" gift from my mother's family, especially as I never met them. I wonder about them as I squeeze my tubes of oil colours every day. I am the custodian of these genes, which I keep in trust for my heirs.

We all have done our sorting this year. From sorting through how he handled all the challenges along the way, Issy now has a better understanding of his successes and the importance of a first impression and why he deserves the continuous accolades from the press and from us.

As *Luxe* magazine put it: "Isadore Sharp is arguably the most innovative hotelier of the century."

Issy gave nobility to the word "service." When the business pages of newspapers heralded that the company's success derived from superior service, the service factor then became an important agent in North American business.

The company, now valued at $10 billion U.S., has had some formative moments. In August of 2006, Martin Zieff came to Issy with a proposition to take the Four Seasons private. He was financial advisor to investors interested in buying into the company. On reflection Issy saw that an orderly transition of the ownership would serve the stakeholders well. So he flew to Paris to discuss the idea with our largest shareholder, Prince Alwaleed, who was very supportive. "What about Bill Gates?" he said, "since his company Cascade already owns shares?" So after some months of negotiating, the company went private on February 12, 2007, for $3.8 billion U.S. — the Prince and Cascade each owning 47.5 percent and our family 5 percent, Isadore to remain in control of operations and strategy as CEO and chairman. This was a unique deal — Kingdom and Cascade brought an expertise that would ensure the Four Seasons legacy. Issy sent out a letter to all the employees to explain why this deal would secure their future and why we would continue to be the leader of luxury hotels and residences, ending with a thank-you for their continued commitment. The next major happening at the company was just last month when Cascade bought another 25 percent of the company from Prince Waleed, making Bill Gates the controlling shareholder — Isadore Sharp to keep 5 percent and remain chairman of the multi-billion dollar Four Seasons. Issy has a great relationship with the owners' representatives Michael Larson, Randy Jack, and Sarmad Zok. They even have fun. And I say that after 69 years, my husband continues to be very kind, very wise, and a business prestidigitator — an unbeatable combination. And as long as there is a Four Seasons, Isadore Sharp will be remembered as the man who made the company.

Meanwhile, back to the business of me, the wife-of, some say matriarch. I have missed our every other Friday family dinners — where I get to connect eye-to-unflinching-eye with my great-grandkids, chat with my girls about what's new on Netflix, hear our two geniuses Tony and Jay match wits, debate science theories, or stage a push-up contest.

Why is it that I have enjoyed the solitude of this pandemic with an almost too happy heart? I hope it's not masochism. Maybe it's just embracing misfortune with the "it could be worse" attitude, or perhaps it suits my anti-social declivities.

Last night, Friday, August 20, 2021, we had our first Friday family dinner since the pandemic began more than 18 months ago. I dressed in a long bouffant skirt with a hoop, and almost wore my celebratory cocktail hat.

Me and my girls sang the blessings over the Sabbath candles, and the boys made the prayers over the wine and the bread. Just like my distant grandmother Breindela Tishler, who in 1786 as a two-year-old would have stood in front of Friday night candles with her mother and perhaps even with her great-grandmother who might have been born in 1699 and escaped from the Spanish Inquisition to Ożarów as some did. Tonight, we sat around our dining table with the centrepiece along its 20-foot length of cactus garden in hills of sand, which I invented in the year 5771 of the Jewish calendar to represent the land of Israel for the Passover dinner. At the table we reminisced, told stories, and laughed as much as possible spurred on by the grateful glow of glasses of wine and the new fun of being together. We hoisted in a huge meal from a lavish buffet, but I forgot to ask them to sing a Yiddish song. Jordy, Emily, Ann, Aaron, and families Zoomed in, except our six great-grandchildren who were by then asleep. It was a historic event, even surreal, after this long quiet year of solitude and discovery while poking around in our childhood, still happily just a few steps from the shtetl.

POSTSCRIPT

ISADORE JUST TURNED 90 and such a rush of good wishes arrived — by phone, by mail, and online. Notes from friends and staff, fans and followers, and the winner is: Shinan Govani in the *Toronto Star*. "Even now at 90 I like to think of him [Isadore] as the world's oldest influencer. . . . What he lacked in knowledge he made up for in perspicacity . . . Sharp embodies the purposeful courtliness for which Four Seasons is universally known . . . ever the *mensch*, the word could have been invented for him."

Well said, Shinan. Me? I couldn't have described him better.

ACKNOWLEDGEMENTS

Again I thank my dear and constant publisher Jack David for his coaching, coaxing, and many suggestions such as including more about Issy and placing a painting facing every chapter. He called me a tinkerer after the hundredth addition or change. A nice word for a nuisance. Jack and Issy happily plotted daily on the best distribution. The brilliant Emily Schultz was my gentle editor whose praise made me feel like a real writer.

With gratitude to all the folks at ECW Press: Sammy Chin for her pleasant patience during production. Troy Cunningham, David Caron, Aymen Saidane, and also Tania Craan for consultation on the cover.

Thanks to my sons and family for humouring me on yet another book.

My son Greg was my daily helpmate and spent weeks working on the photos and paintings, even creating my own handwriting font for photos. And Isadore, always my muse, was a daily inspiration, constantly coming up with new stories to include. Me and him had a happy time conspiring together, and when the book was a wrap we missed it.

This book is also available as a Global Certified Accessible™ (GCA) ebook. ECW Press's ebooks are screen reader friendly and are built to meet the needs of those who are unable to read standard print due to blindness, low vision, dyslexia, or a physical disability.

At ECW Press, we want you to enjoy our books in whatever format you like. If you've bought a print copy just send an email to ebook@ecwpress.com and include:

- the book title
- the name of the store where you purchased it
- a screenshot or picture of your order/receipt number and your name
- your preference of file type: PDF (for desktop reading), ePub (for a phone/tablet, Kobo, or Nook), mobi (for Kindle)

A real person will respond to your email with your ebook attached. Please note this offer is only for copies bought for personal use and does not apply to school or library copies.

Thank you for supporting an independently owned Canadian publisher with your purchase!